Contemporary Science and
Natural Explanation

Contemporary Science and Natural Explanation

Commonsense Conceptions of Causality

Denis J. Hilton
Editor

NEW YORK UNIVERSITY PRESS
Washington Square, New York

First published in the USA in 1988 by
NEW YORK UNIVERSITY PRESS
Washington Square
New York, N.Y. 10003

Library of Congress Cataloging-in-Publication Data

Contemporary science and natural explanation.

    Includes bibliographies and index.
    Contents: Introduction, images of science and common-
sense explanation/Denis Hilton—The problem of
causal selection/Germund Hesslow—Logic and causal
attribution/Denis Hilton—✕etc.⅛
    1. Causation. 2. Explanation (Philosophy) I. Hilton,
Denis J.
BD541.C63   1988   122   87-11142
ISBN 0-8147-3443-X

This volume is dedicated to

Jos Jaspars
(1934–1985)

"Soldier, scholar, horseman, he,
As 'twere all life's epitome."

Contents

The Contributors

Denis J. Hilton
Department of Psychology, University of Illinois at Urbana-Champaign.

Germund Hesslow
Department of Physiology and Biophysics, University of Lund.

William Turnbull and Ben Slugoski
Department of Psychology, Simon Fraser University.

David R. Shanks
MRC Applied Psychology Unit, Cambridge.

Anthony Dickinson
Department of Experimental Psychology, University of Cambridge.

Rom Harré
Sub-faculty of Philosophy, University of Oxford.

Charles Abraham
Department of Business Studies, Dundee College of Technology.

Robert P. Abelson
Department of Psychology, Yale University.

Mansur Lalljee
Department of External Studies, University of Oxford.

William D. Wattenmaker
Glenn V. Nakamura
Douglas L. Medin
Department of Psychology, University of Illinois at Urbana-Champaign.

Preface

This book was prepared whilst I was at the Department of Psychology, University College, Cardiff and was completed at the Department of Psychology, University of Illinois at Urbana-Champaign. I should like to express my appreciation for the facilities provided by both departments, and in particular for the secretarial help provided at Cardiff by Alison Roberts. I should also like to acknowledge the advice and encouragement provided by John Spiers and the staff of Harvester Press during various stages of the preparation of the book.

The evolution of the book was facilitated by the holding of a symposium entitled *Knowledge-based strategies in causal attribution* under the auspices of the British Psychological Society (Social Section) at Clare College, Cambridge in September 1985, which was attended by Charles Abraham, Anthony Dickinson, Germund Hesslow, David Shanks, Ben Slugoski and myself. Also, I should like to acknowledge the diligence with which all the contributors undertook revisions to their original manuscripts in order to produce a volume with some coherence in both style and content. Any undue shortcomings on this account are my responsibility.

Finally, I should most like to acknowledge the contribution of Jos Jaspars to this volume. Jos was instrumental to the inception of this book in ways both intellectual and practical, and was to have contributed to it. His sudden death prevented him from contributing a chapter, but his presence can still be felt in the "bridge-building" nature of this volume.

By way of explanation of this last remark, I offer the following story. At the time of his death, Jos was completing an undergraduate course in engineering with the Open University, with a view to perhaps making a direct contribution to problems in the Third World. As part of this course, students assemble for summer schools where they are set practical tasks. One such task set for engineering students was to build the lightest possible bridge to support a given weight. Jos designed a bridge whose weight was actually less than that prescribed by the examiners. But when he and his mate built his bridge, they found that it was strong enough to do the job required. The reason for the discrepancy between his and the examiners' calculations was that the formula given to the students includes a "fudge factor" which systematically overestimates the weight required for the bridge. Jos, on the other hand, had gone back to first principles in calculating the weight required. Although his mate was evidently outraged that they did not win the class prize for their bridge, Jos was, as was his way, more content simply to be proven correct.

In his penultimate paper on the psychology of causal explanation, *Mental models of causal reasoning,* Jos urged his fellow social psychologists to "look over the fence" at work on causal explanation being done in disciplines such as philosophy, law and cognitive science. This book concords with this exhortation in including contributions which draw extensively from such a variety of disciplines. Although informed by empirical research, the contributions seek to crystallize out the fundamental features of each of the respective approaches more clearly than is customary in conventional research reports. The hope is that by explicating and questioning the axioms of each paradigm of research, the essential similarities and differences between them can be recognized. Any integration of these paradigms that is consequent on such recognition should then rest on surer foundations.

It is in this spirit that this volume is offered.

1 Introduction Images of Science and Commonsense Explanation

Denis J. Hilton

SCIENCE AND THE STUDY OF COMMONSENSE KNOWLEDGE

The scientific study of commonsense explanation: A central paradox

It seems incontrovertible that causal explanation is ubiquitous in both our informal everyday attempts to understand the world that we live in and in the practice of that formal institution of inquiry called science. It also seems plausible that the concept of causality used in scientific explanation is hewn from the same stone as that used in commonsense explanation. Hence the proliferation of "man the scientist" models in psychological studies of commonsense reasoning and judgement.

Yet, in making these analogies, a fundamental paradox immediately reveals itself. This is that philosophers of science differ fundamentally as to what constitutes the essential properties of scientific explanation. Hence, in analogizing commonsense inference to scientific inference, we are importing quite different "ways of seeing" to our object of inquiry. Thus, through the analogy, our characterization of commonsense conceptions of causality grows out of our characterization of the scientific concept, whereas in the growth of the individual scientist, the concept of causality would seem to develop out of the commonsense one.

An examination of uses of the "man the scientist" analogy in social psychological models of causal attribution and person perception illustrates divergences in what is understood by the "man the scientist" model of causal explanation that could hardly be wider. Thus Harold Kelley (1967), following Fritz Heider (1958), proposed a "man the scientist" model of causal attribution that characterized the layperson as an inductive statistician who performed intuitive "analyses of variance" on condition-effect changes in the manner prescribed by J.S. Mill. By way of contrast, George Kelly (1955) proposed a "man the scientist" model of trait attribution that characterized the layperson as a hypothesis-tester, who is subject to pressures of internal consistency to keep his theories about his own and others' personalities intact. Thus, according to which model of science is brought to the comparison, the same analogy of the layperson to the scientist conveys quite different views of the focussed object of inquiry.

The lay scientist analogy in psychological inquiry

The seeming similarities but substantial differences between the "man the scientist" models proposed by Kelly (1955) and Kelley (1967) thus underscore the importance of earnest attention to the nature of the source models employed in the comparison. It is worth noting that similar concerns can be expressed about the use of the "lay scientist" analogy in other areas of psychological inquiry.

For example, Tukey (1986) suggests that implicit adherence to the "falsificationist" Popperian model of science in a programme of research into concept formation (Wason and Johnson-Laird, 1972) obscured the fact that subjects did rule out hypotheses in the task that they were given. Adopting a model of concept formation based on Mill's methods of eliminative induction, Tukey (1986) showed that the majority of subjects could be shown to have eliminated falsified hypotheses.

In related vein, Cohen (1981) has argued that psychologists (e.g. Tversky and Kahneman, 1974) have adopted inappropriate normative models taken from standard treatments of probability in mathematics to study the layperson's likelihood judgements. Note that Cohen's argument is not that ordinary people are bad statisticians, but that it is inappropriate to use standard scientific conceptions of probability to solve some of the experimental tasks that they are given.

In developmental psychology, one can note another example of a particular image of the scientist providing a potentially misleading normative model of ordinary inference. Piaget proposed an image of the "child scientist" who learns many logical concepts through interaction with and "experiments" on the world. One such concept was that of "reversible operations", whereby the inverse transformation of an operation should result in equivalence. Thus, one learns that if one pours water from a short fat glass into a tall thin glass and then back into the short fat glass, one should have the same amount of water at the end that one started out with. At first it was thought that children generally do not learn this concept until the age of seven years. However, a series of studies which explicitly recognized the "conversational" rather than purely "scientific" nature of the questions asked the child in such studies, showed that children were able to show understanding of conservation and other properties of reversible operations at the age of four years (Donaldson, 1978). Here the child had logical abilities which were not revealed because he was not asked the appropriate questions.

No doubt other examples of inappropriate use of a "lay scientist" analogy that biases psychologist's perceptions of the ordinary person's logical abilities could be adduced. But I hope that the central point is clear: uncritical acceptance of normative models of scientific inference may obscure rather than illuminate the object of inquiry.

At the same time, such analogies constitute "ways of seeing" a problem that provide the conceptual glue that holds research problems together, that motivate the generation of new questions and that enable members of the same scientific research community or "paradigm" to communicate with each other (Kuhn, 1970).

Scientific paradigms and the study of commonsense explanation

If the root analogies or metaphysical assumptions that define the collective "way of seeing" that each scientific paradigm uses to characterize its object of inquiry are not shared by researchers from other disciplines interested in the same problem, failures of understanding and communication may result. The concomitant fragmentation and isolation of research efforts that one would expect to be consequent upon such failures does indeed seem to be evident in the study of commonsense causal explanation. Thus the perception of the striking fragmentation of work on commonsense explanation in philosophy, social psychology, developmental psychology, experimental psychology, decision theory, linguistics and cognitive science is shared by many writers (e.g. Einhorn and Hogarth, 1986; Jaspars, in press; Kelley and Michela, 1980).

The isolation of these research paradigms from each other provides part of the justification for this book. There exists considerable specialization of expertise on commonsense causal explanation which no one person could readily master. Hence the reason for inviting authors from a number of disciplines to contribute to this volume. Thus, the present collection includes chapters from scholars who have distinguished themselves in fields as seemingly divergent as the philosophy of science and animal learning theory.

However, the contributions in this book were solicited for two reasons in particular. The first is that all the contributions seemed to me to have relevance to problems in that domain of social psychological research known as attribution theory. They can all be read, in some sense, as being *about* the same thing. Notwithstanding the relevance of the chapters for many other research problems, this shared focus provides an important integrative theme for the whole book. Thus, most of the chapters explicitly signal the relevance their authors perceive their work to have to attribution theory. The relevance of these and other chapters is also implicitly signalled by their being read in the context of the other chapters in the book. I will suggest some points of mutual relevance further below.

The second reason that the present contributions were solicited was that I felt that all the authors would be able to communicate their ideas to workers outside their own speciality through a combination of clear writing and an ability to place their work in a common philosophical framework where similiarities and differences between approaches can readily be noticed and remarked upon. The contributors were encouraged to give illustrative examples of their research methods and procedures, but only insofar as this would enable them to crystallize out the essential features of their work.

Below I detail some of the themes that I detect as running through the contributions, as well as indicating where I see the contributions diverging as to the type of questions that they address.

AN OVERVIEW OF THE BOOK

Themes of the book

The book is divided into two parts, one concerned with what I have termed *explanations,* the other with what I have termed *theories.* This distinction reflects the differing orientations of the contributions. Whereas the first set of contributions seems to me to be concerned with the commonsense explanation of particular events, the second set seems to be concerned with the explication of commonsense theories about the generative mechanisms whereby these events are produced. I see no incompatibility between the two approaches, seeing each as addressing different types of question (cf. Hesslow, this volume).

Although I consider the above distinction between explanations and theories to be a fundamental one, there is much cross-cutting of themes running through contributions placed in both parts of the book. Below, by way of an explanation of the overall conception guiding the book, I offer a selective review of the interlocking similarities and differences to be found in the various contributions.

Contrasts and causal explanations

According to Mackie (1974), there are two major accounts of the psychological processes of causal induction. The first, originating with Hume, is the associationist account in terms of the experience of "constant conjunction" of an antecedent and consequent event. The second, originating in Mill's method of difference, is counterfactual reasoning about the comparison case where the antecedent does not occur. Between them, these accounts inform the contributions to the first part of the book.

Thus, Hesslow presents a general model of causal explanation as involving the selection of necessary conditions that make the difference between the target case and the comparison case presupposed in the causal question. Appropriate answers therefore explain *differences* between a focussed event and its relevant reference class.

Hilton examines the history of the "man the scientist" analogy in attribution research from its inception by Heider (1958). He considers problems with the covariational definition of causality as given by Kelley (1967) as a model of commonsense attribution. He suggests that a model that relativizes Mill's method of difference to presupposed norms or contrast cases, in the manner proposed by Hesslow, may provide a more adequate description of commonsense explanation.

Turnbull and Slugoski consider everyday causal explanation in the context of social interaction. They show how the same principles of explaining contrasts adduced by Hilton for intrapsychic explanation also govern the formulation of interpsychic explanations. They also discuss the effect of deviations from general conversational norms on the attribution process.

Using models originally developed as theories of animal conditioning, Shanks and Dickinson examine the role of factors such as contiguity and "surprise value" in human associative learning about event contingencies. They argue that their model offers a better account of human judgement than various models using "covariational rules". Although their work is in the Humean framework of associative learning, the role of "information gain" in both suggests some fundamental affinities between inductive associative learning about causes and the neo-Millian process of selecting causes from conditions described in the previous three chapters.

In sum, the chapters offered in this section can be read as offering refinements and developments of the basic Humean and Millian frameworks presupposed in much psychological research on causal explanation and associative learning. These approaches have little to say about the role of conceptual structures in causal explanation. Below, proposals that emphasize these factors are presented.

Conceptual structures and theories

Harré leads the charge against the empiricist philosophies of science presupposed in the first section, with a round indictment of Hume and Mill. Nor does he spare their philosophical descendants, in the form of logical positivists such as Hempel. He outlines an alternative model of causal explanation in science, which proposes that conceptual frameworks constitute the glue that holds the mental universe together.

Abraham uses Harré and Madden's (1975) analysis of causal powers to propose that we use three basic conceptual frameworks to account for the nature of human behaviour. In so doing, he argues that he is reviving basic distinctions in Heider's original work that are not incorporated in Kelley's (1967) formulation.

The influence of Heider's thinking is emphatically acknowledged in Schank and Abelson's (1977) book on discourse comprehension. Here, Abelson and Lalljee continue their inquiry into how knowledge-structures generate causal connections between events by outlining a theory of how "explanatory prototypes" guide the explanation process. In so doing, they lay especial emphasis on the role of event categorization in this process.

Finally, Wattenmaker, Nakamura and Medin discuss shortcomings in associationist accounts of concept learning, thus indicating the necessity to posit the existence of underlying "core theories" to hold concepts together. Categories thus become "explanation-based", and examples that appear to be different to each other be explained as the products of a common underlying template, and may hence be classified as being of the same essential kind.

CONCLUSIONS

The perspectives represented in this volume are diverse in their orientation. Although it is my belief that all are necessary elements of the story that science will have to tell about the nature of everyday human explanation, at the present time it is still hard to say definitively how the parts will be put together. Hopefully, this book will facilitate such a development, and future students of natural explanation will find themselves in a better position.

REFERENCES

Cohen, L.J. (1981). "Can human irrationality be experimentally demonstrated?". *Behavioral and Brain Sciences, 4,* 317–30.

Donaldson, M.E. (1978). *Children's Minds.* London: Fontana.

Einhorn, H.E. and Hogarth, R.M. (1986). "Judging probable cause". *Psychological Bulletin, 99,* 1–19.

Harré, R. and Madden, E.H. (1975). *Causal Powers.* Oxford: Basil Blackwell.

Heider, F. (1985). *The Psychology of Interpersonal Relations.* New York: Wiley.

Jaspars, J.M.F. (in press). "Mental models of causal reasoning". In D. Bar-Tal and A. Kruglanski (Eds), *The Social Psychology of Knowledge.* Cambridge: Cambridge University Press.

Kelley, H.H. (1967). "Attribution in social psychology". *Nebraska Symposium on Motivation, 15,* 192–238.

Kelley, H.H. and Michela, J.L. (1980). "Attribution theory and research". *Annual Review of Psychology, 31*, 457–503.

Kelly, G.A. (1955). *The Psychology of Personal Constructs:* New York: Norton. (2 vols).

Kuhn, T.S. (1970). *The Structure of Scientific Revolutions.* (2nd edition). Chicago: University of Chicago Press.

Mackie, J.L. (1974). *The Cement of the Universe.* London: Oxford University Press.

Schank, R.C. and Abelson, R.P. (1977). *Scripts, Plans, Goals and Understanding: An Enquiry into Human Knowledge Structures.* Hillsdale, N.J.: Lawrence Erlbaum.

Tukey, D.D. (1986). "A philosophical and empirical analysis of subjects' modes of inquiry in Wason's 2-4-6 task." *Quarterly Journal of Experimental Psychology, 38A*, 5–34.

Tversky, A. and Kahneman, D.A. (1974). "Judgement under uncertainty: Heuristics and biases." *Science, 125*, 1124–31.

Wason, P.C. and Johnson-Laird, P.N. (1972). *Psychology of Reasoning: Structure and Content.* London: Batsford.

Part I:
Contrasts and Causal Explanations

2 The Problem of Causal Selection

Germund Hesslow

I THE PROBLEM OF CAUSAL SELECTION

1 Introduction: the plurality of causes

The problem to be discussed in this chapter arises from the fact that most of those events, facts, states or properties for which causal explanations are appropriate, have infinitely many causes. There are three reasons for this. Firstly, an event will normally depend on the immediately preceding occurrence of several different events. Secondly, it will usually be possible, at least in principle, to trace a causal chain backwards in time. Thirdly, it is generally possible to conceptualize the causes in infinitely many different ways.

To take a simple example, consider the event of my lifting a cup of coffee to my lips. Immediately preceding this there are several important conditions, such as the weight of the cup, its position in my hand, the position of my hand and arm, the contraction of the appropriate muscles etc., all of which are necessary conditions for the final event's taking place. If we attempt to trace the causal chain backwards, complexities increase exponentially. There will be causes of the cup's having the position it has, and causes of my arm's having the position it does. The muscular contraction will be preceded by calcium ions flowing into the muscle cells, because of the cell's being depolarized, because of the binding of acetylcholine to the receptors on the muscle cell membrane, because of transmitter release from nerve endings etc. And we still have a long way to go before reaching the neural events behind the intention to lift the cup.

However, when we explain why an event occurs, we never mention more than a few, usually just one, of the events making up

11

this complex web of causal antecedents. No one, for instance, would explain my action by mentioning the release of acetylcholine from the motor nerve endings. Nor do we explain the collapse of a bridge by the action of gravity or a fire by the presence of oxygen.

It could, of course, be maintained that gravity is not a cause of bridges collapsing or that oxygen does not cause fires, but this answer is unsatisfactory. One reason is that all philosophical theories about the nature of the causal connection would assign the same role to, for instance, the presence of oxygen, a heat source, inflammable material etc. as causes of a fire. Moreover, intuition suggests that, although there is certainly a difference between, say, oxygen and a lighted match, we nevertheless recognize *some* role for oxygen. Even if we are reluctant to do this in ordinary situations, like the fire in a house, we can easily imagine situations in which the presence of oxygen would be regarded as the crucial condition. Suppose, for instance, that we have a highly inflammable substance at very high temperature in an oxygen-free container. If we then were to let oxygen into the container, and the substance caught fire, we would surely regard the entry of oxygen into the container as an important cause.

Thus we are faced with the situation that a normal event has many, perhaps infinitely many, causes, but that only some of them are selected and cited in causal explanations. Sometimes we even speak of *the* cause of an event which actually has several causes. Why is this so? What determines the selection of the most important cause from the complete set of causal conditions? This is the selection problem with which we shall be concerned in this chapter.

It will be assumed, without detailed argument, that the selection of a cause from a set of conditions is a special case of the weighting of causes according to their relative importance. For instance, although we might explain someone's alcohol problems by their biochemical susceptibility to alcohol dependence, we might also concede that other factors, such as personal problems, were contributory. When the selection criterion unequivocally picks out one condition we call this *the* cause, but when other conditions come close to satisfying the criterion these are termed contributory, and the condition which best fits the criterion is considered more important than the others.

It should be stressed that the problem of understanding what is involved in causal selection is of double relevance to researchers in psychology. It is a theoretical problem in cognitive psychology, because it concerns the way that common sense conceptualizes causes, but it is also a central methodological problem, because causal attribution is among the central activities of the scientist. Since any causal hypothesis in science depends on causal selections, one cannot understand the epistemological status of such hypotheses without an understanding of causal selection. Since it has been claimed that these selections are arbitrary and governed by subjective factors, the existence of causal selection constitutes a challenge to scientific objectivity. (see e.g. the exchange by Martin, 1974, 1978a, 1978b and Frey, 1976, 1978a, 1978b)

In the following, various attempts by philosophers to formulate criteria which govern causal selections and weightings will be reviewed. An alternative theory will also be outlined which, it will be argued, unifies these attempts but avoids some of their difficulties.

2 Two basic distinctions: selections versus connection, individual versus generic

Much of the philosophical discussion of the selection problem is based on the assumption that a causal statement rests on two distinct judgments, each with its corresponding conceptual problem, one concerning the existence of a causal relation between two events, the "connection problem", and one concerning the relative importance of these causes, the "selection problem". The connection problem is the problem of understanding the process by which we determine that, say, the presence of oxygen, combustible material and a heat source are all necessary conditions for houses catching fire. When the causal relevance of these conditions has been ascertained, there remains, however, the question of determining which of these conditions was, in a concrete individual case, the most important one. We do not say that a fire was caused by oxygen, in spite of the fact that we know that there is a causal connection between oxygen and fire.

The assumption that the two problems can be separated is not trivial and has been denied by some writers e.g. (Hart & Honoré 1959). We will return to this question later; for the time being our task is only to understand how and why, out of the set of causal conditions, the *complete cause*, we select one as *the* cause or as the most important cause.

A second important distinction is that between individual and generic causal relations. The first kind are those relations which obtain between concrete individual occurrences of events, such as the house's catching fire at 9.05 pm yesterday because of the explosion in the television set a moment earlier or the fact that Smith's recent death was caused by a heart attack. The second kind are the relations which obtain between kinds of events (generic events) or between properties, such as the general propensity of explosions to cause fires, or the fact that heart attacks cause death.

There are differing views on the relationship between these two kinds of causal relation. The most common one is that we arrive at generic causal relations by generalizing from individual cases of co-occurrence and then apply this general knowledge to other individual occurrences. Thus, since a large proportion of those who have heart attacks die, we conclude that the disease is deadly. If Smith has an infarction and dies, we use our knowledge of the general causal relation to justify the belief that his death was caused by the infarction. (Note, however, that a general causal statement can be true while a corresponding individual statement is not. Smith's heart attack may not have killed him and he may have been killed by something else. Cf. Hesslow, 1981b)

Statements about the relative importance of causes may apply to both generic and individual causal relations, although the meaning of such statements will be very different. If it was said, for instance, that short-circuits are more important causes of fires than are explosions, the meaning would be that short-circuits cause a greater number of fires than explosions do, and it would be assumed that only one cause was important in each individual fire. Statements of this kind do not involve any theoretical problems beyond those of individual selection.

On this view, the connection problem is identical to the problem of how we arrive at general causal statements, while the selection problem is, in a sense, the problem of justifying various applications of general causal knowledge to particular individual events.

II EARLIER APPROACHES TO THE SELECTION PROBLEM

3 Review of selection criteria
The first philosopher to recognize that the conditions which

causally determine an event usually far outnumber the conditions mentioned in a causal explanation, was John Stuart Mill. In *A System of Logic* he advanced an analysis of causality which was essentially a development of Hume's so called "regularity theory". An event *A* is a cause of the event *B*, according to this theory, if events of the kind *A* are always followed by events of the kind *B*. One problem with this analysis is that few causes are invariably followed by their effects as the theory requires. It may be true that a fire was caused by a short-circuit, but short-circuits are not normally followed by fires. Mill recognized that "It is seldom, if ever, between a consequent and a single antecedent that this invariable sequence subsists." However, "It is usually between a consequent and the sum of several antecedents; the concurrence of all of them being requisite to produce . . . the consequent. In such cases it is very common to single out one only of the antecedents under the denomination of Cause, calling the others merely Conditions." (III, v, 3). Mill stressed that, from a scientific point of view, there could be no justification for a differential treatment of the causal conditions. "We have, philosophically speaking, no right to give the name of cause to one of them, exclusively of the others." (III, v, 3). It is important that causal selections, according to Mill and to many other philosophers, are logically *arbitrary*. Nevertheless, Mill did offer an explanation for the selections we actually make.

(a) Unexpected conditions. According to Mill,

> If we do not . . . enumerate all the conditions, it is only because some of them will in most cases be understood without being expressed, or because for the purpose in view they may without detriment be overlooked. For example, when we say, the cause of man's death was that his foot slipped in climbing a ladder, we omit as a thing unnecessary to be stated the circumstance of his weight, though quite as indispensable a condition of the effect which took place (III, v, 3).

Thus, on this view some conditions are not mentioned because they are presumed to be already known to the listener, and stating them explicitly would be superfluous. Consequently, we select as causes only such conditions that are unknown or unexpected.

A similar criterion, but with a different rationale, is given by William Dray. "To explain a thing", according to Dray, "is sometimes merely to show that it need not have caused surprise" (1957, p. 157). The idea is that we do not generally require explanations when things behave normally. We ask "why" mainly when something unexpected happens, and a relevant explanation will then state those events which were unexpected, but which would have enabled us to predict the surprising event if we had known about them (see Gärdenfors, 1980 for a theory of explanation along these lines). The conditions which explain unexpected occurrences will generally themselves be unexpected, hence the selection of unexpected causes.

(b) Precipitating causes. In discussing the example of the man slipping on the ladder, Mill also notes that in this as in many other cases, "the fact which was dignified with the name of cause, was the one condition which came last into existence" (III, v, 3). It is often possible to divide the complete cause into more or less permanent *states* and instantaneous changes or *events*. We usually select the events immediately preceding the effect which we are trying to explain (cf. MacIver, 1952). This is one of the few selection criteria for which there is direct support in ordinary language, namely when we talk of "precipitating" causes. In such cases, we explicitly use the distinction between permanent conditions and the instantaneous event which "last came into existence". Furthermore, the fact that we explicitly qualify the causal statement by calling the cause precipitating, suggests that we are aware that the other conditions are also causes of a kind. Note that precipitating conditions are not necessarily the same as unexpected conditions. When a match catches fire, the precipitating cause will normally be the striking of the match, but this need not be unexpected.

(c) Abnormal conditions. A similar view is that we select conditions which are abnormal or unusual. This criterion was proposed in H.L.A. Hart and A.M. Honoré's book *Causation in the Law* which contains a very penetrating discussion of the distinction between causes and "mere" conditions with legal problems in mind.

> In a railway accident [mere conditions] . . . will be such factors as the normal speed and load and weight of the train and the routine stopping and acceleration. These factors are, of course, just those which are present alike both in the case where such accidents occur and in the normal cases where they do not; and it is this consideration that leads us to reject them as the cause of the accident, even though it is true that without them the accident would not have occurred.

It is important to notice the motivation given by the authors, that "to cite factors which are present both in the case of disaster and normal functioning would explain nothing: such factors do not 'make the difference' between disaster and normal functioning, as the bent rail [does]" (Hart & Honoré, 1959, p. 32). It may seem over-sophisticated to make a distinction between unexpected and abnormal events, but these words reflect a substantial difference. Firstly, abnormality refers to objective facts; things are normal or abnormal independently of our knowledge of them, while unexpectedness refers to a subjective state. Secondly, the motivation given by Hart & Honoré in terms of explanatory relevance is quite different from that given by Mill, and it depends on an objective feature of situation. The weakness of the train's speed as an explanation for the accident is that it is the same both in cases where accidents occur and in cases where they do not. It is not that we expect the speed to be high.

(d) Variability. Selection of those conditions which are variable in contrast to more permanent conditions (cf. Nagel, 1961) is a blend of the first three, and it is doubtful if a defence of such a criterion could be made that would not also support the others.

(e) Deviation from theoretical ideal. A relevant observation, in this context, is that certain abstract theoretical concepts often guide causal selections. Examples are provided by Weber's concept of "ideal types", equilibrium models in social science, e.g. the perfectly working market economy in neo-classical economics, the definition of a "wild type" in bacterial genetics, the physiology of the healthy human organism in medicine etc. These *theoretical ideals,* as we may call them, define appropriate causal selections. For instance, in explaining a deviation from the market equilibrium or from physiological health, we select causes which are also deviations from the market or deviations from physiological health. This is very similar to Hart & Honoré's conception of selecting deviations from the normal course of events by causes which are also abnormal, but it differs in that no assumption need be made that market equilibrium is normal or that perfect health is normal.

Theoretical ideals are very similar to what Toulmin has called "ideals of natural order". In Aristotelian physics, a material body strives towards a state of rest on the ground, and the theory attempts to explain why certain bodies deviate from this state. The fact that a body is at rest on the ground does not need an explanation and, indeed, cannot be explained by the theory. Only deviations can. In Newtonian physics, a corresponding ideal of natural order is given by the first law of motion as "a state of rest, or of uniform motion in a right line". The theory does not explain the motion of a body which conforms to this ideal, except in the vacuous sense that a body cannot change its state of motion because no force is acting on it. In a sense, forces are equivalent to causes in Newton's theory, and a state of motion in a straight line has no causes. These are defined away by the theory. Only deviations from this kind of motion have causes and can be explained.

(f) Responsibility. It has frequently been noted that causal statements may have an evaluative component. Indeed, the Greek word for cause, *aitia*, also means guilt. According to some historians (e.g. Kelsen, 1943) the Greeks modelled their idea of causation in nature by analogy with ideas about social organization. A cause was thought of as something that brings about a disturbance in state of harmonious equilibrium in nature, and the effect as something that restores this equilibrium, much as a punishment restores the social harmony after a crime. The idea that cause and effect somehow must equal each other also has a moral counterpart in the idea that the punishment should be proportional to the seriousness of the crime. The Latin word *causa* was originally a legal term. The moral term "responsibility" has a similar double meaning. In a scientific laboratory one may hear it said that "this or that factor was responsible for the failure of an experiment", even when it is clear that the issue is one of causality. If there is a standard view about this, it is that we identify the cause of a tragedy before assigning blame. However, it may be claimed that in selecting among the causal conditions we pick out those events or actions which deviate, not from what is normal, but from what is good, reasonable or appropriate. For instance, Dray maintains that "A cause will often be an omission which coincides with what is reprehensible by established norms of conduct" (1964, p. 56). Thus, when we say that a fire was caused by negligence of the authorities (who failed to notice the special dangers in the building), we are not denying that oxygen, a heat source etc. had something to do with it. Neither are we saying that negligence is abnormal. We are, rather, specifying what went wrong.

(g) Predictive value. According to a widespread view, an explanation for a certain event consists of information that, had we had access to it before the event to be explained occurred, would have enabled us to predict it (see e.g. Hempel, 1965; Gardiner,

1952; Gärdenfors, 1980; Nagel 1961; for critical discussions of this theory see e.g. Dray, 1957; von Wright, 1971; Toulmin, 1961). In view of this, and also for other reasons, a natural and intuitively compelling selection criterion would be that we select as the most important causes those that most effectively predict the effect. In formal terms, this means that C_1 is a more important cause of E than is C_2 if and only if,

$$P(E/C_1) \; \rangle \; P(E/C_2)$$

i.e. if the probability of E is greater when C_1 occurs than when C_2 occurs. Criteria of this sort have been defended by Nagel (1961) and Martin (1972) (see also Hesslow, 1983 for a critical discussion).

(h) Replaceability and necessity. Most of us think about certain historical figures like Napoleon, Hitler or Lenin as being important causal factors in history. Historians sometimes take a different view and argue against the role of the individual in history that even if the person X had not done this or that, someone else would have done it instead, and therefore history would not have been much different. This argument does not deny that X did bring about certain things, only that X was not necessary. X's character, motives etc. may have been sufficient in the circumstances for whatever happened, but there were also other people with similar characters, motives etc., such that these too would have been sufficient. X was, we might say, *replaceable,* and therefore not as important a cause for historical developments as causes which were irreplaceable (cf. Mackie, 1974, p. 128).

Replaceability may be a matter of degree. In a famous and controversial book Robert Fogel (1964) argued that the American railroads were not as important as had previously been thought for the rapid economic development of the nineteenth century. The central argument was that if there had been no railroads, other means of transportation, for instance canals, would probably have replaced railroads and fulfilled the same role. Clearly, the strength of Fogel's argument hinges on the estimated probability that, in the absence of railroads, canals would be developed and would be able to take care of the necessary transportation. The more probable this is, the less important will the existence of the railroads seem. Causal importance in this situation will be inversely related to probability of replacement.

But a condition which is likely to be replaced is also one which is a bad predictor of the effect. If railroads are likely to be replaced by some other condition which would have the same effect, then knowledge about the railroads is useless for predicting economic development. Thus the replaceability criterion reduces to the criterion of predictive value. The main difference between them is that predictive value focusses on the probability that the effect occurs, given the causal candidates, whereas replaceability focusses on the probability that the effect does not occur in the absence of the causal candidates. But, under normal conditions, these formulations are equivalent. (Another obvious difference is that the replaceability criterion is couched in "counterfactual" terms. That is, it requires a judgment about what *would* have happened, if something else *had* happened which in fact did not happen. Such judgments are not universally accepted as legitimate. For a discussion of the methodological problems involved, see Gerschenkron, 1968 and Lewis, 1973).

(i) Instrumental efficacy. Manipulability was suggested by Collingwood (1940) as a selection criterion. It is based on an instrumental view of the causal connection where cause and effect are related as means to ends. Thus, Collingwood refers to causes as levers by means of which we can produce or prevent certain effects. If causality is viewed in this way, it is very natural to think that we select those conditions which enable us to manipulate effects. If we want to bring about something, we will select conditions which come as close as possible to being sufficient for a desired end, and if we want to prevent something, we select conditions which come as close as possible to being necessary for whatever it is we wish to avoid. A related formulation, although not put forward as a selection criterion, is that of von Wright (1974). For von Wright, a cause is something that can be introduced as an intervention in nature by human action and that can be used to bring about other things, the effects. This is congenial to the view of the experimental scientist, who intervenes in nature by experimental manipulations and who typically selects the interventions to explain the experimental outcomes.

Instrumental effectiveness is similar in some ways to predictive value. The condition which is most likely to bring about a desired effect will usually, of course, be the one that gives the effect the highest probability. This is not quite the same thing as instrumental effectiveness, however, for some conditions, although they may be very reliable predictors, may also be humanly impossible to influence, and thus useless as instruments.

(j) Interest. Carnap (1966) probably expresses a common view when he claims that causal selections are arbitrary and governed by the particular interests of the person giving an explanation. He gives the example of a car accident and the different explanations given by different people. Thus, a road engineer might point out that the road had a poor surface and that the cause of the accident was the slippery highway. A policeman might instead pick out some other factor, like the excessive speed of the car, and a psychologist yet another factor such as the driver's disturbed state of mind. According to Carnap, each person looks at the situation from a special point of view and singles out that factor that interests him or her most.

In a sense, Carnap's view amounts to a denial of one of our central presuppositions, namely that selection follows rules with a certain rationale. If this was correct, there would not be any *logical* problem of causal selection at all, only the trivial, from the logical point of view that is, problem of finding out how people's interests are shaped.

This list could no doubt be extended further, but I think that it is sufficient to illustrate the main approaches to the selection problem. It is clear that many of these suggestions are highly similar and it is probable that other suggestions will turn out to be variations on the themes outlined above.

4 Problems raised by theories of causal selection

There are two main problems raised by these proposed selection criteria. One concerns their epistemological status and a second their rationale.

Status and correctness of selection criteria. When it is said that selection proceeds according to some criterion or rule, it is implied that different people select causes in similar ways and that in doing this they adhere to some sort of convention. Thus, the idea of selection criteria is incompatible with the view that selection is arbitrary, and it was not quite correct in the review section to present as a proposed criterion the view that causal selection is guided by personal interests. However, most of the entries in the list have been proposed as criteria, and we must now address the question of how to evaluate them. Are any, or perhaps several, of them true or correct?

It is not self-evident what it would mean to say that any of the proposed criteria is "true" or "correct". One possibility is to interpret them as purely empirical, or "behaviouristic", *descriptions* of the causal attributions made by common sense. Most observers, when confronted with the list of selection criteria above, would probably find some truth in each of them. To those of us who like compromises, it is tempting to conclude that all, or at least most, of the criteria are true but that different criteria are used in different contexts (cf. van Fraassen, 1980). However, if we were to take this approach we would be faced with a new selection problem: how do we select, in each situation, the appropriate criterion of causal selection?

It seems clear that, although each criterion correctly describes selection in some contexts, none of them, taken by itself, correctly describes all causal selections. For each criterion, it is easy to find examples of causal selections which cannot be justified by that criterion alone (see e.g. the criticism of the "abnormality" criterion in Dietl, 1970). In a complete account, therefore, they would have to be supplemented by a description of which criteria are employed in which circumstances. But this would leave us in position scarcely better than the one we started from, for now we have to find out, not how causes are selected, but how causal selection rules are selected, and this is not very impressive progress.

Moreover, when the word "criterion" is employed, it is usually implicit that it is not meant only as description of "selection behaviour", but also that we somehow actually "use" the criterion. Rules of grammar, to take a simple analogy, are not just descriptions of the language actually produced by members of a linguistic community; the rules are also "employed", "followed" or "adhered to". It is for this reason that they are thought to have explanatory value. Claims of this sort are usually very difficult to support, however. Linguistic conventions are generally not consciously adhered to and are inferred from uniformities in linguistic behaviour. This problem is made worse by the fact that, although there are exceptions to most criteria, the majority of causal selections probably satisfy several criteria at once, and it will be a difficult task to say in such a case which criterion was actually operative. Again we will need an account of how selection criteria are selected.

A subsidiary issue concerns the epistemological status of those conditions which are not selected. It is assumed by many writers, and explicitly maintained by some, that the individual normally knows about all the conditions. Indeed, it is implicit in the standard formulation of the problem as a problem of *selection*, that we are generally cognizant of those conditions from which the selection is supposed to be made. Thus, for instance, Carnap's suggestion that we select those conditions in which we are interested would be pointless if these were the only conditions we knew about.

This may often be the case, but quite as often, obviously, it is not. Some people probably do not know that oxygen is a necessary condition for a fire, but everyone knows several common causes of fires. According to Hart & Honoré (1959) it is not possible to separate the establishment of causal connections from the selection of causes, because we only discover the abnormal causes. For the experimental scientist, this is a natural view. In order to establish a causal connection between *A* and *B*, we need cases both where *A* is present and where *A* is absent. It is impossible to demonstrate the causal efficacy of permanent conditions.

This argument clearly has merit, but it does not solve the problem. It may be used to support several of the competing selection criteria. Proponents of variability, unexpected causes and manipulability could all use this argument. Nevertheless, a satisfactory theory of causal selection must account for the fact that although we often only know about one causal condition, we also continue to view this as the most important when science reveals other conditions.

Rationale of selection criteria. Assuming that one criterion is true in the sense that we really do select causes according to it, why do we do this? What purpose is served by focussing on, say, abnormal or manipulable conditions?

The "unexpectedness" criterion is mainly motivated by considerations of informational economy, at least as it is presented by Mill. Most of the others concentrate on one particular use of causal knowledge. There are three main reasons why the knowledge that *A* causes *B* is interesting to us. Firstly, knowledge of *A* may be used to *predict B*. Secondly, by manipulating *A* we may introduce or prevent, that is *manipulate, B,* and thirdly, *A* can be used to *explain B*. Some of the selection rules are straightforwardly explained in this way, e.g. manipulability and predictive value. Other cases are more problematic. It is difficult to see, for instance, why abnormal causes should be particularly suited for any of these purposes.

The rationale of selection rules is interesting also because it might help us to explain the fact that we make different selections in different circumstances. It may be thought, for instance, that in a situation where the problem is to predict the future, predictive causes should be selected. When the problem is of a practical nature, such as determining the causes of disease, we should choose manipulable causes which will enable us to deal with these problems etc.

This suggestion has some initial plausibility, but it fails to solve the problem. Many causal problems are motivated by all potential uses, and causal selections have to be made before any specific use is thought of. Typically we look for an explanation for something that is important, and whose importance makes us want to both predict and manipulate it. The physician, for instance, seeks an explanation for the patient's symptoms, in order to be able to predict the course of the disease as well as to manipulate it. One selection must thus satisfy all three desiderata. I think it is clear then that the uses of causal knowledge cannot be separated.

III A NEW APPROACH TO THE SELECTION PROBLEM

5 The nature of events

In the following sections I will outline a different approach to the problem of causal selection and weighting which, it will be argued, better explains the selections we actually make, and which also overcomes the difficulties discussed above for other theories of selection. (Some aspects of the theory, including technical details, are omitted for reasons of space; cf. especially Hesslow, 1983 and also 1981a and 1984)

This theory rests on two ideas. The first is that the effect or the explanandum, i.e. the event to be explained, should be construed, not as an object's having a certain property, but as a *difference* between objects with regard to a certain property. The second idea is that selection and weighting of causes is determined by *explanatory relevance*. This may strike the reader as yet another addition to the already overlong list of proposals for selection criteria, but, as will be clear shortly, explanatory relevance is different.

In most writings on causality and explanation, philosophers have more or less taken it for granted that an event can be represented as a statement (or a "proposition", i.e. the meaning of a statement) having the form Fa, where F is a property and a is the individual object which has the property F. If we consult everyday languge, this may seem plausible. We ask why the bridge collapsed, the barn caught fire, the patient recovered etc. In these cases, objects (bridge, barn, patient) have properties (collapsing, catching fire, recovering), and it does seem to be the object's having these properties which we want to have explained.

However, if we think about it carefully, it is easy to find complications with this view. Consider, for example, a typical explanation for a friend's alcoholism, in terms of unemployment, depression or marital problems. We are not normally satisfied with such explanations, and the reason is that problems of this kind are very common, most of us have them to some extent; yet only some of us develop alcoholism. One way of putting it is that things like unemployment are at best partial explanations, and they do not, at least not completely, explain why this person became an alcoholic while that person did not. That is, they do not completely explain the difference between alcoholics and others.

But if we agree that this is a legitimate objection, then we must also agree that the explanandum is not simply one object's having a certain property, such as John's being an alcoholic, but a difference, such as John's being an alcoholic while Bill is not. We are, it seems, making a comparison between John and Bill. What I want to suggest, then, is that the explanandum should be construed as a relation which involves three things: an *object a*, an *object of comparison b* and an *explanandum property E* which a has and b does not have. We may abbreviate this

$$\langle a, E, b \rangle$$

In some cases the comparison will be between an object and a whole class of objects of comparison. When asking about Bill's alcoholism, we would normally compare him to all people who are not alcoholics. We may call this class of objects the *reference class*, and write the explanandum

$$\langle a, E, R \rangle$$

where R is the reference class.

Let me illustrate this point further with the help of another example. Consider the two fruit flies (M1 and N1) in the upper row of Fig. 1 which have been raised under identical environmental conditions. If we now ask the question "Why does M1 have such short wings?", the natural answer is that the cause is genetic. Since the environment is the same, only genetic factors differentiate between M1 and N1. But suppose that we had never seen the normal flies, and that M1 had only been observed together with the mutant flies M2 and M3, both of which are genetically identical to M1 but have been raised in higher temperatures (27°C and 32°C respectively as compared to 22°C for M1). If we look at these flies and again ask why M1 has such short wings, the natural answer will be that it was raised in a lower temperature.

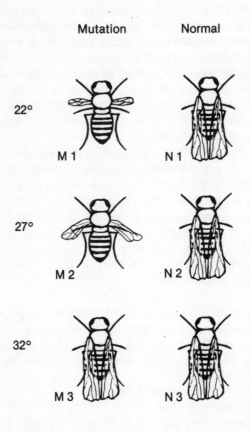

Figure 1

The apparent contradiction between these two different answers is resolved when it is realized that they are really answers to different questions. In the first case we are explaining, not why M1 has short wings, but why M1 has shorter wings than N1. In the second case we are explaining why M1 has shorter wings than M2 and M3. That is, different objects of comparison are related to different questions which in turn have different answers. (Cf. van Fraassen, 1980 for a different but related way of analyzing events.)

6 Explanatory relevance

Given the nature of explananda as differences, it is easy to see why some causal conditions, even if they are necessary conditions for the effect and even if they play a physical role in the outcome, should still lack explanatory relevance. Let us first consider the logical or formal aspects of the situation. Suppose that what we are interested in is Ea, and suppose that there are three conditions jointly sufficient and individually necessary for Ea, i.e. together they bring about Ea and the absence of any of them would ensure the absence of Ea ("$\neg$" indicates negation and "$\rightarrow$" the causal relation):

$$
\begin{array}{lll}
\text{I} & \left.\begin{array}{l} C_1a \\ C_2a \\ C_3a \end{array}\right) & \rightarrow \quad Ea
\end{array}
$$

Clearly, from a formal point of view, any selection from the set of conditions would be purely arbitrary. But suppose that we are interested in the difference between the above situation and the following specific case:

$$
\begin{array}{lll}
\text{II} & \left.\begin{array}{l} \neg\, C_1b \\ C_2b \\ C_3b \end{array}\right) & \rightarrow \quad \neg\, Eb
\end{array}
$$

Now our explanandum is not Ea but $\langle a, E, b \rangle$, i.e. the difference between I and II. If we want an explanation for the fact that a is different from b with respect to E, it is clear that C_1 is the only relevant explanation, for C_1 is the only condition that differs between the two situations. Clearly we cannot explain a difference between two cases with a condition that is present in both. Furthermore, if we are explaining the difference between a and b with respect to E, we are not only explaining why a has E, but also why b does not have E, and we cannot explain why b does not have E with the presence of a condition that causes E.

For instance, if we want to explain why the fly M1 has shorter wings than N1, then the temperature in which the flies were raised is explanatorily irrelevant, since the temperature was the same in both cases. The mutated gene on the other hand was present in one case and absent in the other. It is, therefore, explanatorily relevant.

It is noteworthy that there is nothing arbitrary or subjective about this causal selection. Given that we construe the explanandum as a difference, the relevant selection becomes not only obvious but logically compelling. I have argued elsewhere (Hesslow, 1983) for the following analysis of what it means to explain a difference:

Ca explains the difference between a and b with respect to E, $\langle a, E, b \rangle$, if and only if,

(i) if Cb had been true, then Eb would have been true, and

(ii) if $\neg Ca$ had been true, then $\neg Ea$ would have been true.

For instance, that a condition C explains the difference between this barn, which caught fire, and that barn, which did not, implies that if C had not been present in this barn, it would not have caught fire, and if C had been present in that barn, then that barn would have caught fire.

7 The nature of causal selection

The advantage of this way of looking at explanation is that it dispenses with selection. This is not quite true, for I do claim that we select the explanatorily relevant conditions, but this is selection in a different sense from that discussed above. Let me explain this by discussing in turn traditional selection criteria and the choice of objects of comparison.

Many of the selection criteria listed in Section 3 can be construed as the result of choosing different objects of comparison or reference classes. Let us consider again the fire in the barn, and let us suppose that we have in the back of our minds the picture of a normal barn. This picture has been formed by previous experience and thus represents a kind of crude statistical average. If we ask why this barn caught fire, we will, unconsciously, be comparing this barn with the statistically normal barn. Since the normal barn has not caught fire, it follows that an explanatorily relevant condition for this barn's catching fire must be abnormal. Thus, selection of abnormal conditions can be viewed as the result of comparing the explanandum object with a normal object.

Other criteria may be treated similarly. If we were comparing the barn that caught fire with the same barn before it caught fire, we would have to use a condition which was explanatorily relevant to the difference between this barn now and this barn yesterday, i.e. we would be selecting a precipitating cause. Selection of the unexpected may be viewed as the result of explaining the difference between an expected and an actual outcome. Selection according to responsibility follows from a comparison between actual and morally ideal behaviour. Selection of conditions which cause a deviation from a theoretical ideal involves a comparison between an actual and a theoretically ideal situation, and so on (cf. Hesslow, 1983).

A more difficult case is the situation where several conditions are explanatorily relevant. Say that we want to explain why the fly M1 has short wings, and that we compare M1 to the rest of the fly population. In such a case the explanandum may be broken down into a number of unique differences, $\langle M1, E, N1 \rangle$, $\langle M1, E, M2 \rangle$, $\langle M1, E, N2 \rangle$ . . . It is plausible to say that the condition which explains the greatest number of such unique differences is the one that has the greatest explanatory power and should be chosen as the "most important" cause of the short wings. It has been shown (Hesslow, 1983) that under fairly reasonable assumptions, that condition which has the greatest explanatory power, in this sense, will also be the one with the greatest predictive power, i.e. it will be the one that most raises the probability of the effect.

So far, little has been said about how we choose the objects of comparison or the reference class. This is mainly because the reference class is often an unconscious entity, which is formed by a variety of logically irrelevant factors of which experience, norms and educational indoctrination are examples. We will often compare the explanandum object with what we perceive as normal, but we may also be biased by our education towards using a certain theoretical ideal as a reference class. An economist, when explaining unemployment, might compare the actual situation to a hypothetical one where perfect market equilibrium obtains, whereas a politician is more likely to compare the situation today with that during the previous government.

Notice, however, that this does not make casual explanation subjective. It is not claimed that subjective factors make people answer the same questions differently, but rather that subjective factors *make people ask different questions* (see also Turnbull and Slugoski, this volume). Furthermore, nothing compels us to make a certain comparison or to ask a certain question. It may be true that our intellectual habits and expectancies tend to make us ask certain questions and not others, but we can and do understand questions of an unusual kind when they are explained to us. The important point is that different objects of comparison correspond to different explananda and give rise to and arise from different questions.

For these reasons it is misleading to construe the main problem we have been dealing with in this paper as a problem of selecting causes from a set of objectively equal conditions. What are being selected are essentially questions, and the causal selection that follows from this is determined by the straightforward criterion of explanatory relevance.

REFERENCES

Carnap, R. (1966). *The Philosophical Foundations of Physics*. New York: Basic Books.

Collingwood, R.G. (1940). *An Essay on Metaphysics*. Oxford: Oxford University Press.

Dietl, P.J. (1970). "Abnormalism". *Theoria, 36,* 93–9.

Dray, W. (1957). *Laws and Explanations in History*. Oxford: Oxford University Press.

Dray, W. (1964). *Philosophy of History*. Englewood Cliffs, N.J.: Prentice-Hall.

Fogel, R. (1964). *Railroads and American Economic Growth: Essays in Econometric History*. Baltimore: Johns Hopkins University Press.

Frey, R.G. (1976). "Judgements of causal importance in the social sciences". *Philosophy of the Social Sciences, 6,* 245–8.

Frey, R.G. (1978a). "Contributory causation and the objectivity of the social sciences". *Philosophy of the Social Sciences, 8,* 175–9.

Frey, R.G. (1978b). "Contributory causation and objectivity: a final instalment'. *Philosophy of the Social Sciences, 8,* 182–3.

Gardiner, P. (1952). *The Nature of Historical Explanation.* Oxford: Oxford University Press.

Gärdenfors, P. (1980). "A Pragmatic Theory of Explanations". *Philosophy of Science,* 47, 404–23.

Gerschenkron, A. (1968). *Continuity in History and other Essays.* Cambridge, Mass: Belknap Press.

Hart, H.L.A. and Honoré, A.M. (1959). *Causation in the Law.* Oxford: Oxford University Press.

Hempel, C.G. (1965). *Aspects of Scientific Explanation.* New York: The Free Press.

Hesslow, G. (1981a). "The transitivity of causation". *Analysis 41,* 130–3.

Hesslow, G. (1981b). "Causality and determinism". *Philosophy of Science,* 48, 591–605.

Hesslow, G. (1983). "Explaining differences and weighting causes", *Theoria,* 49, 87–111.

Hesslow, G. (1984). "What is a genetic disease? On the relative importance of causes". In L. Nordenfelt and B.I.B. Lindahl (Eds) *Health, Disease and Causal Explanations in Medicine,* Dordrecht: Reidel.

Hume, D. (1739). *A Treatise of Human Nature.*

Kelsen, H. (1943). *Society and Nature,* Chicago: University of Chicago Press.

Lewis, D. (1973). "Causation". *Journal of Philosophy,* 70, 556–67.

MacIver, R.M. (1952). *Social Causation,* Boston: Ginn & Co.

Mackie, J.L. (1965). "Causes and conditions". *American Philosophical Quarterly,* 2: 245–64.

Mackie, J.L. (1974). *The Cement of the Universe,* Oxford: Oxford University Press.

Martin, M. (1974). "Causal importance and objectivity". *Philosophy of the Social Sciences,* 4, 157–68.

Martin, M. (1978a). "Judgements of contributory causes and objectivity". *Philosophy of the Social Sciences,* 8, 173–75.

Martin, M. (1978b). "Contributory causes again". *Philosophy of the Social Sciences,* 8, 180–1.

Martin, R. (1972). "On weighting causes". *American Philosophical Quarterly,* 9, 291–9.

Mill, J.S. (1973). "System of Logic" (8th edn). In J.M. Robson (Ed.) *Collected Works of John Stuart Mill* (Vols. VII and VIII). Toronto: University of Toronto Press. (Original work published in 1872).

Nagel, E. (1961). *The Structure of Science.* New York: Harcourt, Brace and World.

Toulmin, S. (1961). *Foresight and Understanding.* London: Hutchinson.

van Fraassen, B.C. (1980). *The Scientific Image.* Oxford: Oxford University Press.

von Wright, G.H. (1971). *Explanation and Understanding*. London: Routledge & Kegan Paul.

3 Logic and Causal Attribution

"The logic of science is also that of business and life"

John Stuart Mill

Denis J. Hilton

The fundamental model for research in attribution theory has been the "man the scientist" analogy. First introduced by Heider (1958), it received its most influential statement in Kelley's (1967) comparison of ordinary causal explanation to the scientific analysis of variance. The basic tenets of the so-called ANOVA model are that ordinary causal explanation involves the partitioning of the causes underlying an event into internal and external factors and the observation of covariation between the occurrence of these factors and the occurrence of the target event. These tenets have been adhered to in most of the subsequent major formulations of attribution theory (e.g. Kelley, 1972, 1973; Ajzen and Fishbein, 1975; Jones and Davis, 1965; Jones and McGillis, 1976; Jones and Nisbett, 1972; Ross, 1977; Nisbett and Ross, 1980; Weiner, 1985a).

However, deficiencies in the covariational definition of causality offered by Kelley (1967) have been noted by Jaspars, Hewstone and Fincham (1983) and Hilton and Slugoski (1986) which invite an explicit reconsideration of how the commonsense conception of causality is constituted. In particular it will be suggested that the commonsense ascription of cause depends on the operation of two elements, the *counterfactual* criterion and the *contrastive* criterion, as unified in the notion of an *abnormal condition* (cf. Hart and Honoré, 1959; Hilton and Slugoski, 1986). These two criteria allow critical associated distinctions to be made, such as that between *necessary* and *sufficient* conditions, which the unitary *covariational* criterion does not allow. It will be shown that such distinctions are of fundamental logical and psychological importance, and require a reconceptualization of commonsense explanation in terms other than those specified by the prevailing "man the scientist" model.

33

Thus, although it will be shown that the ANOVA model of Kelley (1967) can be formulated in terms that demonstrate its formal equivalence to the abnormal conditions focus model of Hilton and Slugoski (1986) by presupposing the use of statistical contrast cases, it will be shown that the abnormal conditions focus model has a more general scope. In particular, the abnormal conditions focus model can explain types of causal explanation that use non-statistical contrast cases as "norms" (cf. Hesslow, 1983), and cases where conditions are interdependent, as in complex causal networks (Kelley, 1983). The abnormal conditions focus model will thus be shown to have an explanatory power which enables it to account parsimoniously for a wide range of usages of the concept of causality in natural settings, particularly everyday discourse.

First of all, I consider how Mill's model of scientific practice was applied as an analogy for ordinary causal explanation.

THE LOGIC OF THE LAY SCIENTIST

Psychological investigations of the layman's use of Mill's methods

The "man the scientist" model of causal attribution grew out of Heider's (1958) suggestion that the layman uses a procedure akin to Mill's experimental methods in analysing causality. The suggestion that the layman analyses condition-effect changes was taken up by Kelley (1967) in his comparison of the lay process of causal attribution to the scientific analysis of variance in the so-called ANOVA analogy. Kelley adopted Heider's (1958) distinction between factors internal and external to the person producing the behaviour, and suggested that analysis of the covariation of these factors with the behaviour in question would reveal which one was its cause. Experimental studies appeared to confirm that subjects did use covariation information to make causal attributions, as expected (McArthur, 1972; Orvis, Cunningham and Kelley, 1975).

However, the above empirical studies did not test the full logical implications of Kelley's original proposal (Hilton and Jaspars, 1987). Indeed, it was not until Jaspars, Hewstone and Fincham (1983) produced the inductive logic (sometimes called natural logic) model of causal inference that a fully specified procedure for applying Mill's method of differences to the information that subjects are given in such experiments was formulated. In critical tests, using improved response methodology (Hilton and Jaspars, 1987; Jaspars, 1983; see also Hilton and Slugoski, 1986), the predictions of the inductive logic model were shown to be superior to those made by McArthur (1972) and Orvis, Cunningham and Kelley (1975).

The basic format of the typical social psychological experiment on causal attribution is simple. Subjects are given a skeletal verbal vignette describing an event, and are supplied with three dimensions of covariation information. Thus, they might be told about a *target event*, such as *John laughed at the comedian* which describes the reaction of a particular *person* to a particular *stimulus* on a particular *occasion* (sometimes called *the circumstances*). In addition, they would be given three dimensions of covariation information: *consensus* information, describing whether the behaviour generalizes over other persons; *distinctiveness* information, describing whether the behaviour generalizes over other stimuli; and *consistency* information, describing whether the behaviour generalizes over other occasions. The function of the covariation information can thus be interpreted as indicating whether the target behaviour *generalizes* over the relevant categories of persons, stimuli and occasions (Hewstone and Jaspars, 1983). If, for example, low consensus information indicates that the occurrence of the behaviour does not generalize over other people, then the target person is judged as *necessary* for the occurrence of the target event (Jaspars, Hewstone and Fincham, 1983). The configuration of levels of consensus, distinctiveness and consistency information is sometimes thought of as constituting Kelley's (1967; 1973) "cube".

The inductive logic model therefore instantiates Mill's (1872/1973) definition of causality as being the conjunction of individually necessary but only jointly sufficient conditions. Consider the low consensus, high distinctiveness and high consistency (LHH) configuration below:

John laughs at the comedian (target event).
Hardly anyone else laughs at the comedian (low consensus).
John laughs at hardly any other comedian (high distinctiveness).
In the past, John has almost always laughed at this particular comedian (high consistency).

The LHH configuration indicates that the target behaviour (laughter) does not generalize over other persons (low consensus) or other stimuli (high distinctiveness) but does generalize over other occasions (high consistency). Consequently, the inductive logic model picks out *something about the combination of the person and the stimulus* as the cause of the event, a prediction confirmed in experiments which used appropriate response methodology (Hilton and Jaspars, 1987; Jaspars, 1983).Thus we might infer that John likes the particular comedian's type of joke, although it must be stressed that attribution experiments typically do not solicit the contents of an attribution (but see Abraham, this volume).

The full predictions of the inductive logic model of causal attribution are detailed in Table 1. These predictions were confirmed in an experiment by Jaspars (1983), and extended to the explanation of non-occurrences as well as occurrences, by Hilton and Jaspars (1987).

Finally, it is important to remark that the inductive logic model does *not* perform an intuitive analysis of variance or its naive equivalent. A little reflection should suffice to reveal that to conduct a proper analysis of variance with three factors (target person vs. other persons, target stimulus vs. other stimuli, target occasion vs. other occasions), a $2 \times 2 \times 2$ experimental design is necessary. As Jaspars, Hewstone and Fincham (1983) and Pruitt and Insko (1980) point out, subjects typically receive information about only four of the eight "experimental cells" that are formally required. They thus receive: The *target event* which indicates whether the target behaviour occurs in the joint presence of the target person, the target stimulus and the target occasion; *consensus* information, indicating the occurrence of the target behaviour in the presence of other persons; *distinctiveness* information indicating that the target behaviour occurs in the presence of other stimuli; and *consistency* information indicating that the target behaviour occurs on other occasions. Thus, for example, subjects do *not* receive information about whether the target behaviour occurs in the *joint* presence of *other people* and *other stimuli* (Jaspars, Hewstone and Fincham, 1983; Pruitt and Insko, 1980). The "experimental design" given to subjects is thus incomplete, and a full analysis of variance or its formal equivalent is therefore impossible on the information given to subjects. This last point will be returned to below.

Table 1: *Proportion of attributions made to each causal locus as a function of consensus, distinctiveness and consistency**

Locus of causality	Information pattern †‡							
	$\bar{C}sDCy$	$CsDCy$	$\bar{C}s\bar{D}Cy$	$Cs\bar{D}Cy$	$\bar{C}sD\bar{C}y$	$CsD\bar{C}y$	$\bar{C}s\bar{D}\bar{C}y$	$Cs\bar{D}\bar{C}y$
Stimulus	0.20	**0.45**	0.08	0.11	0.22	0.06	0.14	0.13
Person	0.23	0.00	**0.48**	0.02	0.05	0.11	0.05	0.00
Circumstance	0.03	0.08	0.03	**0.22**	0.03	0.06	0.20	0.19
Stimulus × person	0.27	0.16	0.17	0.20	**0.44**	0.17	0.03	0.11
Stimulus × circumstance	0.06	0.11	0.05	0.13	0.02	0.02	**0.22**	0.14
Personal × circumstance	0.13	0.06	0.06	0.16	0.09	**0.39**	0.14	0.11
Person × stimulus × circumstance	0.08	0.14	0.13	0.17	0.16	0.19	0.22	**0.33**

* Total number of attributions in each condition is 64.

† Cs = high consensus
  $\bar{C}s$ = low consensus
  D = high distinctiveness
  $\bar{D}$ = low distinctiveness
  Cy = high consistency
  $\bar{C}y$ = low consistency

‡ Predicted loci of causality are set in bold type.

Source: J.M.F. Jaspars (1983) "The process of attribution in common sense" in M.R.C. Hewstone (Ed.) *Attribution Theory: Social and Functional Extensions* (Oxford: Basil Blackwell). Reprinted by permission.

Information and the definition of abnormal conditions
The inductive logic model fares reasonably well in predicting subjects' responses to all but one of the eight information configurations made possible by combining high and low levels of consensus, distinctiveness and consistency information. The problematic configuration is the high consensus, low distinctiveness and high consistency (HLH) configuration, for which the inductive logic model predicts no attribution at all, since the target behaviour appears to generalize over all people, stimuli and occasions. Subjects do, however, reliably make 70% of their attributions in this cell to one of the person, the stimulus or the combination of the person and the stimulus. Their responses in this pattern indicate that they were following some rule of inference different from that prescribed by the inductive logic model.

A solution can be found by applying concepts of causation developed in legal philosophy. According to Hart and Honoré (1959), we select that necessary condition which is *abnormal* relative to the target event's context of comparison. Whereas the *counterfactual* criterion determines whether a factor is necessary or not for a given effect, the *contrastive* criterion evaluates whether the feature is "sufficient in the circumstances" by, for example, comparing the target event to the normal case. Subjective presuppositions may play a role in defining *abnormal conditions,* as can be illustrated with reference to the otherwise anomalous HLH configuration described above.

Thus, if given the target event *Ralph trips up over Joan dancing,* the HLH configuration *Almost everyone else trips up over Joan dancing, Ralph trips up over everyone else dancing, In the past Ralph has almost always tripped up over Joan dancing,* subjects make attributions to qualities of the person and the stimulus as multiple sufficient causes (e.g. *Ralph is a clod* and *Joan is a clod*) because both are *abnormally* clumsy, i.e. clumsier than the average person (Hilton and Slugoski, 1986). This is because, in general, the presupposed norm is that, at most, *Some people trip up over some other people dancing.*

By way of contrast, consider the highly normative event *Sally bought something on her visit to the supermarket.* In this case, the HLH configuration is uninformative because it is redundant with subjects' own presuppositions. In other words, saying *Almost everyone else buys something on their visit to this supermarket, Sally buys something on her visit to almost every other supermarket, In the past Sally has almost always bought something on her visit to this supermarket* doesn't tell the competent listener, as characterized by Grice (1975), anything useful, as that person can deduce this information from his general knowledge of the cultural norm that *Almost everyone else buys something on their visit to almost every other supermarket.* In such cases, subjects choose the default option "Nothing special about Sally, this supermarket, the present occasion" (or any combination of the three) caused her behaviour (Hilton and Slugoski, 1986). Indeed, the subject is probably left wondering why the experimenter asked such a non-question (see also Turnbull and Slugoski, this volume).

Notwithstanding the conversational absurdity of the position that the experimenter has placed the subject in, the results do account for subjects' behaviour in the HLH configuration. If the target event and the consensus and distinctiveness information are abnormal, then the person and the stimulus are identified as abnormal conditions, and are dignified as causes. If the target event and consensus and distinctiveness information are normal, then no abnormal condition can be identified, and indeed there seems nothing to explain except why the question was asked in the first place.

So the abnormal conditions focus model of Hilton and Slugoski (1986) explains anomalies in Jaspars' inductive logic model of causal attribution by relativizing the logic of counterfactual reasoning to subjective presuppositions about the statistically normal case in the HLH information configuration. By further assuming that consensus, distinctiveness and consistency information given by the experimenter serve to define contrast cases that may focus aspects of the target event as abnormal, the abnormal conditions focus model of causal attribution can predict the same responses as the inductive logic model in the other seven information configurations. Thus, low consensus throws the target person into focus as abnormal, high distinctiveness throws the target stimulus into focus as abnormal, and low consistency throws the target occasion into focus as abnormal. These predictions were supported by subjects' ratings that these levels of information "tell you something new" about the focussed elements (Hilton and Slugoski, 1986, Experiment 1).

However, having emphasized the differences between the ANOVA model of Kelley, the inductive logic model of Jaspars, and the abnormal conditions focus model of Hilton and Slugoski, I now want to point out some similarities between the models that may not have been apparent in the above discussion, with a view to proposing a framework that integrates the core assumptions of all three.

Norms and the missing dimension of covariation

The crucial insight is that the presupposed norms utilized by the abnormal conditions focus model in effect constitute an extra dimension of variation in Kelley's cube, in other words, *other people producing the target behaviour with other stimuli on other occasions.* Consequently, we may regard such presuppositions as providing values for the missing cells in Kelley's cube, thus enabling the computation of a commonsense analysis of variance (cf. Jaspars, Hewstone and Fincham, 1983, p. 13).

It is useful to work through an example. To simplify matters, we can disregard the less theoretically interesting dimension of consistency, by assuming high consistency in all our examples. This leaves us with a 2×2 design with two factors, the person and the stimulus. The *target event* tells us what happens when this person is combined with this stimulus; the *consensus* information tells us what happens when other people are combined with this stimulus; the *distinctiveness* information tells us what happens when the target person is combined with other stimuli.

We can plot our "experimental observations" in 2×2 tables (see Figure 1). By scoring the occurrence of the target event as 1, high consensus as 1, and low distinctiveness as 1, we fill three of the four experimental cells identically in our two examples, *Ralph trips up over Joan dancing* and *Sally buys something on her visit to the supermarket.* The difference between the two examples comes in how we fill the fourth cell. The presupposed norm *Some people trip up over some other people dancing* indicates a value of ½ in the table associated with the first example, whereas the presupposed norm *Almost everyone buys something on their visit to almost every supermarket* indicates a value of 1 in the table associated with the second.

It then becomes quite easy to see that an ANOVA would calculate two main effects (multiple sufficient causes) in the *Ralph trips up over Joan dancing* example, and would calculate no effects at all in the *Sally buys something on her visit to the supermarket* example.

"Ralph trips up over Joan dancing"

	S	$\bar{S}$
P	Distinctiveness 1	Target event 1
$\bar{P}$	Consensus 1	Norm ½

"Sally buys something on her visit to the supermarket"

	S	$\bar{S}$
P	Target event 1	Distinctiveness 1
$\bar{P}$	Consensus 1	Norm 1

$\underline{P}$ = Target person present
$\bar{P}$ = Other target persons present
$\underline{S}$ = Target stimulus present
$\bar{S}$ = Other target stimuli present

Figure 1: 2×2 Data matrices for high-consensus, low-distinctiveness events as a function of presupposed norms

"Sue is afraid of the dog"

	S	S̄
P	Target event 1	Distinctiveness 0
P̄	Consensus 1	Norm ½

"Tom is enthralled by the painting"

	S	S̄
P	Target event 1	Distinctiveness 0
P̄	Consensus 1	Norm ¼

P = Target person present
P̄ = Other target persons present
S = Target stimulus present
S̄ = Other target stimuli present

Figure 2: 2×2 Data matrices for high-consensus,
high-distinctiveness events as a function of presupposed norms

This, of course, corresponds exactly to the findings of Hilton and Slugoski (1986). So whilst subjective presuppositions about what constitutes normal behaviour enable the identification of abnormal conditions, they also enable the calculation of an ANOVA or its formal equivalent, as Kelley originally suggested. All that has happened is that we understand better what the logical requirements for calculating an intuitive ANOVA are, and how subjects "complete the experimental design" with their subjective presuppositions where they are not given explicit information.

Indeed, viewed as a reformulated ANOVA model, the abnormal conditions focus model can make very specific predictions about the *strength* of attributions as a function of the values entered in the "experimental cell" associated with the presupposed norm. For example, take the events *Sue is afraid of the dog* and *Tom is enthralled by the painting*. Intuitively, the former seems to be more common than the latter, so let us enter values of ½ and ¼ in the cells associated with the presupposed norms associated with each event. We enter the scores associated with high consensus (indicating a value of 1) and high distinctiveness (indicating a value of 0) in the appropriate cells of the matrix in Figure 2. If this were so, then we would expect strong attributions to the stimulus in both cases, as Hilton and Slugoski (1986) found. But we can make *quantitative* predictions on the basis of the matrix values: Attributions to the stimulus should be *stronger* for the example of *Tom is enthralled by the painting* than for the example *Sue is afraid of the dog*, and this was indeed what was found (means of 6.28 and 5.50 on seven-point response scales).

The above kind of analysis can, of course, be applied to all eight configurations of consensus, distinctiveness and consistency information, crossed with high, medium and low values of presupposed normativeness. In theory, it should be possible to make precise quantitative predictions about the relation between *degrees* of perceived abnormality, informativeness of covariation information, and dispositional attribution.

Although not fully tested, the advances of the present formulation on those of Kelley (1967) and Jaspars, Hewstone and Fincham (1983) are considerable. The relevant informational dimensions for the intuitive analysis of variance have been fully specified; interactional attributions can be predicted accurately; the interaction between implicit and explicit covariation information in the causal attribution process explained; and precise quantitative predictions about strengths of attributions made possible.

Indeed, it may be asked whether we have turned full circle. Now that the ANOVA model has been formulated properly, is it adequate to describe ordinary causal attribution? In other words, do ordinary people make causal attributions by performing analyses of covariations in the sense originally intended when Kelley (1967) proposed the ANOVA model?

Below, I consider a number of problems for the covariational definition of causality as a model of ordinary causal ascription. These problems suggest limitations in the covariational model, which prompt a more general formulation of the logic of the causal attribution process. This more general formulation will include the analysis of covariation as a special case.

PROBLEMS WITH THE COVARIATIONAL DEFINITION OF CAUSALITY

Necessary and sufficient conditions

Heider's (1958, p. 152) suggestion that causal attribution proceeds through the analysis of condition-effect changes as formulated in Mill's (1872/1973) methods of experimental inquiry was formulated by Kelley (1973 p. 194) as follows:

> A naive version of J.S. Mill's method of difference provides the basic analytic tool. The effect is attributed to that condition which is present when the effect is present and which is absent when the effect is absent.

The first problem with Kelley's (1967; 1973) definition of the method of difference is that it does not allow the distinction between *necessary* and *sufficient* conditions, a distinction which Mill himself (1872/1973) clearly makes. However, as Mackie (1974) points out, to all intents and purposes Hume did not make this distinction either. Nor, as will be shown below, do psychological researchers on contingency judgment following in the associationist tradition originated by Hume.

Thus Kelley's (1967; 1973) definition of causation in terms of covariation is widely shared by other researchers (for a review, see Alloy and Tabachnik, 1984). For example, using a contingency

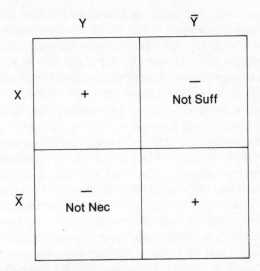

X = The antecedent occurs
X̄ = The antecedent does not occur
Y = The consequent occurs
Ȳ = The consequent does not occur
+ = Occurrences taken as confirming causal relationship by contingency
    rule
— = Occurrence taken as disconfirming causal relationship by
    contingency rule
Not Nec = Occurrences indicating X is not a necessary condition for Y.
Not Suff = Occurrences indicating X is not a sufficient condition for Y.

Figure 3: A comparison of contingency and conditional judgments

judgment paradigm, Schustack and Sternberg (1981) showed that
judgments of causation were positively related to the number of
occurrences in the condition-present/effect-present and condition-
absent/effect-absent cells, but inversely related to the number of
occurrences in the condition-present/effect-absent and condition-
absent/effect-present cells. In terms of Figure 3, where X is the
condition and Y the effect, judgments of causality *qua*
contingency/correlation/covariation are positively related to
occurrences in the X, Y and Not X, Not Y cells and inversely related
to occurrences in the X, Not Y and Not X, Y cells. Although
researchers fit varying weights to each cell as an *a posteriori* function
of experimental procedure (e.g. Chatlosh, Neunaber and

Wasserman, 1985; Schustack and Sternberg, 1981; Wasserman, Chatlosh and Neunaber, 1983), they do not make *a priori* distinctions between the condition-present/effect-absent and condition-absent/effect-present (X, Not Y and Not X, Y) cells: both are treated as negatively correlated with judgments of contingency, and hence evidence against the existence of a causal relationship.

However, a consideration of the philosophical literature on causation provides clear grounds for distinguishing the condition-present/effect-absent (X, Not Y) and condition-absent/effect-present (Not X, Y) cells (Mackie, 1974). The presence of the condition and the absence of the effect warrant the conclusion that the condition is *not sufficient* for the occurrence of the effect, though it may be *necessary*. Conversely, in the counterfactual case, the absence of the condition but the presence of the effect warrant the conclusion that the condition is *not necessary* for the presence of the effect, though it may be *sufficient*. Strictly speaking, occurrences in both the condition-present/effect-absent (X, Not Y) and the condition-absent/effect-present (Not X, Y) do *not* warrant the conclusion that there is no causal relationship between condition X and effect Y as both the ANOVA model (e.g. Kelley, 1967; 1973) and the contingency judgment approaches (e.g. Schustack and Sternberg, 1981) suggest. Rather, they warrant the conclusion that if causal relationships exist, they are of different *types*.

The difference in significance of occurrences in the condition-present/effect-absent (X, Not Y) and condition-absent/effect-present (Not X, Y) cells is recognized in the psychological literature on conditional reasoning (e.g. Staudenmayer, 1975; Rips and Marcus, 1977), but this literature appears to have passed those on causal attribution and contingency judgment by. It is only recently, for example, that theoretical integration has been attempted (e.g. Einhorn and Hogarth, 1986; Hilton and Slugoski, 1986). Einhorn and Hogarth (1986) have indicated how covariational information may be represented in conditional analyses which utilize counterfactual reasoning about the condition-absent/effect-present (not X, Y) case.

The logic of counterfactuals
The second problem with Kelley's (1967; 1973) definition of Mill's method of difference is that although covariational analysis can be represented as a special case of counterfactual reasoning,

counterfactual reasoning does not require covariational information to proceed. Mackie (1974) criticized Hume's regularity theory of causal induction on such grounds, arguing that ordinary causal explanation depends on counterfactual reasoning about the contrast case where the antecedent case does not occur, and that a single contrast case will suffice.

This point can be illustrated with reference to attribution theory with respect to the inductive logic model of Jaspars (Jaspars, Hewstone and Fincham, 1983; Jaspars, in press). Jaspars showed that consensus, distinctiveness and consistency information could be encoded to signify whether the target behaviour occurred or not in presence, respectively, of the target person, stimulus and occasion. The consensus, distinctiveness and consistency information could be viewed as providing experimenter-given "norms" against which to evaluate the particular characteristics of the target person, stimulus and occasion (cf. Hilton and Slugoski, 1986).

Logically viewed, however, subjects could use single cases of consensus, distinctiveness and consistency information and derive the same implications as when they were given statistically quantified information. Thus the information that *On a previous occasion, Jane was not afraid of the white poodle* warrants the conclusion that *Jane is afraid of the white poodle* because of "something special about the present occasion".

This observation suggests that it is the logical relation between the entities involved in the target event and comparison entities that matters for such inference. This point was implicitly recognized by Jaspars (in press) when he points out that his inductive logic model defines an eight-fold truth-table. In addition, in a personal communication, he acknowledged that the function of consensus, distinctiveness and consistency information in his model could be viewed as the provision of counterfactual contrast cases for the person, the stimulus and the occasion respectively.

Thus, whilst the existence of many co-occurrences between conditions and effects indicating a high degree of association may encourage *confidence* that there is a causal relation, it does not logically entail it. This, of course, is the problem that Hume started from, and which has vexed philosophers ever since.

From the psychologist's point of view, it may be objected that using single instances of consensus, distinctiveness and consistency information as contrast cases does not obviate the covariational definition of causality. Hume's doctrine that it is the experience of "constant conjunction" between two events that gives rise to the impression of causality is, as Mackie (1974) points out, a *psychological* theory of how the mind gains such an impression. Mackie's claim is that counterfactual reasoning is another plausible account of how the mind might (rightly or wrongly) gain the impression of a causal relationship. According to this view, from a single comparison case the mind may simply get a weak impression of whether a causal relationship exists.

However, this argument becomes more problematic when the contrast case is an event which has *never* occurred. In everyday discourse, explanations are furnished quite naturally on the basis of such cases. Thus, the U.S. decision to drop an atom bomb on Japan in 1945 is quite felicitously explained by reference to the counterfactual case of what might have happened if they had *not* dropped the bomb. Scientific explanations may also refer to hypothetical entities, as when an economist explains real-life behaviour through its deviation from an idealized model situated in a computer (Hesslow, 1983). Such explanations, although natural, are not readily explained as the simple products of covariational analysis.

Combinations of conditions and combinations of causes

The third problem for the covariational definition of causality concerns the distinction between combinations of causes and combinations of conditions. This is discussed by Kelley (1972; 1973) in terms of what he terms the multiple necessary causes (MNC) and the multiple sufficient causes (MSC) schemata. However, they represent different *types* of causal combination. Indeed, the term "multiple necessary *causes* schema" is something of a misnomer given the distinction between causes and conditions, as will be shown below.

In the case of the MNC schema, each of the conditions is *necessary but not sufficient* for the outcome to occur, whereas in the case of the MSC schema each of the conditions is *sufficient but not necessary* for the outcome to occur. To use McArthur's (1972) example, if Ralph trips up over Joan because *Ralph and Joan do not swing together*, then it is the *combination* of Ralph and Joan that causes them to trip up over each other. The conjunction of the individually necessary but only jointly sufficient conditions constitutes the cause "philosophically speaking" in the sense of Mill (1872/1973, *System of Logic*, Book III, Ch. 5, Section iii). Thus the low consensus, high distinctiveness and high consistency (LHH) pattern of information indicating that outcome (tripping up) does not generalize over other people (other men in the case of Ralph) or stimuli (other women in the case of Joan) but does generalize over other occasions that Ralph dances with Joan indicates an attribution to the *conjunctive* combination of Ralph and Joan (Hilton and Jaspars, 1987; Hilton and Slugoski, 1986).

The multiple sufficient cause (MSC) case is quite different in nature. This indicates the inclusive disjunction of *causes*, not the conjunction of *conditions*. Thus, Ralph's tripping up over Joan could be because either *Ralph is a clod* or *Joan is a clod* or *both*. It is indicated by the high consensus, low distinctiveness, high consistency (HLH) configuration indicating that the behaviour generalizes over other persons (men in the case of Ralph), other stimuli (women in the case of Joan), and over other occasions when Ralph and Joan dance together. Hilton and Slugoski (1986) showed that subjects attributed the occurrence of the outcome to a disjunctive combination of the causes, in contradistinction to similar studies which failed to distinguish conjunctive from disjunctive combinations of factors in their response formats (e.g. Hilton and Jaspars, 1987; McArthur, 1972; Orvis, Cunningham and Kelley, 1975).

Experimental subjects clearly distinguish the types of combination when given the opportunity in experimental procedures. Indeed, there is evidence that they do so even when they are given no explicit opportunity. Hilton and Jaspars (1987) found that subjects were likely to make attributions to the combination (whose nature was unspecified) of the person and the stimulus in response to both the LHH and HLH information configurations. But they were also significantly likely to make attributions singly to *either* the person *or* the stimulus in the HLH configuration but not the LHH configuration. This could reflect the application of the discounting of one of the factors as the cause in the MSC case (cf. Kelley, 1973), or it could be that subjects believe that it is only necessary to cite one cause that is "sufficient in the circumstances" (Mackie, 1974) to satisfy the experimental requirement of explaining the event. Indeed, by citing *two* sufficient causes, subjects may even be breaking Grice's (1975) conversational maxim of quantity by overburdening the experimenter with redundant information.

In sum, the MNC and MSC cases should properly be distinguished as the multiple necessary *conditions* schema (collectively indicating one Millian cause), `and the multiple sufficient *causes* schema (where each condition is individually a Millian cause). This distinction attracts a great amount of attention in the law, as witnessed by the fact that Hart and Honoré (1959, 1985) devote a whole chapter to this issue. The importance of the issue arises in the context of problems of legal attributions of responsibility where there is simultaneous causation, as in the MSC case. Thus, can we hold any single member of a firing squad responsible for the death of a political prisoner, when no single man's shot is necessary to kill the prisoner? The problem for the covariational definition of cause given by Kelley (1967, p. 154) is that one cause of death may plausibly be said to be a condition (Private No. 351's shot) which may be absent where the effect (death) is present. It should be noted, however, that the overdetermination of an event causes considerable problems for any theory of causation (Hart and Honoré, 1959, 1985; Mackie, 1974; see also Hesslow, this volume).

Exclusive disjunctions of conditions

I turn now to the fourth problem for the covariational definition of causality, the non-conjunctive combination of conditions. As Jaspars (in press) and Mackie (1974) note, explanations in terms of exclusive disjunctions ("either the one or t'other, but not both") are quite possible. Consider the predicament of a hostess planning a dinner-party who wishes to occasion an agreeable evening for all concerned. Two possible guests would both contribute materially to the success of the *soirée*, but being recently divorced from each other, would not enjoy each other's company. Inviting both of them together would inhibit the production of the requisite *bonhomie*, although either alone would combine conjunctively with the same set of guests to produce the desired outcome. Consequently, the same condition (e.g. the ex-husband) could both be present when the effect (a charming evening) is present and also be present when the effect is absent due to the presence of his ex-wife. Although the presence of the ex-husband would have to be cited as part of the explanation of the dinner party's success in the first case, note that it does not satisfy Kelley's requirement that a cause be that condition which is absent when the effect is absent.

The selection of causes from sets of interdependent conditions

The fifth problem for the covariational definition of causality is posed by cases where there is interdependence among conditions. As Kelley (1983) notes, this is true of causal networks where attribution of responsibility is traced through a chain of intermediate connections to a distal cause in the sense of Heider (1958). For example, we may judge a child's failure at school to be due to insufficient motivation (a personality factor). However, we may trace the cause of this lack of motivation to lack of encouragement in the child's home (an environmental factor). Internal and external causes are thus interdependent, and may even be recursively embedded in each other in an extended causal chain. How, then, may we select the cause from such a complex set of interdependent conditions?

Various answers have been proposed, most notably by Hart and Honoré (1959; 1985) in legal theory, and by Lehnert (1978) and Schank and Abelson (1977) in artificial intelligence. Both sets of replies involve the prioritizing of certain types of connecting conditions, namely abnormal conditions, voluntary actions and goal states. It remains to be established to what extent these types of connection have the same essential features with respect to causal selection. All may be said to be "operative causes" (Mackie, 1974; Trabasso and van den Broek, 1985; Trabasso and Sperry, 1985; Trabasso, Secco and van den Broek, 1984) in that once established, they normally result in the target outcome assuming that "the world runs on from there". That is, of course, simply another version of the requirement of the *ceteris paribus* assumption that there are no exceptional circumstances holding true.

To take a concrete example. Hart and Honoré (1959) show that causation in law is traced through an abnormal condition if there is an intention lying behind it. The intention is thus designated as the "operative cause". For example, we may attribute a car crash to iced-over roads *qua* abnormal condition, but not to the antecedent physical abnormal condition of a thunderstorm that caused the ice. However, if we learn that the reason that the road is iced over is that some criminal sprayed the road with a hosepipe, then we trace the responsibility for the crash through the ice on the road to the voluntary action behind it of spraying the road. Behind the criminal's voluntary action may lie the goal-state of causing the car driver some harm. If this is so, then the icy roads and the spraying may be judged as immaterial to the effect of *causing harm to the car driver*. They are just the local preconditions necessary to the effect as described. This can be seen if one assumes that if the criminal failed to achieve his goal this way, then he would try some other means to his end, such as putting arsenic in the car driver's meal on some other occasion. The icy road and the action of spraying it are only material to the instantiation of the event described as *causing the car crash*. This feature of intentional actions, that they vary in means according to local circumstances but not in ends, is the characteristic of *equifinality* as described by Heider (1958). The example also illustrates the importance for causal analysis of the exact description chosen for the outcome.

One approach to formalizing this kind of causal inference would be to say that where we have conditional interdependence among factors, we do a naive form of "multiple regression analysis". In the car-crash case, the iced-over road predicts the occurrence of harm to the car driver. However, when the action of spraying the road is taken into consideration, it also predicts the outcome, rendering the iced-over road redundant. In terms of the analogy with multiple regression, the abnormally icy conditions are "partialled out" of our predictor equation since they no longer have any predictive power above and beyond that provided by entering the factor of spraying the road into the equation. And this procedure may be repeated stepwise by "entering" the goal of causing harm to the car driver into the equation, and so on, until no more predictive variables are found.

Multiple regression analysis is of course the covariational or correlational method used to analyse interdependent sets of conditions. By way of contrast, analysis of variance is appropriate to cases of conditional independence, as presupposed by the independent manipulation of variables in experiments. Indeed, analysis of variance can be regarded as a special case of multiple regression (Cohen and Cohen, 1975). However, two points should be noted.

The first is that the analyst's knowledge of conditional

dependencies is already given, for example by his knowledge of what is possible and not possible in the world. For example, we regard it as impossible for an antecedent event to be caused by a temporally subsequent event, and this constrains the kind of causal networks we consider in the first place (Spiegelhalter, 1986), whereas in experiments we constrain the direction of causation by experimental manipulation of conditions and by observing their effects on behaviour. In either case, knowledge of conditional dependencies comes from sources extraneous to the analysis of covariations, such as prior theories. It is of course true, however, that the pattern of covariations concerned may fit one causal model better than another, a fact exploited by causal path analysis.

The second point is that "mere conditions" which would be present when the effect is present and, were they absent, would result in the effect being absent, are not designated as causes in ordinary explanation, even though they satisfy the covariational definition of causality. Consider the explanatory status of the abnormally icy road conditions in the case of the road accident given above, and of the presence of oxygen in the case of any normal fire. Both are not felicitously cited as "causes" in ordinary speech.

This last point allows us to suggest why the covariational definition of causality presupposed by the "man the scientist" model, is *by its very nature* unsuited to describe ordinary causal explanation.

Particular and general explanation

The distinction between causes and conditions can be used to illustrate the reason why the covariational definition of causality is irrelevant to most commonsense concerns. Suppose that we have to explain someone's death. Typically, in a murder case we refer to the *abnormal condition* which caused the death (e.g. the act of poisoning, or shooting, or whatever), not to the necessary conditions for death consequent on the act of shooting or poisoning. Thus, after being shot, the victim may not have been able to breathe, resulting in death. However, lack of oxygen causes death in all cases, and has the status of a covering law. But appeal to this *general* covering law is uninformative as to why this particular man died how and when he did. The general law, although true of all deaths, by the same token only identifies a normal condition of death which cannot therefore qualify as a "cause" in everyday explanation. The lack of oxygen is thus a "mere condition" and only constitutes part of the causal chain connecting the "proximate cause" (the shooting) to the outcome.

As Hart and Honoré (1959) point out, the layman, the court and the historian ask *particular* questions about *specific* people, places, times and events, whereas the scientist asks *general* questions about the relationship between *types* of events, independent of specific persons, places and times. For this reason, "scientific" generalizations are irrelevant to the pragmatic, localized concerns of much everyday explanation.

The only exceptions to this rule would seem to be where our presuppositions about what the normal world is like have to change because the nature of the world under consideration is different. For example, let us take the covering law *oxygen causes fires*. Consider a manufacturing process where oxygen has to be excluded. If oxygen leaks in and causes a fire, we would ascribe the cause of the fire to the oxygen in this case, because its presence in the world of the spacecraft compartment is abnormal (cf. Hart and Honoré, 1959; Hesslow, 1983; also Mackie's discussion of "causal fields"). This example also illustrates the role of changing the context (i.e. the relevant comparison or reference class) in causal explanation.

Thus, in explaining an effect, we have to ask: "What does this difference make a difference to?" Differences between the target case and the statistical norm do not necessarily make a difference to the question in hand, thus rendering the analysis of covariation irrelevant. Thus, if we ask why a fire happened, we know that oxygen would qualify as a condition which has to be present for the effect to be present and which, if absent would result in the fire being absent. Yet, despite thus qualifying as a cause according to Kelley's (1967, p. 154) covariational definition of causality, it would not count as a cause in any ordinary explanation of why the fire occurred. An ordinary explanation would explain why *this particular* fire occurred as opposed to, for example, some other particular fire. Both fires depended on the presence of oxygen, so that cannot count as a differentiating explanation. However, one fire may have been caused by gas leakage and the other by arson. Ordinary explanation would focus on these particular distinguishing characteristics in accounting for each fire.

Differences between scientific and lay explanation

The problems outlined above indicate that the covariational

definition of causality as given by Kelley (1967) is inadequate as a model of ordinary explanation. Indeed, the covariational model is inadequate as a model of scientific induction in the sense intended by Mill. For example, Mill distinguished necessary from sufficient conditions. In addition, Mackie (1974) shows how the methods of agreement and difference may successfully be applied to localizing the cause in complex sets of conjunctive and disjunctive conditions. Ordinary people do distinguish necessary from sufficient conditions, and in this sense resemble the scientific model given by Mill. Nevertheless, two major problems may be found with the Millian notion of causality as a model of ordinary causal explanation, and these are discussed below.

The first problem is that ordinary people may make a causal explanation without having any regularity in mind to support it (Mackie, 1974). They simply know that in the counterfactual case the target event would not have happened, that Bob would not have got drunk if his football team had not lost. Counterfactual reasoning of this kind is essentially the application of Mill's method of difference in its simplest form (Mackie, 1974, p. 56). They do not mean to assert that everybody always gets drunk after their football team loses, or even that Bob always does so. As Mackie shows, application of Mill's experimental methods may eventually reveal a regularity that can be used to support the counterfactual. But, in the first instance of the application of the method of difference, the subject may not yet know the relevant regularity although he may assume that there is *some* relevant regularity.

The second problem is that although ordinary people may be aware of the set of individually necessary but only jointly sufficient conditions that constitute the cause "philosophically speaking", they omit to mention presupposed factors in explanations given in natural discourse. This amounts to saying that although they may be aware of regularities which support their causal explanation and which yield "invariant succession" of the effect given the fully specified cause, they omit them in ordinary explanation. This claim is expanded below.

Thus it is pertinent to note that the critique applied in this essay to the Millian definition of causality "philosophically speaking" as the conjunction of individually necessary conditions sufficient for the occurrence of the target event would also apply to other models of scientific explanation. For example, Hempel (1965) proposes that a scientific explanation should be constituted of a *covering law* indicating a generalization or regularity which, taken together with a set of *antecedent conditions*, allows the explanandum to be deduced. Using the examples familiar in this essay, we might state a covering law saying *All people buy things on their visit to all supermarkets,* which requires the antecedent conditions that someone be a person, be visiting a supermarket etc. for the act of shopping to occur. Thus, we would cite as our explanation the covering law and the individually necessary but jointly sufficient set of conditions. Here, the reason Sally bought something is that people always buy things in supermarkets, that Sally is a person, and she was in a supermarket.

Althouth these conditions may fairly be considered trivial, they meet the formal requirements of Hempel's schema of causal explanation (see Harré, this volume, for another criticism of Hempel's model). However, such explanations would only be offered in conversations where one would presuppose no knowledge of such a regularity in the mind of the inquirer, such as when accounting for such events to a child, a foreigner or an anthropologist.

In sum, commonsense explanations are offered to explain differences between some target event and some contrast case. This may be done by a primitive method of counterfactual reasoning, of "imagination and analogizing" as Mackie says, which is but a special case of Mill's method of difference. Explanations explain by distinguishing the factor(s) that *make the difference* between the target and the contrast case.

I now turn to a consideration of the relation between types of causal question, counterfactual contrast case, and causal explanation.

CONTRAST CASES AND THE EXPLANATION OF DIFFERENCES

Toward a conversational model of causal explanation

As Turnbull and Slugoski (this volume) suggest, the proper unit of analysis should be the question-answer *pair*. In this way, we would recognize the inherently *social* nature of explanation. Unlike "categorization" or "perception", "explanation" is a three-place predicate describing a social interaction. An explanation *of* something is given *by* someone *to* someone. Intrapsychic explanation is analogous to interpsychic explanation in that the same person takes the role of both explainer and explainee, of giver and of recipient. This isomorphism is marked in languages other than English, where *I wonder* is rendered as the reflexive *I ask myself*. Thus, in French one says *Je me demande*, and in German *Ich frage mich*.

Consequently, the "man the scientist" model might profitably be subsumed under the "man the conversationalist" model for two reasons. The first is that it hides the inherently social or dialectical nature of explanation. Explanations are given in dialogue, whether that dialogue be inner (cf. Vygotsky, 1962) or outer. The second is that the scientist typically only asks a certain type of question in his search for generalizations. This type of question may by no means be representative of those that get posed in ordinary thinking and discourse.

Altogether, the recognition that different types of question may be asked enables a unifying framework for psychological models of causal explanation to be proposed. It is to this issue that I now turn.

The explanation of differences: Commonalities between models of causal attribution

Causal explanations account for the differences between the target case and some comparison case to which it is contrasted (Hesslow, 1983; this volume). Diverse models of the process of causal attribution may thus differ not in terms of logic of the process they describe, but in terms of the contrasts that subjects are asked to explain.

Thus, the inductive logic model answers the question *Why did this event occur rather than not occur?* (Why *X* rather than *Not X?*), implicit in Kelley's (1967) definition of a cause as "That condition which is present when the effect is present and absent when the effect is absent". By way of contrast, the abnormal conditions focus model answers the question *Why did this event occur rather than the normal case?* (Why *X* rather than the default value for *X?*) Jones and Davis's (1965) analysis of the explanation of choices in terms of non-common effects answers the question *Why choose this action rather than that action?* (Why *X* rather than *Y?*) Attributions of responsibility may ask the question *Why did this actor do this rather than what he should have done?* (Fincham and Jaspars, 1980; Hart and Honoré, 1959). Schank and Abelson's (1977) model of explanation-based understanding answers questions like *Why did this plan fail rather than succeed?* (cf. Weiner, 1985b) and *Why did the actor value this goal rather than that goal?* (Carbonell, 1979; 1981; Wilensky, 1983).

This general formulation of the problem of causal attribution can be accommodated within the framework of the abnormal conditions focus model of causal attribution proposed by Hilton and Slugoski (1986) provided that non-statistical contrast cases may function as "norms" against which the target event is evaluated. What is common to all the above examples is that the explanations all answer a question as to why there is a *difference* between a target case and a counterfactual comparison case. As Hesslow (1983; this volume) argues, to understand a request for an explanation, we must know the implicit contrast that it presupposes. The rest is logic.

The automatic perception of contrasts

For any event, there is a plethora of necessary conditions that, if they had not occurred, would have prevented the target event from happening. Questions give or imply contrast cases which constrain the selection of causes from conditions. But what if no explicit question is asked?

First of all, when are *implicit* questions asked by nature? In other words, when are causal explanations spontaneously made? This is a much under-researched area. In a review, Weiner (1985b) suggests that two common cases are when something unexpected happens, and when a goal is not fulfilled. This analysis amounts to differences from two types of contrast cases, namely the statistically normal and the subjectively anticipated, and conforms with the general treatment given above.

The second question, given the perception of a difference worthy of explanation, is which necessary condition is focussed on in default of an explicit question focus? Kahneman and Tversky (1982) gave subjects descriptions of a fatal car accident, and asked their subjects to engage in counterfactual reasoning about the scenario by completing "if only" sentences which would "undo" one of the necessary conditions for the accident. Subjects showed a very strong tendency to focus on abnormal conditions for the accident ("he did not go home by his normal route") and to "undo" those ("If only he had gone home by his normal route, he would never have arrived at the traffic junction where the crash happened") than to focus on "normal" conditions ("he left his office at the regular time") and undo those ("If only he had not left his office at the regular time") in their sentence completions. Subjects thus naturally and spontaneously focussed on abnormal conditions in undoing the causes of the tragedy in their imagination.

Note that there is no logical reason why they should do this. Kahneman and Tversky suggest, on the analogy with ski-ing, that people seem to find it easier to make "downhill" changes from abnormal to normal conditions than "uphill" changes from normal to abnormal conditions. It would seem that, in some sense, the brain is "wired" to focus on abnormal features, a possibility that Kahneman and Miller (1986) explore in some detail.

Finally, the work of Shanks and Dickinson (see this volume) can be read as indicating how the brain may be "wired up" to initiate attributional processes when unexpected events occur. Learning about covariations only occurs when some effect is unpredicted, and the pattern of such learning in humans is predicted by models of animal learning about such contingencies. The work of Shanks and Dickinson thus raises the intriguing possibility that the human propensity for "selective attribution" is rooted in basic cognitive mechanisms that we share with other animals. Learning, like good explanations, may serve to render an event less surprising (cf. Gärdenfors, 1985). Indeed, it is worth pointing out in this context that much of what we learn is from what we are told.

In sum, what evidence that there is to hand suggests that explanatory processes are indeed initiated when deviations from some "norm" or expectancy occur, and that these explanations tend to focus on abnormal rather than normal conditions for the occurrence of the target event. The explanation of differences by reference to deviations would thus seem to be a natural process.

CONCLUSIONS

Summary
The aim of this chapter has been to understand the logic of ordinary causal explanation. First of all, experimental subjects followed the

predictions made by Mill's method of difference in properly designed experiments (Hilton and Jaspars, 1987; Jaspars, 1983), and were thus shown to be more rational than might have been concluded from earlier formulations and tests of Kelley's (1967) ANOVA model. Secondly, deviations from the predictions made by the inductive logic model nevertheless suggested that subjects were focussing on *abnormal conditions* as causes (Hilton and Slugoski, 1986). Although it was shown that the abnormal conditions focus model could be reformulated as an updated covariational model, several problems with the covariational definition of causality indicated that it was insufficient to describe all aspects of ordinary causal explanation. These shortcomings centred around problems in the generalization of causal claims. Consequently, Mackie's (1974) view, that commonsense causal explanation makes the weaker claim of "sufficiency in the circumstances", was adopted. Following Hesslow (1983; this volume) it was then shown that the logic of the explanatory process generalizes over the types of contrast cases used, but that the typical contrast cases presupposed by various models of the attribution process vary. Finally, a brief review of the relevant literature in cognitive psychology indicated that spontaneous attribution processes conform in important respects to the idealized models given above.

Theories and ordinary causal explanation
In conclusion, it is important to indicate two things that the present approach does *not* do. Firstly, it does not explain how hypotheses are formed in the first place. Rather, as both Mill and Mackie emphasize, the experimental methods provide means for checking and *ruling out* hypotheses; they are methods, as Mackie (1974) puts it, of "eliminative induction". Thus, if we were to check the hypothesis that "Inflation causes unemployment", we would examine different societies in the manner prescribed by Mill to test the validity of this proposition. In this context it is worth noting that it is no accident that Mill may be regarded as one of the founders of modern empirical social science (Passmore, 1967).

Secondly, it is worth pointing out that the selection of causes from conditions does not *deny* the existence of theoretical hypotheses, but rather *presupposes* them. Thus, if two economists share a common belief in the monetarist theory of economics, then a relevant explanation of high unemployment would not refer to their shared theory that "Inflation causes unemployment", but to an identification of particular policies adopted at a specific time that led to inflation and hence to unemployment in a particular country. It is only in giving explanations to a recipient who does not possess the requisite presuppositions, such as a student who does not know the theory, or another economist who does not believe the theory, that it may be relevant to state the theory itself. Only in such cases does one have to say "Inflation causes unemployment, that's why."

Thus the process of causal selection does not deny the fundamental role of theories in causal explanation. It simply explains why it is natural not to *mention* theories in causal explanations given in ordinary language. The process of causal selection thus accounts for the equivalence of the relationship between logic and conversation (cf. Grice, 1975), and that between logic and causal attribution. In causal explanation, as in other kinds of conversation, we only mention those entities which are relevant to our pragmatic purposes.

NOTE

1. Part of this chapter is the text of a paper read at the symposium *Attitudes and attributions: A symposium in honour of Jos Jaspars*, convened at the Annual Conference of the British Psychological Society, Sheffield, 3–5 April 1986. I would like to thank Edward E. Jones, Harold Kelley, David Shanks, Ben Slugoski and Tom Trabasso for their helpful comments on an earlier version of this chapter.

REFERENCES

Ajzen, I. and Fishbein, M. (1975). "A Bayesian analysis of attribution processes". *Psychological Bulletin, 82*, 261–77.

Alloy, L.B. and Tabachnik, N. (1984). "Assessment of covariation by humans and animals: The joint influence of prior expectations and current situational information". *Psychological Review, 91*, 112–49.

Carbonell, J. (1979). *Subjective Understanding: Computer Models of Belief Systems*. Yale University Department of Computer Science Research Report No. 150.

Carbonell, J. (1981). "POLITICS". In R.C. Schank and C.K. Riesbeck (Eds), *Inside Computer Understanding: Five Programs Plus Miniatures*. Hillsdale, N.J.: Lawrence Erlbaum.

Chatlosh, D.L., Neunaber, D.J. and Wasserman, E.A. (1985). "Response-outcome contingency: Behavioral and judgmental effects of appetitive and aversive outcomes with college students". *Learning and Motivation, 16,* 1–34.

Cohen, J. and Cohen, P. (1975). *Applied Multiple Regression/Correlation for the Behavioral Sciences.* Hillsdale, N.J.: Lawrence Erlbaum.

Einhorn, H.J. and Hogarth, R.M. (1986). "Judging probable cause." *Psychological Bulletin, 99,* 1–19.

Fincham, F.D. and Jaspars, J.M.F. (1980). "Attribution of responsibility: From man-the-scientist to man as lawyer". In L. Berkowitz (Ed.), *Advances in Experimental Social Psychology, 13,* (pp. 81–38). New York: Academic Press.

Gärdenfors, P. (1985). "The dynamics of belief, conditional sentences and explanations". In J. Allwood and E. Hjelmquist (Eds). *Foregrounding Background,* (pp. 107–16). Lund: Doxa.

Grice, H.P. (1975). "Logic and conversation". In P. Cole and J.L. Morgan (Eds), *Syntax and Semantics 3: Speech Acts.* New York: Academic Press.

Hart, H.L.A. and Honoré, A.M. (1959). *Causation in the Law.* Oxford: Clarendon Press.

Hart, H.L.A. and Honoré, T. (1985). *Causation in the Law.* 2nd ed Oxford: Clarendon Press.

Heider, F. (1958). *The Psychology of Interpersonal Relations.* New York: Wiley.

Hempel, C.G. (1965). "Aspects of scientific explanation". In C.G. Hempel, *Aspects of Scientific Explanation and Other Essays in the Philosophy of Science.* New York: The Free Press.

Hesslow, G. (1983). "Explaining differences and weighting causes." *Theoria, 49,* 87–111.

Hewstone, M.R.C. and Jaspars, J.M.F. (1983). "A re-examination of the roles of consensus, distinctiveness, consistency: Kelley's cube revisited". *British Journal of Social Psychology, 22,* 41–50.

Hilton, D.J. and Jaspars, J.M.F. (1987). "The explanation of occurrences and non-occurrences: A test of the inductive logic model of causal attribution". *British Journal of Social Psychology, 26,* 189–201.

Hilton, D.J. and Slugoski, B.R. (1986). "Knowledge-based causal attribution: The abnormal conditions focus model." *Psychological Review, 93,* 75–88.

Jaspars, J.M.F. (1983). "The process of attribution in common-sense. In M.R.C. Hewstone (Ed.), *Attribution Theory: Social and Functional Extensions.* Oxford: Basil Blackwell.

Jaspars, J.M.F. (in press). "Mental models of causal reasoning". D. Bar-Tal and A. Kruglanski (Eds), *The Social Psychology of Knowledge.* Cambridge: Cambridge University Press, in press.

Jaspars, J.M.F., Hewstone, M.R.C. and Fincham, F.D. (1983). "Attribution theory and research: The state of the art." In J.M.F. Jaspars, F.D. Finchman and M.R.C. Hewstone (Eds), *Attribution Theory: Conceptual, Developmental and Social Dimensions.* London: Academic Press.

Jones, E.E. and Davis, K.E. (1965). "From acts to dispositions: The attribution process in person perception". In L. Berkowitz (Ed.), *Advances in Experimental Social Psychology,* (Vol. II, pp. 219–66). New York, Academic Press.

Jones, E.E. and McGillis, D. (1976). "Correspondent inferences and the attribution cube: A comparative reappraisal". In J.H. Harvey, W.J. Ickes and R.F. Kidd (Eds) *New Directions in Attribution Research, Vol. I.,* (pp. 389–420). Hillsdale, N.J.: Lawrence Erlbaum.

Jones, E.E. and Nisbett, R.E. (1972). "The actor and the observer: Divergent perspectives of the causes of behaviour". In E.E. Jones, D.E. Kanouse, H.H. Kelley, R.E. Nisbett, S. Valins and B. Weiner (Eds), *Attribution: Perceiving the Causes of Behavior.* Morristown, N.J.: General Learning Press.

Kahneman, D.A. and Miller, D.T. (1986). "Norm theory: Comparing reality to its alternatives". *Psychological Review, 93,* 136–53.

Kahneman, D.A. and Tversky, A. (1982). "The simulation heuristic." In D. Kahneman, P. Slovic and A. Tversky (Eds), *Judgment under Uncertainty: Heuristics and Biases.* Cambridge: Cambridge University Press.

Kelley, H.H. (1967). "Attribution in social psychology". *Nebraska Symposium on Motivation. 15,* 192–238.

Kelley, H.H. (1972). "Causal schemata and the attribution process". In E.E. Jones, D.E. Kanouse, H.H. Kelley, R.E. Nisbett, S. Valins and B. Weiner (Eds), *Attribution: Perceiving the Causes of Behavior.* Morristown, N.H.: General Learning Process.

Kelley, H.H. (1973). "The process of causal attribution". *American Psychologist, 28,* 103–28.

Kelley, H.H. (1983). "Perceived causal structures". In J.M.F. Jaspars, F.D. Fincham and M.R.C. Hewstone (Eds), *Attribution Theory and Research: Conceptual, Developmental and Social Dimensions.* London: Academic Press.

Lehnert, W.G. (1978). *The Process of Question-answering.* Hillsdale, N.J.: Lawrence Erlbaum.

Levinson, S.C. (1983). *Pragmatics.* Cambridge: Cambridge University Press.

Mackie, J.L. (1974). *The Cement of the Universe.* London: Oxford University Press.

McArthur, L.A. (1972). "The how and what of why: Some determinants and consequences of causal attributions". *Journal of Personality and Social Psychology, 22*: 171–93.

Mill, J.S. (1872/1973). "System of logic" (8th edn). In J.M. Robson (Ed.), *Collected Works of John Stuart Mill* (Vols. VII and VIII). Toronto: University of Toronto Press. (Original work published 1872).

Nisbett, R.E. and Ross, L. (1980). *Human Inference: Strategies and Shortcomings of Social Judgment*. Englewood Cliffs, N.J.: Prentice Hall.

Orvis, B.R., Cunningham, J.D. and Kelley, H.H. (1975). "A closer examination of causal inference: The role of consensus, distinctiveness and consistency information." *Journal of Personality and Social Psychology, 32*, 605–16.

Passmore, J.W.T. (1967). *A Hundred Years of Philosophy*. Harmondsworth, Middlesex: Penguin.

Pruitt, D.G. and Insko, C.A. (1980). "Extension of the Kelley attribution model: The role of comparison-object consensus target-object consensus, distinctiveness and consistency." *Journal of Personality and Social Psychology, 39*, 39–58.

Rips, L.J. and Marcus, S.L. (1977). "Supposition and the analysis of conditional sentences". In M.A. Just and P.A. Carpenter (Eds), *Cognitive Processes in Comprehension*. Hillsdale, N.J.: Lawrence Erlbaum.

Ross, L. (1977). "The intuitive psychologist and his shortcomings: Distortions in the attribution process". In L. Berkowitz (Ed.), *Advances in Experimental Social Psychology, 14*, 173–220.

Schank, R.C. and Abelson, R.P. (1977). *Scripts, Plans, Goals and Understanding: An Enquiry into Human Knowledge Structures*. Hillsdale, N.J.: Lawrence Erlbaum.

Schustack, M.W. and Sternberg, R.J. (1981). "Evaluation of evidence in causal inference". *Journal of Experimental Psychology (General), 110*, 101–120.

Spiegelhalter, D.J. (1986). "Probabilistic reasoning in predictive expert systems". In L.N. Kanal and J. Lemmer (Eds), *Uncertainty in Artificial Intelligence*. Amsterdam: North-Holland.

Staudenmayer, H. (1975). "Understanding reasoning with meaningful propositions". In R.J. Falmagne (Ed.), *Reasoning: Representation and Process*. Hillsdale, N.J.: Lawrence Erlbaum.

Trabasso, T. and van den Broek, P. (1985). "Causal thinking and story comprehension". *Journal of Memory and Language, 24*, 612–30.

Trabasso, T., Secco, T and van den Broek, P. (1984). "Causal cohesion and story coherence". In H. Mandl, N.L. Stein and T. Trabasso (Eds), *Learning and the Comprehension of Discourse*. Hillsdale, N.J.: Lawrence Erlbaum.

Trabasso, T. and Sperry, L.L. (1985). "The causal basis for deciding importance of story events". *Journal of Memory and Language, 24,* 595–611.

Vygotsky, L.S. (1962). *Thought and Language.* Cambridge, Mass.: MIT Press.

Wasserman, E.A., Chatlosh, D.L. and Neunaber, D.J. (1983). "Perception of causal relations in humans: Factors affecting judgments of response-outcome contingencies under free-operant procedures". *Learning and Motivation, 14,* 406–32.

Weiner, B. (1985a). "An attributional theory of achievement motivation and emotion". *Psychological Review, 92,* 548–83.

Weiner, B. (1985b). "Spontaneous causal thinking". *Psychological Bulletin, 97,* 74–84.

Wilensky, R. (1983). *Planning and Understanding: A Computational Approach to Human Reasoning.* Reading, Mass.: Addison-Wesley.

4 Conversational and Linguistic Processes in Causal Attribution*

William Turnbull and Ben R. Slugoski

INTRODUCTION

Two of the most basic assumptions of the ANOVA model of attribution (Kelley, 1967, 1972) are (1) that the naive psychologist explains behavioural events and (2) that this is accomplished by identifying an event's cause—"that condition which is present when the effect is present and absent when the effect is absent" (Kelley, 1967, p. 154). In the present chapter we challenge these assumptions. We argue that everyday explanation involves the resolution of puzzles rather than the explanation of behavioural events. The underlying form of puzzle resolution is that of an answer to a question. Accordingly, the basic unit of analysis of everyday explanation is the question-answer pair. Further, since questions and answers typically occur in conversations, conversational structure and process strongly influence the nature of everyday explanation. An important implication of the conversational nature of everyday explanation is that the appropriate conception of causality for attribution theory is that of an abnormal condition (Hart and Honoré, 1959; Mackie, 1974) rather than constant conjunction (see Kelley's quote above). We outline a conversationally-based model of attribution and present some relevant data.

PUZZLE RESOLUTION: ANSWERS TO QUESTIONS

Clearly, people do not attempt to explain every behavioural event

* Some of the research discussed in this chapter was conducted while the second author was in receipt of a doctoral fellowship from the Social Sciences and Humanities Research Council of Canada.

that confronts them. A conscious and deliberate attempt at explanation occurs only when there is a failure to understand and when understanding is of some importance (Clary and Tesser, 1983; Monson, Keel, Stephens and Genung, 1982; Pyszczynski and Greenberg, 1981; Wong and Weiner, 1981). Failures to understand occur when behaviour is puzzling or surprising. Consider an example. Imagine a perceiver who observes an event encoded as "Mary is eating steak." If the perceiver believes that Mary is a vegetarian, or that Mary knows the steak is poisoned, or that Mary has just finished dessert, the perceiver may not understand Mary's behaviour. In general, a failure to understand behaviour occurs when a perceiver's categorization of the behaviour of a particular person(s) towards a particular entity (entities) under a set(s) of particular circumstances contrasts with what the perceiver would have expected of that person(s) towards that entity (entities) under those circumstances. Perceivers are puzzled by such contrasts and need an explanation. Satisfactory explanations resolve puzzles, thereby eliminating contrasts. In sum, events do not require explanation. Rather, contrasts between observed behaviour and what would have been considered more normal need to be resolved (Kahneman and Miller, 1986; Turnbull, 1986).

In spite of the wide variety of types of puzzles and resolutions (Turnbull, 1986), every explanation/resolution is an answer to a "why" question (Braithwaite, 1959). It should be stressed that puzzles are not necessarily presented explicitly as "why" questions, nor even as any kind of surface question, and an explanation may be given in the absence of a surface question. Indeed, the ways in which "why" questions are encoded and decoded is a challenging issue for attribution theory. But our claim is not a claim about surface structure. It is a claim about deep structure; namely, that the deep structure of everyday explanation is that of an answer to a "why" question.

Every question sets restrictions on the felicitous responses to it, and every felicitous answer reflects the question to which it is addressed (Austin, 1962; Searle, 1969). As a consequence, answers cannot properly be analyzed alone. An answer can be analyzed only with respect to the question that gave rise to it. What this entails for a model of attribution is that the proper unit of analysis is the question-answer pair, or, to put it another way, the puzzle-resolution pair.

The ways in which questions constrain answers and the importance of this for attribution theory can be illustrated by the following example. The head of the British Labour Party is reported to have raised the issue of why Mrs. Thatcher is "out to smash the miners" (*Daily Mirror,* 18 May, 1984, p. 2). Mrs. Thatcher's failure to act was described also on the BBC news as "not wanting to take sides in the dispute". The related "why" questions, "Why is Mrs. Thatcher out to smash the unions?" and "Why does Mrs. Thatcher not want to take sides in the dispute?", suggest very different explanations, in part due to the presuppositions inherent in each. Although both questions presuppose that Mrs. Thatcher's behaviour was intentional, the questions differ with respect to the presupposed goals, character and values of Mrs. Thatcher. In large measure, the presuppositions of a question constrain what counts as a felicitous answer. Similarly, a perceiver may favour a particular explanation of an individual's action and, as a result, pose a question in a way which prompts the favoured explanation. That is, answers constrain questions. This is illustrated in our example, in that it is not surprising that a member of the Labour Party would describe Mrs. Thatcher's action as "out to smash the miners" rather than as "not wanting to take sides in the dispute."

Another important characteristic of the example is that the quoted comments are drawn from conversational exchanges. The conversational nature of the example is not unusual. In everyday life, puzzles are posed and resolutions suggested most typically in conversations or their written equivalents. In these contexts, at least, the structure of conversation exerts a strong influence on the nature of explanation. While we have much more to say about conversational structure and attribution later in the chapter, we note here that a felicitous answer consists of the provision of information unknown to the questioner that can resolve the questioner's puzzle. Thus, the knowledge states of questioner and answerer, including their state of mutual knowledge (Lewis, 1969), are central to the explanation process.

A conversationally-based model of everyday explanation suggests an alternative conception of causality to that proposed by Kelley (see quote on page 66). The constant conjunction notion of causality is inappropriate for attribution theory because what people take for granted and what they find informative influence whether or not a covarying factor is considered a cause. Consider the example of a house that has caught fire. Most observers would assume that both oxygen and flammable material were present. Even though these factors covary reliably with burning houses and are necessary but not sufficient causes of fire, they are unlikely to be identified as the cause of a fire. On the other hand, an arsonist who has set fire to the house, or decayed insulation on an electrical wire, might well be identified as the cause of the fire. In other words, the covarying factor that is not taken for granted, which is unusual or abnormal in some way, is typically identified as the cause. Those causal factors that are taken for granted have been referred to as "mere conditions" while the unusual factor, *the* cause, has been referred to as the "abnormal condition" (Hart and Honoré, 1959). Thus, an abnormal condition conception of causality seems to be the appropriate conception for everyday explanation.

The abnormal condition conception of causality fits well into a conversationally-based attribution theory. "Mere conditions" correspond to assumptions that questioner and answerer mutually take for granted, while the abnormal condition corresponds to information the answerer believes the questioner does not know and which, when known, will resolve the questioner's puzzle. For example, if a questioner knows that a fire started in a laboratory believed to be free of oxygen, being told that oxygen was present will constitute a satisfactory explanation because oxygen *in those circumstances* constitutes an abnormal condition that could have led to a fire. In general, when asked why an event occurred, answerers identify as the cause that factor or set of factors from the total causal field that best complements the questioner's presupposed knowledge (see Mackie, 1974).

CONVERSATIONAL PROCESSES IN CAUSAL ATTRIBUTION

We have claimed that everyday explanation is best conceived of as a form of puzzle-resolution and hence that the proper unit of analysis of everyday explanation is the question-answer pair. Since questions and answers have their canonical forms in conversations or their written equivalents (e.g. novels, editorials) it follows that an understanding of conversational structure should provide important clues about the requisite form of explanations. Even J.S.

Mill, so frequently cited as having provided the logical foundation for the ANOVA model, appears to have recognized the importance of conversational factors in causal attribution. However, in attributing the selection of the cause from the range of conditions necessary for the occurrence of an event to "the purpose of our immediate discourse", Mill (1872/1973) discerned only capriciousness in such causal selection. Recent research in discourse analysis undertaken in philosophy (Austin, 1962; Searle, 1969; Grice, 1975), cognitive science (Schank, 1977; Winograd, 1977), and linguistics (Brown and Yule, 1983; Levinson, 1983) suggests, on the contrary, that the conditions under which a single event is spoken of as a cause are indeed orderly and rule-governed. In this section we focus on one strand of this work, that of conversational pragmatics grounded in ordinary language philosophy.

A COGNITIVE CONCEPTION OF CONVERSATION

People converse in order to attain goals. The goals of speaker and hearer can be attained only if conversation is a cooperative, reflexive process (Winograd, 1977; Clark, 1985). In order for a speaker to get across an intended message to a hearer by making an utterance (or set of utterances), the speaker must tailor utterances to that specific hearer in that specific context. That is, when designing utterances for the hearer, the speaker must consider the conversation from the hearer's point of view. In a similar vein, in order for the hearer to comprehend the speaker's message, the hearer must construct an interpretation of the speaker's utterances on the assumption that the speaker tailored those utterances for that specific hearer in that context. That is, when constructing an interpretation of an utterance(s), the hearer must consider the conversation from the speaker's point of view.

From a cognitive perspective, designing/interpreting an utterance "from the other's point of view" implies that speakers and hearers process utterances on the basis of mental models of the knowledge states of the other. These mental models are themselves reflexive—the speaker's model of the hearer includes, at least, assumptions about the hearer's model of the speaker and the hearer's model of the speaker's model of the hearer. That is, the mental models contain assumptions about what is *mutally known* (Lewis, 1969; Levinson, 1983).

We can identify two general classes of content in the mental models of speakers and hearers. Mental models must contain assumptions about knowledge of the general structure of conversation, such as general principles of communication, rules of discourse and rules of politeness. But knowledge of general principles is insufficient for producing/comprehending specific conversations. Additionally, mental models must contain assumptions about knowledge of the *specific* conversation at hand, such as knowledge of the personal characteristics of speaker and hearer, of their relationship and past experiences; and knowledge of the specific events and objects under discussion and of the physical, social and cultural context. Speakers and hearers must process these different types of content of mental models to create and interpret utterances. Conversational processes operate at different levels, from high-level processes that are engaged to keep utterances within the limits of appropriate general conversational structure, down through intermediate processing levels (e.g. processes for establishing reference to particular objects), to the lowest level of choosing/interpreting the meaning of the specific words and phrases in an utterance. In the following three sections of the chapter we examine the influence of both higher and lower-level conversational processes on the explanation process.

HIGHER-LEVEL CONVERSATIONAL PROCESSES AND EXPLANATION

The philosopher Grice (1975) provides the most general set of guidelines for determining the acceptability of utterances in conversation. According to Grice's Cooperative Principle, conversational participants try to cooperate with each other so as to maximize their joint outcomes. To do this, speakers must attempt to follow certain conversational conventions or maxims, including fashioning their utterances so that they are clear (maxim of manner), informative (maxim of quantity), truthful (maxim of quality), and relevant (maxim of relation). (For more rigorous formulations of Grice's maxims, see Kempson, 1975; Gazdar, 1979). Hearers, for their part, are obliged to assume that speakers are following these maxims and to intepret the conversation as if they were. As a consequence, in order to maintain the assumption that the speaker is being cooperative and that the maxims are being preserved, hearers must occasionally interpret an utterance non-literally. Consider an example:

A. What time is it?
B. Well, the postman's already been.

(Brown and Levinson, 1978: p. 63).

Only if A assumes that B has intentionally violated the maxim of relation can A infer that B is providing an answer to the question, and that the conveyed or intentional meaning ("implicature") is, for example, that it is past 9.00 am.

Of the four components of the Cooperative Principle, the maxim of quantity plays a particularly significant role in determining the form of conversationally conveyed explanations. The constraint on questioners not to ask for information of which they are already aware (Searle, 1969), plus the Gricean demand that speakers provide only informative contributions, places restrictions on felicitous explanations. Cooperative speakers should, in response to a request for an explanation for some event, provide information that will "fill the gap" in the inquirer's knowledge state. In general, this is accomplished by singling out as cause the factor or set of factors about which the inquirer is ignorant.

The influences of conversational principles on everyday explanation are not incorporated into traditional attribution theory. This can be seen most clearly in a central distinction made in such theories—that between personal and situational causality. Ever since Heider (1958) proposed that lay causal inference proceeds according to a form of "psychological factor analysis", it has been assumed that attributions of causality to either personal or situational factors could be determined purely in terms of the original information input and abstract principles of logical induction (cf. Jones and Davis, 1965; Kelley, 1967, 1972; Nisbett and Ross, 1980; Weiner, 1982). By contrast, the present pragmatic-purposive analysis suggests that whether a personal or situational factor is identified as causally relevant should depend on the answerer's beliefs about the knowledge being presupposed by the inquirer. Two experiments were conducted in order to evaluate this proposition empirically.

Slugoski (1983) had subjects read a detailed case history of a youth who had committed a crime. The case history included personality information about the youth, and situational information about the circumstances in which the crime occurred. Subjects were then led to believe that they would be conversing with a partner who (a) knew nothing at all about the case; (b) knew only about the youth, or (c) knew only about the situational background. Subjects then provided explanations for the crime in response to a "why" question from their partner. These explanations were scored by raters, blind to the experimental hypothesis, to determine the number of propositions containing personal and situational information.

As would be expected from the conversational convention of informativeness, subjects who believed their partner to have knowledge about the person conveyed relatively more situational information than did subjects in the no information or situational information conditions. There was a marginally significant difference in the predicted direction between explanations provided by the subjects in the no information and situational information conditions. These different explanations presumably reflect different puzzles subjects believed they were resolving, based on their beliefs about mutual knowledge. In the person information condition, it is likely that subjects recognized their partner's puzzle as "Given that type of person, why that crime?" whereas in the situational information condition the puzzle was "Given that type of situation, why that crime?" The results of the study provide firm support for the idea that speakers tailor the content of their explanations to suit the presupposed knowledge of the inquirer.

In a second experiment, Slugoski, Lalljee and Lamb (1985) employed a within-subjects design to test the proposition that people will *change* the explanation they give to inquirers understood to be sharing *different* types of knowledge about the same target event. This experiment was similar to the previous one except that subjects participated in two conversations rather than one. Subjects first memorized an information sheet consisting of personality and situational information about a student who had received a very high grade in a national examination. The personality information described the student as intelligent and industrious, while the situational information extolled the merits of the particular school the student had been attending. These two sources of information had been pre-tested so that, taken together in the absence of any manipulation of mutual knowledge, they would produce a balanced person and situation attribution for the student's success.

Subjects were given a profile of their prospective partner, in which he was described as being familiar either with the student's dispositional qualities or with the merits of the school. Subjects then provided explanations for the student's success. About half an hour after the first conversation subjects engaged in a second conversation, this time after having received the complementary profile of their prospective partner. Again they were asked for and provided an explanation for the student's success. All explanations were tape-recorded and transcribed for subsequent scoring of the degree to which they incorporated personality or situational factors as presented in the original information sheet.

Despite some individual differences in conversational rule-following, a significant tendency was found in both the first and second conversations for subjects to provide as an explanation to their partner information that complemented what he already knew. More importantly, subjects revealed a strong tendency to *change* their explanations across the conversations; they provided relatively more situationally oriented explanations when they believed their partner knew about the student rather than about the school. Again, we suggest that these different explanations correspond to different deep structure questions or puzzles; namely, in the former instance, "Given that type of student, what was responsible for the high grade?", and in the latter instance, "Given that type of school, what was responsible for the high grade?". Although the target event remains the same, different explanations are appropriate to each case.

The results of these studies demonstrate that speakers act cooperatively by conveying explanations that are informative from the inquirer's point of view. As indicated earlier, this conception of explanation fits well with the analysis of causal inference developed by Mackie (1974; see also Hastie, 1983). Recall that in the second study stimulus material had been pretested to produce a balanced person and situation attribution. Presumably, then, explanation-givers believed that *both* person and situational factors were part of the causal field—the background of insufficient but necessary factors that led to the student obtaining a very high grade on the examination. The factors elevated from the causal field to the status of cause were, as Mackie holds, contingent upon "some conversational or other purpose of the speaker" (p. 36); in particular, the Gricean maxim of quantity.

LOWER-LEVEL CONVERSATIONAL PROCESSES AND EXPLANATION

To this point we have discussed the influence of certain high-level conversational processes on explanation-giving. Conversation also engages lower-level processes; for example, processes to decide on which specific words to utter or on how to interpret specific words. As an illustration of lower-level processes, we consider the influence on puzzle-resolution of the particular verbs employed in behavioural event descriptions.

In a well-known test of the ANOVA model, McArthur (1972) presented subjects with sentences of the form "John laughed at the comedian' along with consensus, distinctiveness and consistency information. Ratings of the causes of behaviour described in the critical sentences offered considerable support for the ANOVA model. However, there was a very strong effect of the category of the verb employed in the event descriptions. When presented without consensus, distinctiveness and consistency information, events encoded by verbs of action and accomplishment were rated as being caused mainly by the person, whereas events encoded by verbs of emotion or opinion were rated as being caused mainly by the stimulus. Following Gilson and Abelson (1965), McArthur proposed that verbs may contain expectancies that subjects use to make causal ascriptions.

The possibility that verbs may contain an implicit causal structure has been examined directly by Garvey and her colleagues (Garvey and Caramazza, 1974; Garvey, Caramazza and Yates, 1976; Caramazza, Grober, Garvey and Yates, 1977). These researchers were interested in the role of verbs in the assignment of referents to ambiguous pronoun antecedents. To study the process of disambiguation, they presented subjects with sentence fragments of the form "NP1 Verb NP2 because Pronoun . . ." (e.g. "George telephoned Harry because he . . ."). Subjects were asked to complete each fragment by supplying a motive for the action or attitude presented. The sentence fragments contained no surface cues, such as differential marking for sex, that would allow disambiguation (as could occur, for example, with the fragment "George telephoned Susie because he . . ."). Completions were scored in terms of whether they indicated that the pronoun referred to the first or second noun phrase (i.e. as NP1 or NP2 completions).

Results from several studies showed a highly significant and consistent pattern. Although there was no strong tendency for some verbs, certain verbs tended to provide NP1 assignment and others NP2 assignment. For example, the verb *telephone* was found to be strongly NP1 (as in "George telephoned Harry because he wanted information about the exam") while *scold* was strongly NP2 (as in "Mary scolded Susie because she was shoplifting"). Garvey *et al.* concluded that to disambiguate pronoun antecedents, subjects used a semantic property of the verb; namely, an implicit causality feature.

Using a somewhat different methodology, Brown and Fish (1983) reached similar conclusions about the implicit causal structure of verbs. Subjects in their studies were presented with sentences of the form "Ted likes Paul" and were asked to rate the extent to which this event was caused by Ted (i.e. Ted is the kind of person that likes people), by Paul (i.e. Paul is the kind of person that people like) or by some other factor. The results indicated that for events encoded by verbs in Agent-Patient constructions (e.g. *criticize*) greater causal weighting was assigned to the Agent, while for events encoded by verbs in Stimulus-Experiencer (e.g. *attract*) or Experiencer-Stimulus (e.g. *admire*) constructions, greater causal weighting was assigned to the Stimulus. These and other results (for example, adjectives derived from action verbs are attributed to the agent while those derived from state verbs are attributed to the stimulus—consider *critical* and *attractive* or *admirable*, respectively) led Brown and Fish to suggest that verbs encode causal ascription, that "a theory of psychological causality is implicit in natural language itself" (p. 238).

Taken together, the results of studies by different researchers employing very different methodologies all lead to a similar conclusion; namely, that the verbs of English contain an implicit causal structure and that observers can "read off" the causal locus of an event from the verb employed in that event's description. Thus, at a micro-structural level of conversation there exists a mechanism that allows observers to explain events by identifying, from the verb used in the event description, whether the person or stimulus was the primary causal factor. This explanation process can occur without recourse to either macro-structural properties of conversation or to explicitly presented patterns of consensus, distinctiveness and consistency information.

Earlier in the chapter we stressed the importance of the way an event is categorized for how it is explained. The studies on implicit causality reinforce this point. Although the process by which behavioural events are categorized, a process at the micro level of conversational structure, is generally ignored by attribution theorists (but see Weary, Rich, Harvey and Ickes, 1980), no less an authority than Heider (1958) stressed the importance of "immediate causal perception." A study of event categorization is a necessary part of a theory of attribution (see also Abraham, this volume).

THE INTERACTION OF DIFFERENT LEVELS OF CONVERSATIONAL PROCESSES ON EXPLANATION

Our discussion of the influence of the different levels of conversational process on explanation should not be interpreted as implying that these levels operate independently. Conversationally-based explanation-giving is a *heterarchical* process, one in which higher levels of structure and process affect lower levels, and vice-versa. Some research we conducted in collaboration with D. Hilton can be used to illustrate this point.

Recall that Garvey *et al.* (1974) and Brown and Fish (1983) argued for an implicit marking of causality in verbs. It was our contention that under normal circumstances causality is only weakly marked by verbs and that nouns are more influential in the determination of causality. Following Gentner (1981), we argued that because verbs are relational terms, they have a greater adjustability than nouns; that is, verbs vary more in meaning under paraphrase, they are harder to remember and they have a greater breadth of meaning than nouns (see also Wattenmaker, Nakamura and Medin, this volume). Of particular importance to us is Gentner's (1981) finding that the meaning of a verb in a sentence can be altered significantly by the noun(s) with which it occurs. If verb meaning can be altered significantly in this way, it seems likely that so too can the implicit causal structure of an event description.

To test this hypothesis, seventy-six subjects completed, for each of eight verbs (four NP1 and NP2 according to Garvey *et al.*, 1971), one of three possible sentence fragments: Control—"Proper Name—Verb—Proper Name—because he/she . . ."; Experimental —"Person Category—Verb—Proper Name—because he/she . . ."; and Reverse Experimental—"Proper Name—Verb—Person Category—because he/she. . .". For the specific example of the verb *hit*, the corresponding sentence fragments were: Control— "Ted hit John because he . . ."; Experimental—"The headmaster hit John because he . . ."; and Reverse Experimental—"John hit the headmaster because he . . .". For this verb, 68% of subjects gave NP1 completions to the Control fragment, 20% gave NP1 completions to the Experimental fragment and 83% gave NP1 completions to the Reverse Experimental fragment. In other words, the particular nouns and their order significantly influenced causal ascription. Reliable and statistically significant differences in pronoun assignment were obtained for all eight verbs as a function of the order and type of person category noun presented in the sentence fragments.

Our explanation for these results is based on the contention that subjects constructed scenarios or mental models of the situation described in the sentence fragments (c.f. Bransford, Barclay and Franks, 1972; Bransford and Johnson, 1973), and that the meaning of the noun in these scenarios remained relatively invariant across sentences for any one verb, whereas the verb often underwent a change in meaning. For example, *hit* suggests *punish* in "The headmaster hit John" and *hit* suggests *strike* in "John hit the headmaster". This explanation of the pattern of results for *hit* receives support from Garvey *et al.* (1976) who report evidence that *hit* and *strike* are strongly NP1 but *punish* is strongly NP2.

The results of our study bear importantly on *everyday* explanation-giving. Note that the stimuli used in our study are ecologically more representative that those of either Garvey *et al.* (1974) or Brown and Fish (1983). In everyday life, people typically know much more than just the names of persons involved in behavioural events. This real world knowledge influences the scenarios perceivers construct. As a consequence, the model of a situation constructed in a conversation will influence lower-level information that can, in turn, influence the process and products of explanation.

CONVERSATIONAL CONSTRAINTS IN TRADITIONAL ATTRIBUTION TASKS

In developing the puzzle-resolution approach to attribution we have relied heavily upon the notions of logical presupposition and focus. The former refers to the background context or "causal field" (Mackie, 1974) of insufficient but necessary factors for the occurrence of an event that is taken for granted by participants, while the latter refers to information that is not taken for granted and that is therefore in some sense "abnormal". So far we have treated the partition between focussed and presupposed information as relatively unproblematic, for example by controlling it directly in the experiments conducted by Slugoski (1983) and Slugoski, Lalljee and Lamb (1985). In other contexts, however, the identification of the contents of presupposed background, and hence what might count as a resolution of the inquirer's puzzle, is not so straightforward. Because presupposed background changes across contexts, the processes and variables that determine what is presupposed (ground) and what is new (figure) need to be identified.

Turnbull (1986) has discussed some of the ways in which figure and ground can be manipulated through variations in the linguistic form in which puzzles are presented. Some information in a sentence/utterance is presented as given, or ground, and some as new, or figure (Haviland and Clark, 1974). New information may be signalled by focal stress, for example "Why did JOHN kiss Mary?" verus "Why did John kiss MARY?" Sentences also have a focus, what a speaker is talking about, and a comment, what the speaker has to say about the focus. Unless specifically marked to the contrary, the subject of a sentence is assumed to be its focus (Clark and Haviland, 1977; Pryor and Kriss, 1977). Thus, "Why did Becker beat Curren at Wimbledon?" presents a different puzzle than "Why did Curren lose to Becker at Wimbledon?" even though both sentences encode the same event. Puzzles can be signalled by negation and, more generally, by markedness. The negation in "Why is Andrea Jaeger not playing tournament tennis?" identifies the norm as "Andrea Jaeger is/should be playing tournament tennis", and in "Why is John unhappy?" the morpheme "un" identifies the norm as "John is/should be happy."

These linguistic means for signalling what is new and what is presupposed background are not merely conventional. They reflect also the cooperative nature of puzzle-resolution exchanges. Hearers identify which puzzle is to be resolved on the basis of the assumption that speakers are acting cooperatively (c.f. Clark and Haviland, 1977; Brown and Yule, 1983). In typical attribution experiments, however, attempts are made to eliminate for the sake of experimental control the cooperative aspect of puzzle-resolution exchanges, including the contextual factors necessary for determining what is presupposed background. In spite of this, as demonstrated by Adler (1984), such attempts generally result in only limited success because it is not possible for subjects to suspend completely the assumption of speaker (in this case, the experimenter) cooperativeness.

Failure to appreciate the conversational pull towards assuming experimenter cooperativeness in attribution experiments can result in difficulties in interpretation. For example, when the behaviours presented to subjects (e.g. sentences of the form "John laughed at the comedian") are comprehensible and, therefore, in no need of explanation, subjects may feel obliged to offer a resolution of some puzzle, but it is not at all clear which puzzle they attempt to explain. Furthermore, if subjects are not puzzled by presented behaviour and if they believe that neither is the experimenter, subjects are faced with the task of identifying and resolving a second-order puzzle. Such puzzles are infrequent and unrepresentative of everyday explanation.

A further difficulty arises if the presented behaviour encodes presuppositions that are in conflict with other information provided by the experimenter. Adler (1984) has shown how such conflicts may contribute to apparent "biases" from normative probabilistic judgments reported by Kahneman and Tversky (1973; Tversky and Kahneman 1983). His argument is easily extended to the traditional attributional paradigm where comparable biases in subjects' inferential reasoning have been reported. Consider the following target event and associated configurations of covariation information as they are typically presented to subjects in experiments designed to test the ANOVA model of causal attribution (c.f. McArthur, 1972; Orvis, Cunningham and Kelley, 1975; Jaspars, 1983; Hilton and Slugoski, 1986):

John hit the teacher. (Target event)

Almost everyone/hardly anyone else hits the teacher. (High and Low Consensus)
John hits almost every/hardly any other teacher. (Low and High Distinctiveness)
In the past, John has almost always/almost never hit the teacher. (High and Low Consistency)

Using this paradigm, McArthur (1972) found, consistent with the covariation principle, that distinctiveness information accounted for 12 per cent of the variance in subjects' causal attributions to the entity, and consistency information accounted for about 41 per cent of the variance in attributions to the circumstances. However, she found that consensus information accounted for only 6 per cent of the variance in causal attribution to the person. Since the effect, or lack thereof, of consensus information on causal attributions is formally equivalent to the neglect of base-rate information demonstrated by subjects in other tasks (c.f. Nisbett and Borgida, 1975), it may be explained in the same terms of subjects' failure to apply a Bayesian decision model to their judgments (Tversky and Kahneman, 1982).

An alternative explanation is based on the operation of conversational principles. According to the principle of selective relevance (Adler, 1984), only when it is not common knowledge that members of a class have a given property is it informative, and hence conversationally felicitous, to mention that someone has that property. Presentation of the focussed behaviour *John hit the teacher* in the McArthur (1972) paradigm should thus lead subjects to believe that something *new* is being expressed about John—that he is unlike other people in some respect. In Adler's (1984) terminology, the statement has to do with John *rather-about* some other individual(s) (i.e., John rather than about Sam, Sue, Jill, etc.). However, subjects are then presented with High Consensus information, information that indicates that in fact there is nothing special (rather-about) John at all (i.e., *almost everyone else hits the teacher*). Under the normative statistical model, subjects are expected to disregard the selective relevance of the target behaviour (and thus to suspend the assumption of experimenter cooperativeness) and base their causal judgments solely on the background covariation information. The conversational pull against doing so is evident in the following mini-conversation.

> *A:* Hey, did you hear who hit the teacher?
> *B:* No. Who was it?
> *A:* John.
> *B:* He must be pretty weird to do that.
> *A:* Not really. He's no different from anyone else. Almost everyone hits the teacher.
> *B:* Oh . . .? So what's this about John then?

It might be objected that this artificial conversation is biased in favour of demonstrating selective relevance with respect to the person (John), whereas an equally plausible case could be made for the selective relevance of the entity (the teacher). In fact, there is nothing in Adler's (1984) formulation that precludes the selective relevance of both the person and the entity in the focussed event. Consider the following analogue of the above conversation.

> *A:* Hey, did you hear who John hit?
> *B:* No. Who did he hit?
> *A:* The teacher.
> *B:* The teacher must have really given him a hard time.
> *A:* Not really. The teacher's the same as all the rest. John hits almost every other teacher, too.
> *B:* Oh . . .? So why did you single out this teacher then?

If the specification of the entity in the target statement was in fact perceived by subjects as selectively relevant to the task at hand, this would help to explain why distinctiveness information accounts for less than one third of the variance in causal attributions as does consistency information.

The above argument does not account for the fact that consensus information accounts for only about half of the variance in causal attributions than does distinctiveness information. But we do have an account of this difference based on the notion of linguistic focus. In the majority (10 out of 16) of McArthur's (1972) vignettes, entities were expressed as definite noun phrases (e.g. *John laughed at the comedian*). Despite their location in the stem of actively voiced constructions, which suggests that this information is new, the definite article would serve to mark the entity as given information (Clark and Haviland, 1977). As a consequence, focus would be attached to the heads of the sentences; that is, the agent would be singled out for special causal status (see Klenbort and Anisfeld, 1974; and Hornby, 1974, for research demonstrating the effect of passivization in creating pragmatic presuppositions about causal agency). If this analysis is correct, we have an explanation in terms of linguistic form and conversational principles for the rank-ordering in the McArthur paradigm of the sources of variance in causal judgments accounted for by consensus, distinctiveness and consistency information (but see Ruble and Feldman, 1976, for an alternative explanation in terms of order effects).

The "abnormal conditions focus" model of causal attribution (Hilton and Slugoski, 1986; and see Hilton, this volume) takes the above line of reasoning a step further. The model proposes that it is the very function of consensus, distinctiveness and consistency information to provide subjects with a basis for making only *informative* causal attributions; that is, to identify as the cause of the target behaviour the condition that cannot be presupposed from the general knowledge of the world shared by the subject and experimenter. Furthermore, in explicitly instantiating Grice's (1975) maxim of quantity within the attributional paradigm, the "abnormal conditions focus" model is able to account for departures from the normative Bayesian model without positing "biases" in subjects' formal reasoning (*pace* Nisbett and Ross, 1980). Hence it may be concluded that the Cooperative Principle and its maxims operate throughout the attributional system. They must be taken into account in explaining both departures from and conformity to predictions based on content-independent covariational (Kelley, 1967) and formal logical (Jaspars, 1983) models of causal inference (c.f. Hilton and Slugoski, 1986).

CONSEQUENCES OF NON-COOPERATIVE RESPONDING

In this section we consider some possible consequencs for both speaker and hearer of the speaker failing to take a cooperative attitude. A corollary of the pragmatic view of language is that linguistic action is a form of action in general (c.f. Austin, 1962;

Searle, 1969; see also Harré, this volume). More accurately, it is a form of rule or norm-governed action, the observance and non-observance of which has broader implications than the transmission of the direct, propositional content of the message. Unfortunately, we are aware of no empirical work examining these implications with respect to causal explanation. A literature is, however, beginning to accumulate on the topic more generally.

As mentioned earlier, listeners hold strong expectancies that the speaker is taking a cooperative attitude in the exchange, and hence that he or she is observing at some level the more specific conversational maxims. Thus, even when a response is literally in breach of a maxim, listeners generally will tend to make an inference (or "conversational implicature") concerning the meaning of the utterance that will establish its fidelity to the maxim. In support of this, while several studies have established that speakers do attempt to provide only informative answers to inquirers' questions (Higgins, McCann and Fondacaro, 1982; Slugoski, 1983; Slugoski, Lalljee and Lamb, 1985), Turnbull and Smith (1985) demonstrated a strong tendency for subjects to assign non-literal interpretations to *uninformative* answers to inquirers' questions. The comprehension of indirect speech acts (Clark and Lucy, 1975; Clark and Carlson, 1982) and the construction of "bridging inferences" (Clark and Haviland, 1977) are further examples of listeners' attempts to maintain the assumption of speaker cooperativeness in the face of apparent departures from the Cooperative Principle.

Whether the conversational maxims are adhered to also has important consequences for person perception. By deliberately choosing one construction over others, speakers allow hearers to draw inferences regarding their personal characteristics as well as their conception of the relationship between them. This is particularly true when hearers find it impossible to locate a reading of the speaker's utterance that would allow them to maintain the assumption that the speaker is acting cooperatively. For example, Turnbull and Smith (1985, Study II) found that neutral observers perceived the conveyer of a defective answer to be inconsiderate and hostile, and to judge the relationship between the questioner and answerer as negative and distant. Using a political debate format, Davis and Holtgraves (1984) similarly found that the candidate who provided irrelevant answers to interviewers' questions was perceived by subjects as having less clearly understood the questions, as possessing a less adequate response repertoire, and as being less competent than the candidate who provided relevant answers. Further, subjects perceived the "irrelevant answer" candidate to be more evasive and less attractive. Taken together, these studies would appear to establish a strong self-presentational motive for speakers to adhere to Grice's maxims and assume a cooperative attitude in the exchange.

There are also predictable consequences for hearers when speakers fail to conform to the rules of conversation. In the main, these have to do with processing efficiency. When a conversationally defective utterance is encountered, the hearer is under the obligation to process it in such a way that the assumption of speaker cooperativeness can be maintained. Utterances that fail to conform to conversational rules should therefore be processed less efficiently than those that conform to them. In support of this, Planalp and Tracy (1980) found that topics that were made most clearly relevant to their predecessors were rated by subjects as more understandable and communicatively effective. Similarly, Holtgraves and Davis (1983) used Newtston's (1973) unitizing task to demonstrate that responsive answers are parsed into larger chunks than unresponsive answers, thereby indicating greater processing efficiency for the responsive answers. In a subsequent study, these authors found responsive (cooperative) content to be rated as clearer and more organized, and to be better retained in memory (Davis and Holtgraves, 1984).

There is an important qualification that needs to be made with respect to the above findings. Whether breaches of the conversational maxims result in increased cognitive work for the hearer, negative evaluation of the speaker, etc. may depend in part on the social relationship of the participants. Grice's (1975) model of conversation is essentially one of a contract between cooperating equals who set out to transmit information in the most clear and efficient manner possible. However, conversations also contain a phatic dimension. In addition to assuming that their utterances will conform to the conversational maxims, participants also expect that their utterances will not threaten one another's "face" (Goffman, 1976; Brown and Levinson, 1978). Thus, it appears that the conversational maxims need to be relativized to specific aspects of the relationship between the participants. For example, on a straightforward Gricean account a manifest breach of the maxim of quality ("say only what you believe to be true") should automatically cause the hearer to intepret the utterance in such a way that it conforms to the maxim. However, in a study that investigated neutral observers' interpretations of counter-to-fact insults and compliments conveyed within particular social relationships, Slugoski and Turnbull (1987) found that whether an utterance was interpreted literally or non-literally depended more on the affective valence and social distance of the speaker and hearer. For instance, in the literal compliment condition subjects were much more inclined to assign non-literal interpretations to the utterances when the compliments were directed at disliked and socially intimate recipients than when they were directed at liked and socially distant recipients. Furthermore, it was found that subjects' cognitive representations of the relationship between the speaker and the recipient were influenced by the literal meanings of the utterances; even though the relationship had been specified for the subjects, they rated the affective valence between the speaker and recipient to be more negative when literal insults were conveyed than when literal compliments were conveyed.

Taken together, these findings serve to underline a point made earlier; that there exists a dynamic balance between the need to interpret the meaning of a defective utterance so as to make it conform to felicity conditions, and a reciprocal tendency to reconstrue the speaker's state (e.g. perhaps he's angry or inattentive) or disposition (e.g. perhaps he's stupid or crazy) on the basis of the literal meaning of the utterance. Note that whatever the outcome it must be the result of an implicit attribution process. When hearers encounter an utterance that departs (at the level of literal meaning) from normatively grounded felicity conditions, they must seek to eliminate the contrast between what was said literally and what normally would be expected. We speculate that only when it is very difficult or impossible for hearers to interpret the meaning of an utterance so as to fit with the context will they then alter that context (e.g., reconstrue the speaker or the speaker's relationship to the hearer) to accommodate the literal meaning of the utterance (c.f. Slugoski and Turnbull, 1987).

Attribution theorists have paid scant attention to social-structural variables that might mediate the framing of explanations deployed within particular relationships. To be sure, the effect on causal ascription of the need to preserve face in social encounters generally has been well-documented in the attribution literature, particularly that dealing with "self-serving biases" (c.f. Bradley, 1978; Weary and Arkin, 1981). However, there has as yet been no systematic attempt to integrate this work with that on politeness phenomena as studied by discourse analysts. In our view, this is an unfortunate state of affairs, not merely because of a potential reduplication of effort, but because by concentrating on individual motivational (i.e. ego-defensive) factors underlying departures from "logical" explanations psychologists neglect the normatively compelling nature of face-preserving attributions, and hence a *transpersonal* level of explanation that we believe would allow for a more systematic analysis of such departures.

INTRAPSYCHIC EXPLANATION

We have outlined a conversationally-based model of attribution. It might be objected, however, that ours is a model of the communication of explanation rather than a model of the intrapsychic determinants of everyday explanation. Perhaps we have identified factors that influence only the causes of events that speakers convey to listeners but have failed to address the issue of speakers' own beliefs about those causes. In this section we demonstrate that a conversationally-based model of explanation has considerable relevance for an intraphysic model.

Intrapsychic explanation-giving, the explanation of our own and others' behaviour that we give ourselves, can be viewed as occurring in an internal dialogue in which puzzles and resolutions are defined relative to an intrapsychic presupposed background of belief. Effective interpersonal explanation requires speakers to make assumptions about the listeners' goals and beliefs, including listeners' beliefs about speaker's beliefs, and vice-versa for hearers. Since intrapersonal explanation requires only awareness of one's own beliefs, intrapersonal explanation places fewer cognitive demands on explainers than does interpersonal explanation.

In spite of this difference, there is a strong equivalence between interpersonal and intrapersonal explanation. In general, those factors that influence what and how we explain to others determine what explanations we hold subsequently (Higgins, McCann and Fondacaro, 1982; Higgins and Rholes, 1978). Because there are many levels of understanding, explainers often will be able to create or access many potential explanations of a puzzling behavioural event. The potential resolution identified as *the* explanation, *the* cause, will depend on what is presupposed and what is perceived as new or informative. But, as we have seen, "given" and "new" are themselves determined by conversationally-based structures and processes. Thus the structure and processes of conversation will determine what is identified as the causal field, and what is the abnormal condition. In sum, for many explanatory contexts, the explanation conveyed by a speaker will be equivalent to the explanation held by that speaker.

One apparent difficulty with trying to incorporate an intrapersonal model of explanation within an interpersonal model is the observation that explainers sometimes offer different explanations of the same event to different people and/or at different times. Indeed, if the observer of a behavioural event can offer several different explanations, then it is not clear which explanation the observer holds, interpersonal considerations notwithstanding. This criticism is based on the mistaken view that people explain behavioural events. Once we recognize that people resolve puzzles, contrasts between what would have been expected and what was observed, and that different puzzles can underlie the same behavioural event, the criticism loses much of its sting. Thus the fact that someone responds to the same surface question (i.e. surface request for explanation) with different answers does not entail that different explanations have been given for the same puzzle. It is equally plausible to propose that different answers were given in response to different puzzles. In sum, there are good reasons to accept the view that a conversationally-based model of everyday explanation is relevant also to intrapersonal explanation.

SUMMARY

In this chapter we have argued that everyday explanation is determined in large measure by the structures and processes of conversation. This can be seen most clearly in what people attempt to explain and in what they identify as causes in their explanations. People attempt to resolve puzzles, contrasts between what they take for granted and what they observe; and they explain by identifying a cause that is a covarying factor not taken for granted. Because conversationally-based structures and processes exert a major influence on what people take as given and what as new, conversational structure and process determine in part which puzzles will exist and what causes will be identified in the resolution of these puzzles.

We illustrated our conversationally-based model of attribution in three main ways. First, we presented some data supportive of the model from some recent experimental studies. Second, we considered the difficulties in interpreting data from studies based on traditional models of attribution and, more importantly, demonstrated how certain findings, puzzling from the traditional perspective, can be clarified from a conversational perspective. Third, we described some of the serious social implications that can obtain when conversational principles are violated. We concluded the chapter with the claim that a conversationally-based model of attribution is a model of *both* the communication and holding of explanations, that it applies equally to interpersonal and intrapersonal explanation.

REFERENCES

Adler, J.E. (1984). "Abstraction is uncooperative". *Journal for the Theory of Social Behaviour, 14*, 165–81.

Austin, J.L. (1962). *How To Do Things With Words*. Oxford: Clarendon Press.

Bradley, G.W. (1978). "Self-serving biases in the attribution process: A re-examination of the fact or fiction question". *Journal of Personality and Social Psychology, 36*, 56–71.

Braithwaite, R.B. (1959). *Scientific Explanation: A Study of the Function of Theory, Probability and Law in Science*. Cambridge: Cambridge University Press.

Bransford, J.D., Barclay, J.R. and Franks, J.J. (1972). "Sentence memory: A constructive versus interpretive approach." *Cognitive Psychology, 3*, 193–209.

Bransford, J.D. and Johnson, M.K. (1973). "Consideration of some problems of comprehension". In W.G. Chase (Ed.), *Visual Information Processing*. New York: Academic Press.

Brown, G. and Yule, G. (1983). *Discourse Analysis*. Cambridge: Cambridge University Press.

Brown, P. and Levinson, S. (1978). "Universals in language usage: Politeness phenomena." In E. Goody (Ed.), *Questions and Politeness: Strategies in Social Interaction*. Cambridge: Cambridge University Press.

Brown, R. and Fish, D. (1983). "The psychological causality implicit in language." *Cognition, 14*, 237–73.

Caramazza, A., Grober, E., Garvey, C. and Yates, J. (1977). "Comprehension of anaphoric pronouns". *Journal of Verbal Learning and Verbal Behavior, 16*, 601–9.

Clark, H.H. (1985). "Language use and language users". In G. Lindzey and E. Aronson (Eds), *Handbook of Social Psychology* (3rd ed). Reading, Mass.: Addison-Wesley.

Clark, H.H. and Carlson, T.B. (1982). "Hearers and speech acts". *Language, 58*, 332–73.

Clark, H.H. and Haviland, S. (1977). "Comprehension and the given-new contract". In R. Freedle (Ed.), *Discourse Production and Comprehension*. Norwood, N.J.: Ablex.

Clark, H.H. and Lucy, P. (1975). "Understanding what is meant from what is said: A study in conversationally conveyed requests". *Journal of Verbal Learning and Verbal Behavior, 14*, 56–72.

Clary, E.G. and Tesser, A. (1983). "Reactions to unexpected events: The naive scientist and interpretive activity". *Personality and Social Psychology Bulletin, 4*, 595–9.

Davis, D. and Holtgraves, T.M. (1984). "Perceptions of unresponsive others: Attributions, attraction, understandability, and memory of their utterances". *Journal of Experimental Social Psychology, 20*, 383–408.

Garvey, C. and Caramazza, A. (1974). "Implicit causality in verbs". *Linguistic Inquiry, 5*, 459–64.

Garvey, C., Caramazza, A. and Yates, J. (1976). "Factors influencing the assignment of pronoun antecedents". *Cognition, 3*, 227–43.

Gazdar, G. (1979). *Pragmatics: Implicature, Presupposition and Logical Form*. New York: Academic Press.

Gentner, D. (1981). "Some interesting differences between verbs and nouns". *Cognition and Brain Theory, 4*, 161–78.

Gilson, C. and Abelson, R.P. (1965). "The subjective use of inductive evidence." *Journal of Personality and Social Psychology, 2*, 301–10.

Goffman, E. (1976). "Replies and responses". *Language in Society, 5*, 257–313.

Grice, H.P. (1975). "Logic and conversation". In P. Cole and J.L. Morgan (Eds), *Syntax and Semantics: Vol. 3, Speech Acts*, New York: Academic Press.

Hart, H.L.A. and Honoré, A.M. (1959). *Causation and the Law*. Oxford: Clarendon Press.

Hastie, R.L. (1983). "Social inference". *Annual Review of Psychology, 34,* 511–42.

Haviland, S. and Clark, H. (1974). "What's new? Acquiring new information as a process in comprehension". *Journal of Verbal Learning and Verbal Behavior, 13,* 512–21.

Heider, F. (1958). *The Psychology of Interpersonal Relations.* New York: Wiley.

Higgins, E.T. and Rholes, W.S. (1978). "'Saying is believing': Effects of message modification on memory and liking for the person described". *Journal of Experimental Social Psychology, 14,* 363–78.

Higgins, E.T., McCann, C.D. and Fondacaro, R. (1982). "The 'communication game': Goal directed encoding and cognitive consequences". *Social Cognition, 1,* 21–37.

Hilton, D.J. and Slugoski, B.R. (1986). "Knowledge-based causal attribution: The abnormal conditions focus model". *Psychological Review, 93,* 75–88.

Holtgraves, T.M. and Davis, D. (1983). *Processing Efficiency of Responsive and Unresponsive Content.* Paper presented at the annual meeting of the American Psychological Association, Anaheim, CA.

Hornby, P.A. (1974). "Surface structure and presupposition". *Journal of Verbal Learning and Verbal Behavior, 13,* 530–8.

Jaspars, J.M.F. (1983). "The process of attribution in common sense". In M.R.C. Hewstone (Ed.), *Attribution Theory: Social and Functional Extensions.* Oxford: Basil Blackwell.

Jaspars, J.M.F. (in press). *Mental Models of Causal Reasoning.* In D. Bar-Tal and A. Kruglanski (Eds), *The Social Psychology of Knowledge.* Cambridge: Cambridge University Press.

Jones E.E. and Davis, K.E. (1965). "From acts to dispositions: The attribution process in person perception". In L. Berkowitz (Ed.) *Advances in Experimental Social Psychology.* New York: Academic Press.

Kahneman, D. and Miller, D.T. (1986). "Norm theory: Comparing reality to its alternatives". *Psychological Review, 93,* 136–53.

Kahneman, D. and Tversky, A. (1973). "On the psychology of prediction". *Psychological Review, 80,* 237–51.

Kelley, H.H. (1967). "Attribution theory in social psychology". In D. Levine (Ed.) *Nebraska Symposium on Motivation, 15,* 192–238.

Kelley, H.H (1972). *Causal Schemata and the Attribution Process.* Morristown, N.J.: General Learning Press.

Kempson, R. (1975). *Presupposition and the Delimitation of Semantics.* Cambridge: Cambridge University Press.

Klenbort, I. and Anisfeld, M. (1974). "Markedness and perspective in the interpretation of the passive voice". *Quarterly Journal of Experimental*

Psychology, *26*, 189–95.

Levinson, S. (1983). *Pragmatics*. Cambridge: Cambridge University Press.

Lewis, D. (1969). *Convention*. Cambridge, Mass.: Harvard University Press.

McArthur, L.A. (1972). "The how and what of why: Some determinants and consequences of causal attribution". *Journal of Personality and Social Psychology*, *22*, 171–93.

Mackie, J.L. (1974). *The Cement of the Universe*. Oxford: Oxford University Press.

Mill, J.S. (1872/1973). "System of logic" (8th edn). In J.M. Robson (Ed.), *Collected Works of John Stuart Mill* (Vols. VII & VIII). Toronto: University of Toronto Press.

Monson, T.C., Keel, R., Stephens, D. and Genung, V. (1982). "Trait attributions: Relative validity, covariation with behavior, and prospect of future interaction". *Journal of Personality and Social Psychology*, *42*, 1014–24.

Newtson, D. (1973). "Attribution and the unit of perception of ongoing behavior". *Journal of Personality and Social Psychology*, *28*, 28–38.

Nisbett, R.E. and Borgida, E. (1975). "Attribution and the psychology of prediction". *Journal of Personality and Social Psychology*, *32*, 932–43.

Nisbett, R.E. and Ross, L. (1980). *Human Inference: Strategies and Shortcomings of Social Judgment*. Englewood Cliffs, N.J.: Prentice-Hall.

Orvis, B.R., Cunningham, J.D. and Kelley, H.H. (1975). "A closer examination of causal inference. The roles of consensus, distinctiveness and consistency information". *Journal of Personality and Social Psychology*, *32*, 605–16.

Planalp, S. and Tracy, K. (1980). "Not to change the subject but . . .: A cognitive approach to the management of conversation". In D. Nimmo (Ed.), *Communication Yearbook*, *4*, New Brunswick, N.J.: Transactions.

Pryor, J.B. and Kriss, N. (1977). "The cognitive dynamics of salience in the attribution process". *Journal of Personality and Social Psychology*, *35*, 49–55.

Pyszczynski, T.A. and Greenburg, J. (1981). "Role of disconfirmed expectancies in the instigation of attributional processing". *Journal of Personality and Social Psychology*, *40*, 31–8.

Ruble, D.N. and Feldman, N.S. (1976). "Order of consensus, distinctiveness and consistency information and causal attribution". *Journal of Personality and Social Psychology*, *34*, 930–7.

Schank, R.C. (1977). "Rules and topics in conversation". *Cognitive Science*, *1*, 421–44.

Searle, J.R. (1969). *Speech Acts: An Essay in the Philosophy of Language*. Cambridge: Cambridge University Press.

Slugoski, B.R. (1983). *Attribution in Conversational Context*. Paper presented to the Annual Social Psychology Section Conference of the British Psychological Society, Sheffield, U.K.

Slugoski, B.R., Lalljee, M. and Lamb, R. (1985). *Conversational Constraints on the Production and Interpretation of Explanations*. Paper presented to the Annual Social Psychology Section Conference of the British Psychological Society, Cambridge, U.K.

Slugoski, B.R. and Turnbull, W. (1987). *Cruel to be kind and kind to be Cruel: Sarcasm, banter and social relations*. Unpublished manuscript.

Turnbull, W. (1986). "Everyday explanation: The pragmatics of puzzle resolution". *Journal for the Theory of Social Behaviour*, 16, 141–60.

Turnbull, W. and Smith, E.E. (1985). *Attribution and Conversation: Comprehending Uncooperative Question-answer Exchanges*. Unpublished manuscript.

Tversky, A. and Kahneman, D. (1982). "Judgments of and by representativeness". In D. Kahneman, P. Slovic and A. Tversky (Eds), *Judgment under Uncertainty: Heuristics and Biases*. Cambridge: Cambridge University Press.

Tversky, A. and Kahneman, D. (1983). "Extensional versus intuitive reasoning: The conjunction fallacy in probability judgment", *Psychological Review*, 90, 293–315.

Weary, G. and Arkin, R.M. (1981). "Attributional self presentation". In J.H. Harvey, W. Ickes and R.F. Kidd (Eds), *New Directions in Attribution Research*, (Volume III). Hillsdale, N.J.: Lawrence Erlbaum.

Weary, G., Rich, M.C., Harvey, J.H. and Ickes, W.J. (1980). "Heider's formulation of social perception and attributional processes: Toward further clarification". *Personality and Social Psychology Bulletin*, 6, 37–43.

Weiner, B. (1982). "An attributionally based theory of motivation and emotion". In N.T. Feather (Ed.), *Expectations and Actions*. Hillsdale, N.J.: Lawrence Erlbaum.

Winograd, T. (1977). "A framework for understanding discourse". In M.A. Just and P.A. Carpenter (Eds), *Cognitive Processes in Comprehension*, Hillsdale, N.J.: Lawrence Erlbaum.

Wong, P. and Weiner, B. (1981). "When people ask 'why' questions, and the heuristics of attributional search". *Journal of Personality and Social Psychology*, 40, 650–63.

5 The Role of Selective Attribution in Causality Judgment*

David R. Shanks and Anthony Dickinson

The dominant approach in the study of causal attribution assumes that such judgments are the outcome of some form of inference and that the problem facing psychology is that of specifying the rules of inference by which we arrive at causal interpretations. Such an approach is represented, for example, by attribution theory in social psychology which seeks to determine the inference rules or strategies by which people select personal or situation factors as causal agents (e.g Hilton and Slugoski, 1986; also see Hilton, this volume). Similarly, another body of research has attempted to specify the rules by which covariational or contingency information is used to assess the strength of a causal connection (see Shaklee, 1983, for a recent discussion of this approach). These inferential or rule-based approaches can be contrasted with an associative account deriving from Hume's original thesis that experiencing a causal relationship between two events results in an association or connection between their ideas or representations in the mind. Thus, according to this theory, a causal judgment is seen as reflecting no more than the strength of the relevant association between the cause and the effect, and the principles governing such attributions are those of associative learning.

In spite of its authoritative pedigree, the only area of current research related to the judgment of causation in which associative theory holds any sway is that of conditioning. Although it is not a

* The work reported in this chapter and its preparation was in part supported by grants from the SERC and the MRC. We thank Alisande Martinez-Lainez for recruiting subjects and Paula Durlach and Cliff Preston for their many helpful comments.

common perspective, conditioning can be seen in terms of causality detection; an instrumental or operant conditioning procedure presents the subject with a causal relationship between an action and an outcome, the reinforcer. Performing an action either causes the reinforcer to occur under a positive contingency or prevents its occurrence under a negative one, and the subjects demonstrate a sensitivity to these causal relationships by adjusting their behaviour appropriately. In fact, not only can conditioning be viewed a causality detection task procedurally, but it is also true that a number of its features suggest the operation of a mechanism specifically designed to register causal relationships (see Dickinson, 1980; Testa, 1974).

Although it has been argued that conditioning reflects the application of a concept of contingency (see Alloy and Tabachnik, 1984, and Hammond and Paynter, 1983), the dominant theoretical approach appeals to the role of associative learning. According to such current theories (e.g. Gibbon and Balsam, 1981; Pearce and Hall, 1980; Mackintosh, 1975; Rescorla and Wagner, 1972; Wagner, 1981), conditioning results from increments in the strength of the association between event representations resulting from contiguous pairings of the events with the level of the conditioning being related monotonically to associative strength. In order to extend these theories to causal attribution, all one has to assume is that not only conditioning but also judgments of event relationship are determined by associative strength, an assumption that is bolstered by the general finding that in humans, at least, conditioning only occurs when the subjects have knowledge of the relevant event relationship (see Brewer, 1974, for a review).

There are a number of reasons for the contemporary neglect of an associative approach to causal attribution. Perhaps the most obvious is the limited scope of the theory. Because it appeals to the growth of associative strength across a series of episodes involving the pairing of events in real time, it is clearly not applicable to judgments based upon narrative or abstract representations and summaries of event co-occurrences. But this does not mean we should dismiss the associative approach in the case of judgments based upon real-time observation or interaction with a causal process. In fact, in these cases it may have a distinct advantage in providing an account of how attribution is affected by the dynamics of the causal interaction.

TEMPORAL CONTIGUITY IN CAUSALITY JUDGMENT

One important dynamic aspect of a causal interaction is the temporal relationship between the constituent events. It is well established that the strength of conditioning decreases systematically as the reinforcer is delayed (Mackintosh, 1974), and built into associative theories of conditioning is the basic assumption that the increment in associative strength accruing from event pairings is an inverse function of the temporal interval between the events. Thus, an application of these theories to causal attribution would predict that the judgment of causal effectiveness should also decline as the interval between a putative cause and effect is lengthened. A compelling example of the critical role of the temporal relationship is to be found in Michotte's (1963) classic studies of the perception of mechanical causation. The so-called "launching effect", in which a simulated collision between two objects yields the impression that the movement of one is caused by the impact of the other, shows a progressive degradation as the temporal interval between the collision and the consequent motion is lengthened. However, a role for temporal contiguity is not restricted to the phenomenal impression of mechanical causation but is also to be found in general judgments of causal effectiveness. This point can be illustrated by a recent study from our laboratory, which employed a video game.

In this game the subjects were asked to judge the effectiveness of new types of shells in destroying tanks under battle conditions. They were given forty trials in which to fire a shell of a particular type at the tanks before being required to judge the effectiveness of that type. On each trial the image of a tank emerged from the right-hand side of the screen and passed through a gun sight before crossing the rest of the screen. The subjects were told that if they chose to fire a shell on that particular trial by pressing the space-bar on the computer keyboard while the tank was within the gun sight, the shell would hit the tank and might cause it to explode, an event represented by a fragmentation of the image and the disappearance of the remains. Immediate feedback as to whether the subjects fired on target, thus scoring a hit, was given by the appearance of a marker above the gun sight.

The subjects were explicitly told that the shells, being of new types, might be unreliable or ineffective and thus might hit the tank

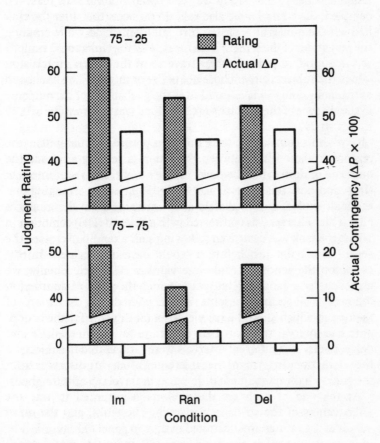

Figure 1

Mean judgment and mean actual contingency (Δ P×100) for the immediate (Im), delayed (Del), and random (Ran) conditions under either the 75–25 (top panel) or 75–75 contingency (bottom panel).

without destroying it. If we regard the destruction of the tank as the outcome *(O)* and scoring a hit as the putative cause, in this case an action *(A)*, we can represent the ineffectiveness of the shells by setting the probability of the outcome given the action, $P(O/A)$, at less than one. In this study we set $P(O/A)$ at a value of 0.75. To complete the scenario, we also told the subjects that after the tank had left the gunsight it passed through a minefield while crossing the remainder of the screen. This meant that the tanks could explode at some random point in their traverse of the screen on trials on which the subjects either chose not to fire or missed. The likelihood of the tanks doing so is referred to as the probability of the outcome in the absence of the action or $P(O/-A)$ and was set at a value of 0.25 in this study.

Given this context, we were now in a position to manipulate the temporal relationship between the action of scoring a hit and the outcome of destroying the tank. In one set of trials, the immediate (Im) condition, this interval was set at 250 msec. by arranging that the tank exploded immediately after emerging from the gunsight after a hit. This set was contrasted with a delayed (Del) condition in which the tank was destroyed following a hit after it had crossed the screen to a point just before it would have disappeared. In this condition the action-outcome interval was 700 msec. Finally, we also included a random (Ran) set in which the point of destruction following a hit occurred at some random point during the traverse of the screen which should have yielded a mean value for the action-outcome interval that was between those for the immediate and delayed sets. The different intervals were rationalized to subjects in the instructions in terms of the tanks being at varying distances from the gun with the consequent differences in travel time for the shells.

At the end of each set the subjects were asked to rate the effectiveness of the shells in destroying the tanks, and the mean values of the ratings are illustrated in the top panel of Figure 1. The judgments were made on a scale from 100, indicating that the shell when fired on target always destroyed the tanks, to zero, indicating that this type of shell was completely ineffective. Also illustrated is the actual contingency between the action and outcome. Because the nominal $P(O/A)$ and $P(O/-A)$ acted as parameter values for a random number generator in the program controlling the display, the actual probabilities experienced by individual subjects could deviate from the nominal values. Consequently, we measured the

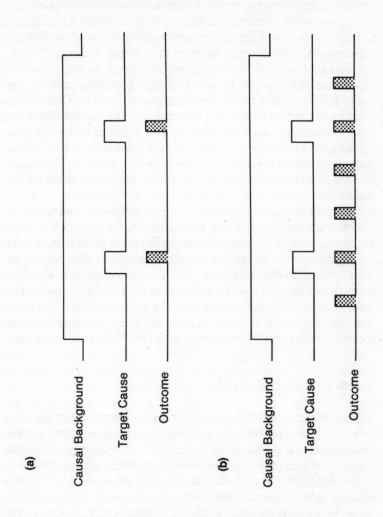

Figure 2

Schematic illustration of the sequence of events for a contingent (a) and non-contingent (b) relationship between a target cause and an outcome in the presence of a causal background.

actual contingency experienced by the subjects in terms of one of the many normative measures (see Allan, 1980), ΔP, that is the change in probability of tank destruction produced by firing on target or, in other words, the difference between $P(O/A)$ and $P(O/-A)$.

As can be seen in the top panel of Figure 1, there was no significant difference in the actual contingency experienced by the subjects in the different temporal conditions. Even so, the subjects consistently produced higher judgments in the immediate condition than in the other two sets, a finding that indicates that a dynamic aspect of the causal interaction plays an important role in causal judgments. More specifically, it points to the operation of the type of contiguity-sensitive mechanism which lies at the heart of the associative explanation, but is outside the immediate scope of inferential and rule-based accounts. Under certain circumstances, of course, such theories may well have to assume the operation of some mechanism that is sensitive to dynamic factors in order to define the information in terms of event conjunctions and disjunctions to which the inferential strategies and rules can be applied. Whether such a mechanism would be expected to discriminate between the immediate and delayed conditions in the present context, however, is far less clear; in both cases the covariation of action and outcome was well defined by the trial structure of the task in all conditions.

EVENT CONTINGENCY

In spite of the evidence for the importance of temporal contiguity in causality judgment, there is one major weakness with any system that determines the causal structure of its environment simply on the basis of pairings of putative causes and effects, namely that it will be prey to superstitious beliefs based upon accidental or fortuitous conjunctions of events. This point is illustrated in Figure 2, which portrays schematically two temporal sequences of a putative target cause and an outcome. In the case of sequence (a) there would be little disagreement that the target is, at least, a good candidate for being the cause of the outcome, and a system sensitive only to contiguous pairings of the events would detect it as such. The problem is that this system would be just as likely to identify the target as the agent producing the outcome in sequence (b), for there are the same number of contiguous pairings in the two sequences.

And yet there is no reason to believe that the target is in fact a causal agent in sequence (b), for the occurrence of this event does not alter the likelihood of the outcome; the outcome is just as probable in the absence of the target cause as in its presence. What distinguishes the two sequences, of course, is the contingency or temporal correlation between the events; in sequence (a) there is a positive contingency between the target cause and the outcome, whereas these events are independent or non-contingent in sequence (b). Thus, in order to acquire veridical knowledge of causal relationships, a system must be sensitive not only to the event contiguities, but also to event contingencies.

There is in fact now considerable evidence that judgments of the effectiveness of an agent based upon interactions with a causal process are sensitive to event contingency (eg. Allan and Jenkins, 1980, 1983; Alloy and Abramson, 1979; Chatlosh, Neunaber and Wasserman, 1985; Wasserman, Chatlosh and Neunaber, 1983), but we shall illustrate this point by considering three further sets of trials received by the subjects in our video-game experiment. In each of these sets the temporal relationship between firing on target and the destruction of the tank was identical to that in one of the sets already described, that is the destruction was immediate, delayed, or occurred at some randomly varying intermediate interval. The only difference was that the contingency between the action and the outcome was reduced in the present sets. Whereas there was a positive contingency in the 75–25 condition already described in that $P(O/A)$ at 0.75 was higher than $P(O/-A)$ at 0.25, this contingency was reduced to zero under the 75–75 condition by raising $P(O/-A)$ to 0.75, the same as $P(O/A)$. This meant that scoring a hit on the tank had no effect at all on the likelihood of the tank's destruction. Formally, the 75–25 condition is similar to the schedule shown in sequence (a) in Figure 2, and the 75–75 condition to that illustrated in sequence (b). The variation in $P(O/-A)$ across these two conditions was rationalized for the subjects in terms of differences in the density of the minefield.

The ratings of the effectiveness of the shells under these two conditions are shown in the top and bottom panels of Figure 1. As can be seen, a reduction in the action-outcome contingency produced a corresponding reduction in judgments in a way that did not interact significantly with the effect of varying the temporal relationship. This finding presents particular difficulties for a simple contiguity theory. Because the mean number of hits per set of forty trials was comparable under the two contingencies (21 for the 75–25 condition and 19 for the 75–75 condition), the subjects should have received a similar number of action-outcome pairings in the two conditions because $P(O/A)$ was the same under the two contingencies. Thus, an associative mechanism that registered only contiguous pairings should yield similar ratings for the two conditions.

The sensitivity to event contingencies is not restricted to the particular event probabilities studied in this experiment, and in fact we (Dickinson, Shanks, and Evenden, 1984, Experiment 1) have already shown that with this video-game procedure ratings of causal effectiveness vary systematically across a range of contingencies. In this study the random temporal action-outcome relationship was employed in all sets so that the temporal and spatial locus of destruction following a hit was on average indistinguishable from that on trials when the subject either chose not to fire or missed. This meant that the only information provided about the causal effectiveness of the shell was the event contingency. As in the previous study, we fixed $P(O/A)$ at 0.75 and degraded the contingency across three sets of trials by raising $P(O/-A)$ from 0.25 (set 75–25) through 0.50 (set 75–50) to the case in which the two conditional probabilities are equal and the outcome and action uncorrelated (set 75–75). Sets 75–25 and 75–75 represent a replication of the contingent and non-contingent conditions of the previous study under the random temporal relationship. A comparison of judgments across these three sets thus provided a further test of whether the subjects are sensitive to contingency in the absence of variations in the probability of contiguous pairings. In addition, we also looked at the effect of bringing about a contingency by employing $P(O/-A)$ that is above rather than below $P(O/A)$. Consequently, in another set, set 25–75, $P(O/-A)$ at 0.75 was three times $P(O/A)$ at 0.25 so that the actual contingency between the action and the outcome was negative; firing a shell on target actually decreased the probability of tank destruction. This possibility was explained in the instructions by pointing out that not only might the shell fail to destroy the tank, but it might also alert the tank driver to the fact that he is in enemy territory and thereby cause him to drive more carefully so as to miss the mines. This set allowed us to study whether subjects can detect what might be called a preventative or inhibitory cause or, in other words, an event that, rather than bringing about the outcome, actually reduces its likelihood. Once again, we compared judgments for this set with a control, non-contingent set (25–25) which was matched with set 25–75 in terms of $P(O/A)$. Finally, we also sought to determine whether subjects are sensitive to the magnitude of a negative contingency by raising $P(O/A)$ to 0.50 in set 50–75 so as to reduce the contingency relative to set 25–75.

Three main features of the results, illustrated in Figure 3, are worth noting. First, when $P(O/A)$ is held constant, judgments decrease as $P(O/-A)$ is raised across sets 75–25, 75–50 and 75–75, thus replicating the sensitivity to the magnitude of a positive contingency even when the probability of action-outcome pairings is held constant. Again there were no significant differences in the number of hits scored by the subjects in the different sets, so that the actual number of action-outcome conjunctions was comparable across the reduction in the positive contingency. Secondly, subjects can detect preventative or inhibitory relationships in that negative contingencies consistently yielded negative judgments. These judgments cannot be explained simply in terms of the number of pairings of firing with destruction because set 25–75 gave a more negative judgment than the non-contingent set 25–25 with a matched $P(O/A)$. In addition, a comparison of sets 25–75 and 50–75 shows that judgments under negative contingencies reflect variations in $P(O/A)$ as well as $P(O/-A)$. Finally, it should be noted that judgments appear to be biased by the overall frequency of the outcome under non-contingent schedules. This bias is represented by the more positive ratings given for the 75–75 set than for the 25–25 set. Although it is true that the actual contingency in the 75–75 set was slightly positive, whereas that for set 25–25 was on average negative (see Figure 3), this difference, unlike that for the ratings, was not significant. Consequently, we do not believe that the discrepancy in the actual contingency can account for the difference, especially as comparable biases have been reported in other studies (see below, and Alloy and Abramson, 1979).

Contingency results such as these have provided the main empirical motivation for the rule-based accounts, for it is not obvious how to explain this sensitivity without appealing to some

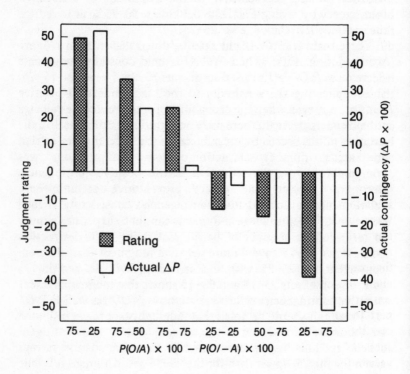

Figure 3

Mean judgment and mean actual contingency (∆ P × 100) for each condition.

concept of covariation. Consequently, in the case of judgments based upon interactions with a causal process, the main empirical strategy has been the attempt to determine the simple statistical rule that best predicts the ratings of causal effectiveness from combinations of information about the frequency or probability of occurrence of various events. For example, Allan and Jenkins (1980) found that the judgments of the majority of their subjects were most highly correlated with the actual contingency as measured by ΔP, thus implying that the subjects were basing their judgments on the difference between $P(O/A)$ and $P(O/-A)$. In a more recent report (Allan and Jenkins, 1983), however, they found that judgments were best accounted for by the ΔD rule in which judgments are based on the difference between the frequency of "confirming" instances, $F(O/A)$ and $F(-O/-A)$, and "disconfirming" instances, $F(-O/A)$ and $F(O/-A)$. A comparable analysis by Wasserman, Chatlosh and Neunaber (1983) found that judgments were significantly correlated with both the ΔP and ΔD rules.

As they stand, however, such rules cannot account for one of our observations, namely that judgments are biased by the overall frequency of the outcome under a non-contingent schedule. One way round this problem is to give different weighting coefficients to the terms in the rule (see Einhorn and Hogarth, 1986, for a recent review of evidence on the differential weightings). In the ΔP rule, for example, giving more weight to $P(O/A)$ than to $P(O/-A)$ will allow the bias to be accounted for. To see what sort of relative weightings of $P(O/A)$ and $P(O/-A)$ are implied by our data, we performed a multiple regression of the judgments upon the actual conditional probabilities experienced by the subjects. Since the subjects' judgments were not independent, we included a subject variable in the analysis, which was the simple average of the judgments for the six sets of trials for each subject. The magnitude of the regression coefficient for $P(O/A)$, 1.05, was about twice that for $P(O/-A)$, 0.42.

Although this weighted ΔP rule can account for the pattern of terminal judgments seen in the experiment, we have recently become dissatisfied with this approach on the basis of further data that we have gathered concerning not the terminal judgments, but rather the way in which causality judgments develop across trials or, in other words, the acquisition process.

ACQUISITION OF CAUSALITY JUDGMENTS

These data come from a study (Shanks, 1985a, Experiment 1) in which the procedure was modified so that the subject had to make judgments throughout each set of trials. A linear scale was displayed at the bottom of the screen going from -100 to $+100$ along with a pointer to register the judgment. At the beginning of the set the subjects were asked to specify a number on the scale to indicate at which point they would like the pointer to start before the first trial. It was explained that there was no rational basis for selecting any particular starting value, but we thought that if the subjects were starting with strong biases towards, for example, positive contingencies, then this would show up in the initial location of the marker. The subjects were then asked to relocate the pointer every five trials during each set. They received one set with a positive contingency (75–25), one with a negative contingency (25–75), and two in which the contingency was zero (75–75 and 25–25).

Figure 4 illustrates the way judgments changed across trials for each of the four sets, as well as the actual contingency as measured by ΔP. The pattern of terminal judgments replicated that seen in the first experiment, including the greater judgments for the 75–75 set than for the 25–25 set. The starting values were all close to zero, which can be taken as evidence that the subjects were not initially biased towards a positive or a negative contingency. The principal aspect of the results, however, is that judgments appear to reach their terminal value via the cumulation of increments or decrements. In the 75–25 set, for which the action-outcome contingency is positive, judgments start close to zero and then slowly increment until they reach an asymptote very close to the actual contingency. The same is true for the 25–75 set in which the contingency was negative, except that here the judgments slowly decrement towards an asymptote. Judgments were fairly constant across trials for the two non-contingent sets with the full bias being evident after the first five trials. This pattern of results does not depend upon the request for an initial judgment, since the same acquisition profile is observed in the absence of a starting value (see Shanks, 1985a, Experiment 2).

What do these data imply about the process underlying our sensitivity to event contingencies? The ΔP rule clearly has trouble explaining the change in judgments across trials because, as Figure

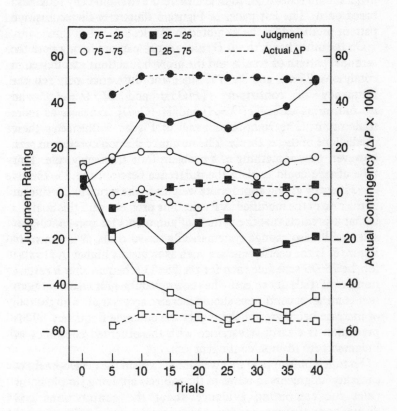

Figure 4

Mean judgment and mean actual contingency ($\Delta P \times 100$) for each condition as a function of number of trials.

4 shows, the actual ΔP was constant across trials for each condition. Although the variance of ΔP should drop with increments in the sample size on which it is based (in this case the number of trials) its mean should remain constant and therefore so should any judgment based on it. The left panel of Figure 5 illustrates the acquisition pattern predicted by the weighted ΔP rule.

On the other hand, the ΔD rule is capable of predicting both the terminal pattern of results and the growth functions manifested in conditions 75–25 and 25–75, since the difference between the frequency of confirming $[F(O/A)$ and $F(-O/-A)]$ and disconfirming cases $[F(O/-A)$ and $F(-O/A)]$ increases as more trials occur. The right-hand panel of Figure 5 illustrates these predictions of the ΔD rule. The results of the non-contingent sets, however, pose something of a problem for a frequency rule. This type of rule could explain the difference between the 75–75 and 25–25 sets by giving appropriate weights to the terms in the rule, as in the case of the modified ΔP rule. The problem with this analysis is that it predicts that the pattern of judgments for non-contingent sets should also change systematically across trials, as is shown in Figure 5. If the coefficients are such as to yield a higher ΔD value for the 75–75 schedule than for the 25–25 schedule after a certain number of trials, it can easily be shown that the judgments for both non-contingent conditions should increase across trials with the rate of increase being greater the higher the outcome frequency.[1] This prediction is clearly at variance with the observed constancy of judgments for the non-contingent sets.

Thus, it would appear that we cannot explain the development of causality judgments in terms of the subjects applying simple linear rules for combining evidence about the conjunctions and disjunctions of events produced by a causal process. Of course, we could have gone on to entertain the possibility that people employ more complex, non-linear metrics, but two observations dissuaded us from doing so. The first is that the acquisition profiles are just those anticipated by the type of incremental (and decremental) processes envisaged by conditioning theory for changing associative strength. Secondly, there is the well-established fact that the humble laboratory rat is perfectly capable of detecting event contingencies, a feat that is very unlikely to be based upon the application of complex correlational rules. As a result, conditioning theory has had to face up to the problem of event contingencies without appealing to such

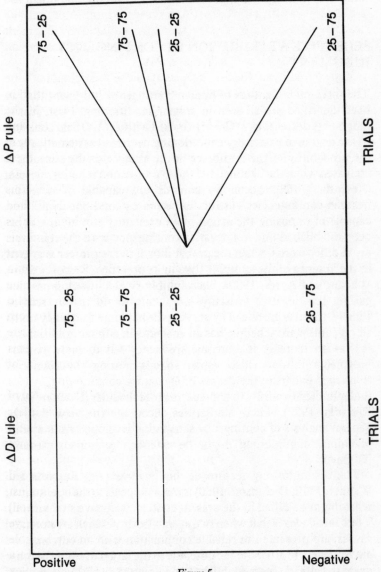

Figure 5
The predicted acquisition profiles for judgments according the weighted △P (left-hand panel) and △D rules (right-hand panel).

rules, and this raises the possibility that we could apply the general
solution offered by this approach to human causality judgment.

SELECTIVE ATTRIBUTION IN CONTINGENCY JUDGMENT

The three main features of human contingency judgment that we
have identified are all seen in animal conditioning. First, just as
judgments decrease as $P(O/-A)$ is raised with $P(O/A)$ held constant,
so the degree of excitatory conditioning decreases systematically as
the probability of the reinforcer in the absence of the stimulus is
increased when the likelihood of their conjunction remains constant
(Rescorla, 1968). Secondly, animals are capable of detecting
negative contingencies. A stimulus becomes a conditional inhibitor,
capable of opposing the action of an excitatory stimulus, if it has
been established under a negative contingency with the reinforcer
or, in other words, when the probability of the reinforcer is greater
in the absence of the stimulus than in its presence (Rescorla, 1969;
Witcher and Ayres, 1980). Such inhibitory conditioning parallels
exactly the negative causality judgments found in our studies.
Finally, the bias produced by varying the outcome frequency under
a non-contingent schedule has an analogue in animal conditioning;
just as an increase in outcome frequency led to more positive
judgments in our video game, so augmenting the reinforcer
frequency enhances the degree of excitatory conditioning, at least
under limited exposure to non-contingent schedules (Kremer, 1971;
Rescorla, 1972). These similarities encourage the view that the
general analysis of contingency sensitivity developed from studies
of animal conditioning might be extended to human causality
judgment.

The distinguishing feature of this analysis (e.g. Rescorla and
Wagner, 1972; Dickinson, 1980) is that is appeals to the operation of
what might be called in the present context "selective attribution".
The central idea is that when two events, both of which are potential
causes, are presented in reliable conjunction with an outcome, we
are less likely to attribute the outcome to the target event if the other
event has already been established on its own as an adequate cause of
the outcome. A simple illustration of the operation of this process in
conditioning is seen in a form of selective learning called "blocking"

(Kamin, 1969). For example, Saavedra (reported by Wagner, 1969) conducted one version of a blocking experiment in which two groups of animals received trials on which a compound of two stimuli, stimuli A and B, was paired with a reinforcer. Intermixed with these compound trials were others on which stimulus B was presented alone. The only difference between the two groups was that presentations of stimulus B alone were paired with the reinforcer for one group, but not for the other. Thus, half of the animals received an $AB+,B+$ schedule and the remainder an $AB+,B-$ schedule, where + and − designate the delivery and omission of the reinforcer, respectively. After training on these schedules, the amount of conditioning that had accrued to stimulus A was tested by presenting it alone.

The reliable finding in this type of experiment is that stimulus A shows much less conditioning in the group given the $B+$ trials in spite of the fact that all animals received the same number of contiguous pairings of stimulus A with the reinforcer on compound trials. The reason for this difference must be the schedule of reinforcement associated with stimulus B alone, for this is the only factor that differentiates the two groups. As a result of its independent association with the reinforcer on $B+$ trials, stimulus B is said to be capable of "blocking" conditioning to stimulus A on compound trials. It is as though the animals selectively attribute the reinforcer on compound trials to stimulus B rather than stimulus A when they have independent evidence from the $B+$ trials that stimulus B is an adequate cause or predictor of the reinforcer by itself. By contrast, the reinforcer on compound trials tends to be attributed to stimulus A rather than B when the animals have evidence from $B-$ trials that stimulus B by itself is not an adequate cause of the reinforcer.

The way in which such a process of selective attribution or blocking might mediate sensitivity to event correlation can be illustrated by reference to Figure 2. If we take the target cause as being analogous to stimulus A, the causal background to stimulus B, and the outcome to the reinforcer, there is a formal parallel between the episodes presented by the non-contingent schedule (b) in Figure 2 and the $AB+,B+$ schedule of the blocking study; the non-contingent schedule presents episodes in which a compound of the causal background and the target cause are paired with the outcome $(AB+)$, intermixed with occasions on which the outcome occurs in association with the causal background alone *(B +)*. Similarly, there is a formal correspondence between the contingent schedule (a) in Figure 2 and the *AB +,B −* schedule.

If the same principle of selective attribution operates in conditioning and causality judgment, we should expect the causal background to block the attribution of the outcome to the putative cause under the non-contingent schedule, but not under the contingent one. Set within the scenario of our own studies, the firing of a shell on target acted as the putative cause and the minefield as the causal background. The selective attribution or blocking principle then makes the commonsense claim that subjects should be more likely to attribute a destruction that follows a firing to the minefield rather than to the shell if there is evidence from trials during which they do not fire that the minefield on its own is an effective cause of destruction.

The operation of this process of selective attribution depends critically upon the status of the causal background, or minefield in our studies. If this is thought to be a sufficient cause of destruction, then the process will yield a low judgment for the effectiveness of the shell. By contrast, an ineffective minefield should give a high positive judgment of the causal efficacy of the shell. So, to test this account, we needed to find out whether the appropriate manipulation of the effectiveness of the causal background or minefield results in the appropriate changes in the judgments of the target cause or shell. This had to be done, however, in procedures that affect neither the frequency nor the probability with which the shell is paired with an explosion of the tank, nor the actual contingency between firing and destruction. Unless this is so, any effect of manipulating the status of the causal background on the judgments could be traced to these sources rather than to the process of selective attribution.

In the first study (Dickinson, *et al.*, 1984, Experiment 2) we sought to determine whether the provision of more evidence for the effectiveness of the minefield would reduce the judgments for the shell. This we did by giving the subjects an initial observation stage in one set. During this stage they could not fire the shells but simply observed the tank passing through a minefield that had a destruction probability of 0.75. This observation experience should have enhanced the subject's belief in the effectiveness of the minefield prior to any firings, and consequently should also have increased the extent to which the minefield blocked attributions to the shell when the subjects could fire in a second stage under the non-contingent 75–75 schedule. Judgments of the shell's effectiveness in this blocking set were compared to control conditions consisting only of firing trials under the 75–75 contingency. In fact, we examined judgments in two control sets, one consisting of 30 firing trials (Con30) and the other of 60 firing trials (Con60). The first control condition matched the number of firing trials to that in the blocking condition, whereas in the second the number of trials was the same as in the observation and firing stages combined.

The outcome of this study, illustrated in Figure 6, shows that judgments were reduced in the blocking set relative to both control sets in line with the predictions of the selective attribution account. It is important to note that these differences occurred in the absence of any discrepancies in the actual contingency experienced in each set; Figure 6 shows that the actual ΔP was very close to zero in all three sets. Moreover, the number of pairings of a firing and a destruction should have been similar in the blocking and Con30 sets as there was no significant difference between the number of trials in which the subjects fired in these sets.

On the basis of this result, we should argue that augmenting the subjects' belief about the causal efficacy of the minefield enhances the ability of this causal background to block the target cause, the shell. Such an interpretation would be strengthened if we could also produce a change in judgment in the opposite direction by manipulating the selective attribution process appropriately. To do this, we had to degrade the causal status of the background. The procedure that we employed to bring about this degradation involved presenting the subjects with the non-contingent schedule and "signalling" outcomes that occur in the presence of the causal background but in the absence of the target cause. If the signal is designated by C this schedule has the form $AB+ CB+$ as opposed to the standard $AB+, B+$ non-contingent schedule. The rationale for this procedure is that the presence of event C on $CB+$ trials will serve, at least in part, to block the attribution of the outcomes to the causal background B on these trials. This in turn will reduce the ability of the background to block the target cause A on the $AB+$ trials, thus raising the subjects' judgments of the effectiveness of A relative to the ratings derived from experience of the simple non-contingent schedule.

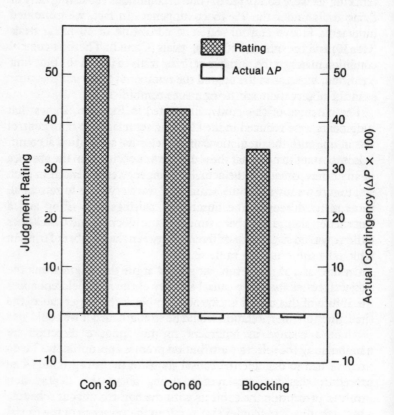

Figure 6

Mean judgment and mean actual contingency ($\Delta P \times 100$) for each condition. Subjects gave judgments after 30 trials in the CON30 condition and after 60 trials in the CON60 condition, in each case under the 75–75 non-contingent schedule. In the blocking condition they were given 30 observation trials during which P(O/–A) was 0.75 prior to 30 trials under the 75–75 schedule.

To instantiate this procedure, we arranged for a representation of a jet plane crossing the screen above the tank to act as event *C*, which then occurred on all occasions when the subject either chose not to fire or missed and the tank was programmed to blow up (*CB*+ trials). The subjects were told that the jet was capable of destroying the tank. This condition is referred to as *SIG(O/−A)* to indicate that the signal occurred on occasions when the outcome happened in the absence of the action. Ratings of the effectiveness of the shells under this condition were compared to those derived from two further sets. The first was a simple non-contingent set. To recapitulate, the selective attribution account predicts that ratings of the shells' effectiveness should have been greater in the *SIG(O/−A)* condition than in the standard non-contingent set, because destructions accompanied by the jet should have been attributed to the plane rather than to the minefield. Consequently, the minefield's ability to block attribution to the shell should have been reduced, and judgments of the shell's efficacy, in turn, increased. If the presence of the jet plane was capable of completely blocking attributions to the minefield, the ratings of the shell's effectiveness in set *SIG(O/−A)* should have been the same as for a matched contingent set. To measure the extent of blocking under these conditions such a contingent set was also run. Whereas *P(O/A)* and *P(O/−A)* were 0.50 in both the non-contingent and *SIG(O/−A)* sets, *P(O/−A)* was reduced to zero for the contingent set.

A final condition controlled for the presence of the jet plane *per se*. In this set [*SIG(O/A)*] the plane again appeared, but in this case on trials when a destruction followed a hit. Thus, the representation of the jet traversed the screen immediately following a firing on target on trials when the tank was programmed to explode. The contrast between the *SIG(O/A)* and *SIG(O/−A)* conditions highlights the fact that the effect of a signal should depend critically upon the trials on which it occurs. Whereas the presence of the jet in the *SIG(O/−A)* condition should have enhanced the judged effectiveness of the shells, if anything, it should have reduced them in the *SIG(O/A)* set. This is because in the latter condition the jet plane is in a position to block attributions to the shell.

The pattern of judgments of the effectiveness of the shells, shown in Figure 7, fits the predictions of the selective attribution account perfectly; in the *SIG(O/−A)* condition the presence of the plane on trials on which tank was destroyed without the subject firing or

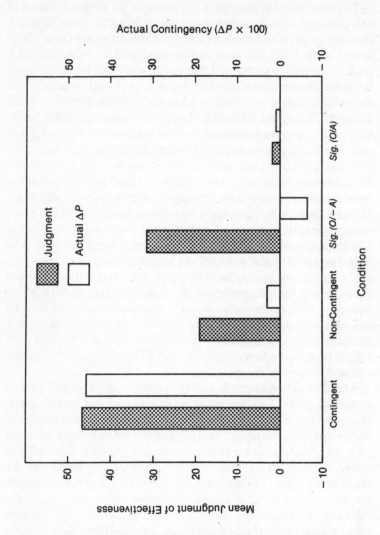

Figure 7

Mean judgment and mean actual contingency (Δ P×100) for each condition. In conditions Contingent and Non-contingent the schedules were 50–0 and 50–50, respectively. In condition Signal (O/−A) the schedule was 50–50, but every outcome that occurred in the absence of the action was signalled. In condition SIG (O/A) the schedule was again 50–50, but all outcomes following the action were signalled.

scoring a hit increased the ratings relative to the non-contingent set. However, the fact that judgments in the *SIG(O/−A)* set remained below those in the contingent set suggests that the presence of the plane did not completely block attributions to the minefield. In contrast to the *SIG(O/−A)* condition, the presence of the plane following a hit in the *SIG(O/A)* set reduced judgments of the shells' effectiveness relative to the non-contingent set. This finding demonstrates that the effect of the plane critically depended upon the type of trial on which it occurred in a manner that reflected the principle of selective attribution. Once again, it should be emphasized that these differences emerged even though the programmed contingencies between the action and outcome were identical in the non-contingent and signal sets. Hitting the tank with the shell had no programmed effect on the likelihood of its destruction in any of these conditions and, moreover, Figure 7 shows that the actual contingencies experienced by the subjects in these sets were all similar and close to zero.

In conclusion, these two studies demonstrate that we can manipulate judgments about a target cause in both directions without altering its actual causal relationship to the outcome. Our ability to do this by manipulating the causal status of the background clearly points to the operation of some process of selective attribution. In addition, it is worth noting that the signalling result extends the parallel between animal conditioning and human contingency judgment, and in fact our study was modelled upon signalling experiments with animals. Just as signalling outcomes in the absence of the action enhanced the judged effectiveness of the action, so signalling reinforcers that occur in the absence of the stimulus increases the level of Pavlovian conditioning (Durlach, 1983; Rescorla, 1984). Perhaps an even closer analogy is to be found in instrumental conditioning where signalling reinforcers that are presented independently of the instrumental action augments the performance of that action (Dickinson and Charnock, 1985; Hammond and Weinberg, 1984).

Finally, it should be made clear that we are not claiming that the results of these selective attribution studies necessarily lie outside the scope of inferential or rule-based models, although it is not clear that their present formulations can encompass our data. In the signalling study, for example, it might be argued that the presence of the signal in the *SIG(O/−A)* set should effectively prevent information derived from outcomes in the absence of the action contributing to rule-based estimates of contingency. This would mean that there was no evidence upon which to base estimates of $P(O/-A)$ and $F(O/-A)$. Although this is a possibility, until the appropriate rules for deciding whether or not to ignore such information are clearly formulated this approach cannot be evaluated. An alternative might be developed from Kelley's (1972, 1973) notion of discounting, according to which we assimilate causal information to a schema for "multiple sufficient causes". This assimilation results in a form of selective attribution by leading us to "discount" one putative cause, say a hit by a shell, in the presence of another, sufficient cause, the minefield. However, the relevance of the discounting principle to the present observations is far from clear, for Kelley offered the discounting principle to explain attributions based on single observations and in the absence of covariational information. In our studies, of course, such information is available.

Recently, Einhorn and Hogarth (1986) have suggested explicitly that the evidence for a causal relationship derived from a variety of sources, including contingency information, should be subject to a discounting rule. According to their rule the net strength of a causal explanation is equal to the gross strength of the explanation derived from these sources minus some weighted value of the gross strength of alternative explanations or causes. Whether or not this formulation can encompass our selective attribution data is not clear, but one can see problems. Presumably one reason why a reduction in contingency decreases judgments of the shell's effectiveness is because the gross strength of the minefield is taken away from the gross strength of the shell in arriving at its net strength and hence the judgment. Increasing $P(O/-A)$ augments the gross strength of the minefield and thus reduces judgments of the shell's effectiveness. So far so good, what but happens when we introduce the plane on trials when a destruction occurs without a hit in the $SIG(O/-A)$ condition of the signalling procedure? According to this formulation, the presence of the plane should not alter the gross strength of the minefield because gross strengths are not subject to discounting. In turn this manipulation should have no effect on the discounting process for the shell, leaving judgments of its effectiveness unaltered.

We shall not belabour rule-based accounts any further as our purpose in the selective attribution experiments was not to discredit such explanations, but rather to test an account of the sensitivity to event contingencies that might be married to an associative theory. This is the issue we finally turn to in our concluding comments.

ASSOCIATIVE THEORY RECONSIDERED

At this point a summary of our arguments and findings is in order. Current analyses of causal attribution and judgment have emphasized the role of inferential and rule-based strategies to the exclusion of the venerable tradition of associationism. While acknowledging that the scope of any associative theory must be limited to judgments based upon the observation of or the interaction with a causal process in real time, in these cases it has a certain *prima facie* merit. It provides, for instance, a ready account of the role of the dynamic aspects of a causal process, such as the influence of temporal contiguity demonstrated in our first study. But the problem with simple associative theory lies in the sensitivity of judgments to event contingencies, the *forte* of rule-based explanations. However, the acquisition profiles that we observed for causality judgments under different event contingencies could not be readily explained by the extant rule-based accounts. Moreover, the incremental and decremental nature of these profiles were of the form that would be anticipated by a process that produces increments and decrements in the strength of an associative connection beween cause and effect on a trial-by-trial or episode-by-episode basis. Even so, this still left us with the problem of how an associative theory, based upon contiguous conjunctions of cause and effect, could explain the contingency effect. Our attempt to show this was derived from the type of process which current associative conditioning theory uses in its analysis of the comparable contingency effects found in animal conditioning. We refer loosely to this process as that of selective attribution.

The main evidence for selective attribution in animal experiments comes from blocking experiments which demonstrate that the conditioning to a target stimulus is reduced when it is reinforced in compound with another, established predictor of the reinforcer. We succeeded in demonstrating a blocking-like effect with our video game and took this as evidence that selective attribution also occurs in human causality judgment. In accord with this claim, we showed that a procedure likely to reduce the causal status of the background increased judgments of the action-outcome contingency. This is a procedure known to illustrate selective attribution in animal conditioning, consisting of signalling those outcomes that occur in the absence of the action, outcomes that would otherwise reduce judgments of action-outcome relationship.

This leaves us only with the problem of marrying the process of selective attribution to an associative theory, a union that has been attempted in a number of different ways within conditioning theory. Rescorla and Wagner (1972), for example, have argued that an outcome will sustain only a limited amount of associative strength and that the increment in the strength of a target event accruing from each pairing with an outcome will be reduced if these pairings occur in the presence of another event, with the size of the reduction being proportional to the associative strength of the competing event. This means that the independent pairing of the minefield with destructions under the non-contingent schedule should increase its associative strength, which in turn will then reduce the increment in the strength of the shell accruing from a pairing of a hit with a destruction in the presence of the minefield. The Rescorla-Wagner model does not represent the only attempt to incorporate a selective attribution process within an associative account of learning. A number of other theorists have appealed to the role of attentional-like processes. The reduced increment in associative strength produced by the presence of the alternative event on a particular trial may be due to a consequent failure to attend to the target either on the same (Sutherland and Mackintosh, 1971) or subsequent trials (Mackintosh, 1975; Pearce and Hall, 1980).

An alternative embodiment of the selective attribution process is to be found in what are called comparator theories. This approach involves the comparison of the associative strength of the target cause with that of the causal background at the time of judgment. Within conditioning theory, such a comparison is embodied in the scalar expectancy model of Gibbon and Balsam (1981). An application of this model to causality judgments would assume that the associative strengths of the target cause and background simply grow as a function of the number of times they are paired with the outcome. The final judgment of the effectiveness of the target cause is then determined by the ratio of these two strengths. We

(Dickinson and Shanks, 1985) have recently proposed a similar type of account specifically within the context of causality judgment.

If we are to argue seriously for these associative accounts, we must demonstrate that they can account for the empirical observations that provided the main stumbling block for the rule-based approach, namely the acquisition profiles that we observed under the different contingencies. We attempted to do so by running a simulation of our own comparator model under the conditions of our acquisition experiment. According to this model, the occurrence of the target cause in the causal background is treated as a single compound element whose associative strength is incremented each time it is paired with the outcome and decremented each time it occurs in the absence of the outcome (see Dickinson and Shanks, 1985, for a formal presentation). Another associative strength is associated with the causal background alone which is similarly affected each time the causal background alone is or is not paired with the outcome. The associative strength of the target cause is then taken to be the difference between that of the compound of the target and background and that of the background alone.

Five hundred simulated sets of trials were run under each of the probabilistically specified contingencies employed in the acquisition study. The parameters of the model used in the simulation were chosen by a non-exhaustive search of its parameter space (see Figure 8). The probability of a hit on each trial was set at 0.5 so as to give equal sampling of both conditional probabilities that define the contingencies, a strategy that was close to the one actually employed by subjects with our procedure. A comparison of Figure 8, which illustrates the results of this simulation, with the acquisition profiles in Figure 3 shows that our model can produce associative strength functions with the main characteristics of these profiles. There is an incremental and decremental growth in the associative strength of the shell under the positive and negative contingencies, respectively. In addition, the simulation can reproduce the effect of outcome frequency on judgments under non-contingent schedules, although the difference in the associative strengths for the 75–75 and 25–25 sets tends to decline with extended exposure due primarily to a reduction in the strength sustained by the schedule with the higher outcome frequency. Although we failed to observe a similar convergence in our acquisition data, it should be pointed out that the rate of

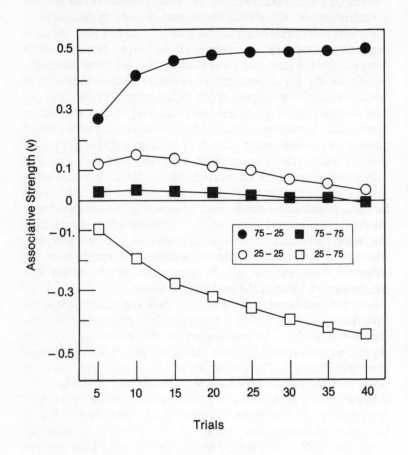

Figure 8

Mean associative strength of the shell predicted by the application of a comparator model (Dickinson and Shanks, 1985) to the procedure for studying the acquisition of causality judgments (see text). The associative strength of the shell (V) equalled the difference between V_{AB}, the associative strength of the shell and minefield combined, and V_B, the strength of the minefield alone. The increments in these strengths were determined by the functions: $\Delta V_{AB} = \alpha_{AB}\,\beta\,(\lambda - V_{AB})$ and $\Delta V_B = \alpha_B\,\beta(\lambda - V_B)$, where the learning rate parameter for the shell and minefield combined, α_{AB} was 0.6 and that for the minefield alone, α_B was 0.3. The asymptote, λ, and learning rate parameter, β, for the outcome were 100 and 0.4, respectively, when the outcome was the destruction of the tank and 0 and 0.6, respectively, when the tank remained intact.

convergence is parameter dependent, and it may well be that the forty trials in our study were insufficient to detect the reduction in bias. In the CON60 set of the blocking study the subjects actually received 60 trials under the high frequency non-contingent schedule, and it may be significant that this condition tended to produce lower judgments than the CON30 set in which only 30 trials were given (see Figure 6). Finally, it is worth noting that our model is not the only associative account that can produce the appropriate acquisition functions; for instance, Shanks (1985a) reports a comparable simulation of the Rescorla-Wagner model which yields very similar profiles.

Whatever the merits of these various theories of selective attribution, and it has to be admitted that there are a number of problems with some of them (see Dickinson and Shanks, 1985; Shanks, 1985b; Shanks and Dickinson, 1987), the identification of the process should, at the very least, encourage us to take associative accounts as serious candidates in understanding certain forms of causality judgment. Protected from the danger of superstition by the process of selective attribution, pre-theoretical beliefs based upon associations brought about by contiguous pairings of events can yield a relatively veridical picture of the causal structure of our environment.

NOTE

1. In a weighted ΔD rule with coefficients a, b, c, and d
$$\Delta D = aF(O/A) + bF(-O/-A) - cF(O/-A) - dF(-O/A).$$
Thus, under a non-contingent schedule the expected value of ΔD after N trials is:
$$\Delta D = aprN + b(1-p)(1-r)N - cp(1-r)N - d(1-p)rN.$$
where p is the probability of the outcome and r is the probability of an action. If $r = 0.5$, as it did approximately in our studies, the expected ΔD is:
$$\Delta D = 0.5 [p(a+d-b-c) + b-d]N.$$
If the coefficients are such as to yield a positive ΔD, then ΔD is an increasing function of N with a slope that increases with p.

REFERENCES

Allan, L.G. (1980). "A note on measurement of contingency between two binary variables in judgment tasks". *Bulletin of the Psychonomic Society, 15*, 147–9.

Allan, L.G. and Jenkins, H.M. (1980). "The judgment of contingency and the nature of the response alternatives". *Canadian Journal of Psychology, 34*, 1–11.

Allan, L.G. and Jenkins, H.M. (1983). "The effect of representations of binary variables on judgment of influence." *Learning and Motivation, 14*, 381–405.

Alloy, L.B. and Abramson, L.Y. (1979). "Judgment of contingency in depressed and nondepressed students: Sadder but wiser?" *Journal of Experimental Psychology: General, 108*, 441–85.

Alloy, L.B. and Tabachnik, N. (1984). "Assessment of covariation by humans and animals: The joint influence of prior expectations and current situational information". *Psychological Review, 91*, 112–49.

Brewer, W.F. (1974). "There is no convincing evidence for operant or classical conditioning in adult humans". In W.B. Weimer and D.S. Palermo (Eds), *Cognition and the Symbolic Processes*. Hillsdale, N.J.: Lawrence Erlbaum.

Chatlosh, D.L., Neunaber, D.J. and Wasserman, E.A. (1985). "Response-outcome contingency: Behavioral and judgmental effects of appetitive and aversive outcomes with college students". *Learning and Motivation, 16*, 1–34.

Dickinson, A. (1980). *Contemporary Animal Learning Theory*. Cambridge: Cambridge University Press.

Dickinson, A. and Charnock, D.J. (1985). "Contingency effects with maintained instrumental reinforcement". *Quarterly Journal of Experimental Psychology, 37B*, 397–416.

Dickinson, A. and Shanks, D.R. (1985). "Animal conditioning and human causality judgment". In L.G. Nilsson and T. Archer (Eds), *Perspectives on Learning and Memory*. Hillsdale, N.J.: Lawrence Erlbaum.

Dickinson, A., Shanks, D.R. and Evenden, J.L. (1984). "Judgment of act-outcome contingency: The role of selective attribution". *Quarterly Journal of Experimental Psychology, 36A*, 29–50.

Durlach, P.J. (1983). "Effect of signaling intertrial unconditioned stimuli in autoshaping". *Journal of Experimental Psychology: Animal Behavior Processes, 9*, 374–89.

Einhorn, H.J. and Hogarth, R.M. (1986). "Judging probable cause". *Psychological Bulletin, 99*, 3–19.

Gibbon, J. and Balsam, P. (1981). "Spreading association in time". In

C.M. Locurto, H.S. Terrace and J. Gibbon (Eds), *Autoshaping and Conditioning Theory*. New York: Academic Press.

Hammond, L.J., and Paynter, W.E., Jr. (1983). "Probabilistic contingency theories of animal conditioning: A critical analysis". *Learning and Motivation*, *14*, 527–50.

Hammond, L.J. and Weinberg, M. (1984). "Signaling unearned reinforcers removes the suppression produced by a zero correlation in an operant paradigm". *Animal Learning and Behavior*, *12*, 371–7.

Hilton, D.J. and Slugoski, B.R. (1986). "Knowledge-based causal attribution: The abnormal conditions focus model". *Psychological Review*, *93*, 75–88.

Kamin, L.J. (1969). "Predictability, surprise, attention and conditioning". In B.A. Campbell and R.M. Church (Eds), *Punishment and Aversive Behavior*. New York: Appleton-Century-Crofts.

Kelley, H.H. (1972). *Causal Schemata and the Attribution Process*. New York: General Learning Press.

Kelley, H.H. (1973). "The process of causal attribution". *American Psychologist*, *28*, 107–28.

Kremer, E.F. (1971). "Truly random and traditional control procedures in CER conditioning in the rat". *Journal of Comparative and Physiological Psychology*, *76*, 441–8.

Mackintosh, N.J. (1974). *The Psychology of Animal Learning*. London: Academic Press.

Mackintosh, N.J. (1975). "A theory of attention: Variations in the associability of stimuli with reinforcement". *Psychological Review*, *82*, 276–98.

Michotte, A. (1963). *The Perception of Causality*. London: Methuen.

Pearce, J.M. and Hall, G. (1980). "A model of Pavlovian learning: Variations in the effectiveness of conditioned but not of unconditioned stimuli". *Psychological Review*, *87*, 532–52.

Rescorla, R.A. (1968). "Probability of shock in the presence and absence of CS in fear conditioning". *Journal of Comparative and Physiological Psychology*, *66*, 1–5.

Rescorla, R.A. (1969). "Conditioned inhibition of fear resulting from negative CS-US contingencies". *Journal of Comparative and Physiological Psychology*, *67*, 504–9.

Rescorla, R.A. (1972). "Informational variables in Pavlovian conditioning". In G.H. Bower (Ed.), *The Psychology of Learning and Motivation* (Vol. VI). New York: Academic Press.

Rescorla, R.A. (1984). "Signaling intertrial shocks attenuates their negative effect on conditioned suppression". *Bulletin of the Psychonomic Society*, *22*, 225–8.

Rescorla, R.A. and Wagner, A.R. (1972). "A theory of Pavlovian conditioning: Variations in the effectiveness of reinforcement and nonreinforcement. In A.H. Black and W.F. Prokasy (Eds), *Classical Conditioning II: Current Theory and Research*. New York: Appleton-Century-Crofts.

Shaklee, H. (1983). "Human covariation judgement: Accuracy and strategy". *Learning and Motivation, 14,* 433–48.

Shanks, D.R. (1985a). "Continuous monitoring of human contingency judgment across trials". *Memory and Cognition, 13,* 158–67.

Shanks, D.R (1985b). "Forward and backward blocking in human contingency judgement". *Quarterly Journal of Experimental Psychology, 37B,* 1–21.

Shanks, D.R. and Dickinson, A. (1987). "Associative accounts of causality judgement". In G.H. Bower (Ed.), *The Psychology of Learning and Motivation,* Vol. XXI. New York: Academic Press. (in press).

Sutherland, N.S. and Mackintosh, N.J. (1971). *Mechanisms of Animal Discrimination Learning.* New York: Academic Press.

Testa, T.J. (1974). "Causal relationships and the acquisition of avoidance responses". *Psychological Review, 81,* 491–505.

Wagner, A.R. (1969). "Stimulus selection and a 'modified continuity theory'". In G.H. Bower and J.T. Spence (Eds), *The Psychology of Learning and Motivation,* Vol. III. New York: Academic Press.

Wagner, A.R. (1981). "SOP: A model of automatic memory processing in animal behavior". In N.E. Spear and R.R. Miller (Eds), *Information Processing in Animals: Memory Mechanisms.* Hillsdale, N.J.: Lawrence Erlbaum.

Wasserman, E.A., Chatlosh, D.L. and Neuanber, D.J. (1983). "Perception of causal relations in humans: Factors affecting judgments of response-outcome contingencies under free-operant procedures". *Learning and Motivation, 14,* 406–32.

Witcher, E.S. and Ayres, J.J.B. (1980). "Systematic manipulation of CS-US pairings in negative CS-US correlation procedures in rats". *Animal Learning and Behavior, 8,* 67–74.

Part II:
Conceptual Structures and Theories

6 Modes of Explanation

Rom Harré

INTRODUCTION

"Explanation" is a commonsense notion or cluster of notions. One way of grasping what is involved in everyday explanations is to use the modes of scientific explanation as some sort of "control". But adopting that strategy lays one open to the danger of picking up some outdated or mistaken philosophical theory, which then distorts one's intuitions. Perhaps more than in any field of psychology, philosophers of science have a vital role to play in attribution theory. It is only by stepping back and surveying the whole field of explanation that one can get a feel for the deleterious effect on this branch of psychology of the methodological and metaphysical assumptions of the Humean account of causality and its immediate descendant, the causal theory of J.S. Mill.

According to Hume, the root ideas in the concept of causation are succession and necessary connection His metaphysics of experiential atoms, impressions and ideas, each independent of its precedent or subsequent impression or idea, fixes causation as a relation between events. Using a strong verificationist (positivist) theory of meaning Hume treats the meaning of each idea as its corresponding impression. The idea of succession derives from empirically presented regularities, but, according to Hume, there is no empirically presented impression of connection since all impressions are atomic, so there can be no empirical presentation of an impression of necessary connection. But the idea of necessary connection must come from somewhere. Having allegedly shown no empirical source of the idea is possible, only a psychological source remains, the habit of expecting the second member of a pair

129

of previously concomitant events when we have had an impression of the first.

There are all kinds of confusions of thought in this doctrine, but two difficulties are outstanding. Basing everything on an event ontology, and simply eliminating any reference to enduring substances in the physical world (the substances we normally refer to in giving causal explanations) begs the question. According to Hume there is no ontological tie that binds causes to their effects. So the scraping of the violin strings is ontologically independent of the heard sound and related to it only by the formal relation of regularity of succession. We know that the air mediates the causal process from violin to ear, and that the physiological mechanisms of audition link vibrations of the air to hearing. As a positivist, Hume will have none of this, since both the vibrations in the air and the electrical impulses in the cochlea are unobservable. We have no impressions of them. Only if one denies theory a role in specifying the nature of reality will this argument go through. So the argument cannot be used in a positivistic denigration of theory, such as that popular amongst certain psychologists. The same point can be made about Hume's treatment of the necessity of causal connections. The scientific "must" has to do with the way substantial causal mechanisms behave, and the variety of dispositions their natures admit. That lemon juice *must* dissolve eggshells *(ceteris paribus)*, is an apodeictic fact whose necessity is grounded in the chemical and physical nature of hydrogen ions and calcium carbonate.

Mill's version of the regularity theory is not essentially different, as the following quotation testifies.

> I premise then, that when in the course of this enquiry I speak of the cause of any phenomenon, I do not mean a cause which is not itself a phenomenon; I make no research into the ultimate or ontological cause of anything. To adopt a distinction familiar in the writings of the Scotch metaphysicians, and especially of Reid, the causes with which I concern myself are not efficient, but physical causes. They are causes in that sense alone in which one physical fact is said to be the cause of another. Of the efficient causes of phenomena, or whether any such causes exist at all, I am not called upon to give an opinion. The notion of causation is deemed by the schools of metaphysics most in vogue at the present moment to imply a mysterious and most powerful tie, such as cannot, or at least does not, exist between any physical fact and that other physical fact on which it is invariably consequent, and which is popularly termed its cause: and thence is deduced the supposed necessity of ascending into the essences and inner constitution of things, to find the true cause, the cause which is not only followed by, but

actually produces, the effect. No such necessity exists for the purposes of the present enquiry. (Mill, 1879).

And, of course, science deals only with the observable.

> The only notion of a cause which the theory of induction requires is such a notion as can be gained from experience. The Law of Causation, the recognition of which is the main pillar of inductive science, is but the familiar truth that invariability of succession is found by observation to obtain between every fact in nature and some other fact which has preceded it, independently of all considerations respecting the ultimate mode of production of phenomena. (Mill, 1879).

On this account of science the study of malaria should have stopped in its tracks when the invariability of succession between the onset of the fever and the presence of swampy conditions was established. Only by adverting to the *mode of production of the phenomenon, namely the plasmodium and the mosquito that is its vector* is one able to sort out even the relevant concomitances. If we followed Mill's recipe there could be no science of the kind we know at all. Gone would be virus theories of disease, electrons from electrical physics and so on. Medicine would be a catalogue of syndromes, and physics would still be at the stage of rubbing bits of amber and playing with iron filings.

Bland talk of necessary and sufficient conditions still leaves one with a pre-scientific account of causality. There are two radically different kinds of necessary conditions in the distinction between which lies the clue to a proper understanding of causation. There are ephemeral events which trigger or release certain tendencies or dispositions. Only conditions of this sort meet the full requirements as set out by Mill in the quotations above in which his "method" is definitively prescribed. Then there are the permanent substances or mechanisms, which have the tendencies or dispositions which are triggered by the stimulus events. For instance there are such entities as electrical charges, chemical ions, blood vascular systems, plasmas, ocean currents. These are the generative bases of causal production of events of various kinds. We can all agree that smoking is correlated with heart disease. But to establish that it is the cause of that unhappy condition calls for two further steps. It must be the most obvious element in the whole causal story that can be picked out as perhaps amenable to human control, from all the other events germane to the occurrence of the effect. But we must also be able to identify the causal mechanism. The latter is harder to do than the former, and this fact makes the absence of a well attested hypothesis about a mechanism a very attractive excuse in the continuous battles between business interests and those attempting to preserve the environment's health. (C.f. the recent discussions of the cause of acid rain.) Knowledge of mechanisms is of a quite different status from knowledge of triggering or unblocking events, and lies at the end of a different kind of process of knowledge acquisition. (See Bunge, 1959 and Harré and Madden, 1975). If one has hit on a correct description of the real causal mechanisms, those inherent constitutions of things which Mill *explicitly* denies are part of the subject matter of science, and by the use of non-inductive existential searches you have revealed such a mechanism to observation, and if you destroy or disable it, the effect won't occur. But this is *not* Mill's method of difference, since that is explicitly confined by Mill to "facts which precede effects".

Explanations, whether lay or scientific, are discourses. There are various ways of classifying discourses, but a preliminary sorting of those that intuitively strike us as explanatory can be accomplished by references to content. Something is given as *explanandum*, that which is to be explained. In one kind of explanatory discourse putative causes of the explanandum are offered. A cause must have an existence and a description independent of its effect. In another kind, the structural, a template is offered in explanation of the structural properties of some outcome, be it a thing (a crystal) or a sequence of events. The template and the explained structure must come, at least in part, under the same description, and may not have an existence independent of one another. In psychology a plan and its execution in a pattern of action are related in such a way that the former is a structural explanation of the form of the latter. Explaining the coming into existence of the action pattern needs a causal or intentional explanation. Then there are teleonomic explanations when function or end are cited in the explaining discourse. To keep up the Latinate terminology, that which does the explaining is referred to as the *explanans*. This might refer to the discourse, or to that which the discourse refers. In this chapter I shall concentrate only on the first of these explanatory formats, that in which the explanans refers to causes.

Some reflection on the kinds of causal explanations typical of the natural sciences leads to a preliminary distinction between what I shall call positive and negative causality. Citing a field potential as the explanation of the accelerating motion of a test body is a case of positive causality. This body is acted on by this field. But biology is full of citations of negative causality. Darwinian theory has it that an organic form is selected not because there is any positive relation between that form and the environmental niche it fills, but because that environment has eliminated all its potential rivals from the effective breeding population. The survivors should not be said to be well adapted to their niche, but should be characterized as those least ill-adapted, of course "on the average". His and her offspring make up the bulk of the next generation because all the other potential parents are either dead or less prolific in that environment. In this chapter I shall concentrate on cases and modes of the citation of positive causes in explanatory discourses.

Positive causality occurs in very complex natural conditions, and a first step is needed to mark out ways of distinguishing causal conditions from other aspects of a causal nexus. We could think of this as an exploration of ways in which scientists pick out genuine from pseudo causes. Two cases spring to mind. There are mere accidental correlations. Perchance we find some cases in which finding a robin in the house has been followed by a trio of deaths in the family. Some cases of this apparently malign influence were cited by an elderly neighbour in the village where I live. They were genuine enough, so why was I not impressed? For the life of me I couldn't imagine what causal mechanism there could have been which, stimulated by the presence of the robin, had such alarming consequences. Then there are side effects which sometimes masquerade as causes. The AIDS epidemic may be a case in point. It has been suggested that the virus, HTVL III, is picked up by those whose immune system is already "down" through the effects of social isolation and depression. The correlation between infection and development of total immune deficiency is weak. It may be that the presence of the virus is a side-effect of a social or psychological cause. The correlation of night and day is a classical example of the same sort of thing. Why is "It was day" not a good answer to the question "Why is it dark now?" In both cases the picking out of causal from noncausal correlates requires attention to the causal mechanisms through which an effect is produced. Only by the development and testing of the relevant theory is knowledge of causal mechanisms enhanced. Only by reference to such enhanced knowledge can accidental correlations or side-effects be set off from causes. No amount of Humean concomitances nor Millian agreements and differences can take us one single step along this road. It is theory which provides the content of explanations, and so enables us to give causal explanations.

EXPLANATIONS AS SPEECH-ACTS

Given that an explanation is a discourse and human beings mostly use discourse to perform speech-acts, what sort of speech-act is explaining? When language is considered within speech-act theory a discourse is examined for its typical "forces". There is the locutionary force, its literal meaning. Then there is the illocutionary force, the social act performed by uttering it. And finally there is the perlocutionary force, the cluster of effects brought about by the utterance of that discourse with that illocutionary force. "There is a bull!" is a description of the environment. It is used to issue a warning, and the effect of the warning is to alert the picnic party, and to send it helter skelter for the nearest cover. I may grasp the literal meaning, but unless I am capable of illocutionary uptake the point of the utterance may be lost. (See Turnbull and Slugoski, this volume, for a related approach).

What are the performative forces of explanatory discourse? We can start with the simplest to identify, the perlocutionary force. There is some effect on the community or some member of it of hearing or reading the discourse. Amongst the proposals for what that effect might be have been a sense of understanding (just what that is is to be further looked into); the removal of puzzlement; the filling of a felt gap in the body of relevant knowledge, and so on. To pick up the illocutionary force is more subtle. Is the act of explaining like the act of warning? That is, is the perlocutionary force of the act just the result of the illocutionary uptake? Is it enough just to take the discourse as explanatory for it to have one or more from amongst the list of perlocutionary effects? Why is "There's a bull!" a warning? We might say that illocutionary uptake depends on our knowing that bulls are often dangerous. The locutionary force of the speech-act is involved. Equally, in the case of explaining we can ask why is this or that discourse explanatory? An answer might be

"Well it has the form of a syllogistic deduction" or "It mentions causes" or some other feature of the discourse considered within the framework provided by a literal reading of it. The problem of explanation seems to be able to be tackled from either of two directions. What sort of perlocutionary effects does a community expect of those discourses it calls explanatory? Given some answer to that question we might then look for the conditions for the achievement of those effects in the locutionary nature of the discourse. Alternatively one might pick on a cluster of discourses that are, within some community, just taken as explanatory, and try to discern what it is about them that is responsible for that reading. Later one might be able to see what sort of perlocutionary effects one would expect from discourses picked out in just these ways. I will follow the latter strategy. (For an interesting attempt to start with what we would now call the perlocutionary effects see Scriven, 1963; and for attempts at taking on the analysis of illocutionary force head on see Bromberger, 1966 and Achinstein, 1983.)

WHAT FEATURES OF DISCOURSE ARE EXPLANATORY?

A rough and ready preliminary distinction can be made between the logical form of a discourse and its content. In general these aspects of discourse seem at first sight to be independent of one another. The same logical form can be found in discourses devoted to all manner of subjects, and the same subject may be set out in a variety of logical forms. Amongst philosophers there has been a long tradition of "logicism". Logicists try to give exhaustive accounts of puzzling concepts in terms of the logical structure of typical discourses alone. For instance the puzzling content of "substance" might be tackled by a logicist by examining the logical structure of predications. One might try to understand the concept of "causality" in terms of the logical structure of the "if . . . then . . ." sentence. The main alternative to logicism is the analysis of content. On the anti-logicist view a causal explanation would be picked out not by how it is structured but by what it says about the process, event or substance under discussion. In recent philosophy of science, logicism has been closely associated with positivism, that general point of view which depreciates theory, and tries to defend a simplistic empiricism.

In adjudicating between a logicist or an anti-logicist account of explanation we will not only be discussing alternative models that an attribution theorist might use for bringing out the main features of everyday explanations, but also touching on a metatheoretical issue: what is the proper way to go about giving an explanation in psychological science? Defects in the logicist account of explanation spill over into criticisms of the positivistic empiricism *still* surviving in tacit form in much academic psychology.

The logicist account of explanation is not new. One of the protective moves made by astronomers in the sixteenth century was to retreat to a logicist account of astronomy. The content of an astronomical theory was unimportant (was the sun *really* at the centre of the universe?), only the form mattered, because it was by virtue of the deductive form of astronomical explanations that predictions of the future appearance of the heavens could be made. Predictive power coincided with explanatory power. By the year 1600 five main astronomical theories were in contention. The Aristotelian, developed from the account of Eudoxus, had each planet attached to a nest of contrarotating, concentric spheres, the whole driven by one outermost sphere, the primum mobile. Ptolemaic astronomy used deferent circles with the planets on epicycles. Tycho Brahe had a sun-centred orbital system, the whole rotating around the fixed earth. Copernicus needed equants and eccentrics to jiggle his sun-centred circles into what Kepler, last of all, spotted were elliptical orbits. Each system was logically satisfactory. It saved the appearances. In a Hempelian framework a decision between them could only be made on such non-physical grounds as simplicity or economy. Kepler insisted that one, plainly his, had to be an accurate representation of the real planetary system. Part of the battle between heliocentrists and geocentrists (progressives and conservatives) was fought out over the nature of explanation. Kepler argued that what distinguished one explanation from another could not be form, as formal structures all explanations were the same, but content. But the most devastating blow to logicism came from Christopher Clavius (1602). Essentially it amounts to the point that if we adopt a logicist account of explanation there are far too many explanations (namely infinitely many) for any data base and there is no way, within the logicist framework of thought, of choosing between them. (This point has been revived, without acknowledgement of its Renaissance origins, by W.V.O. Quine as the problem of the underdetermination of theory by data.) Clavius' argument is very simple. Suppose we take syllogism as the form of explanation, and this looks a very reasonable choice, since many explanations do indeed appear, if spelled out, in syllogistic form. (The particular logical form chosen does not matter since the paradox is perfectly general.) Take a simple example:

> All iron things are magnetic
> Ships are iron things
> *therefore*
> Ships are magnetic

This explains why ships needed to be degaussed during the war to avoid setting off magnetic mines. But if valid syllogistic form (AAA or Barbara) is the heart of the explanatory power of the above story what is wrong with this?

> All ceramic things are magnetic
> Ships are ceramic
> *therefore*
> Ships are magnetic

It would still explain why ships need to be degaussed. "Don't be absurd!" you might say. The second "explanation" is a fraud since its two premises are false. But, the anti-logicist replies, that has nothing to do with logical form. The formal expression of the validity of both arguments is in the tautology

If p then q and if q then r so if p then r

and running through the truth table of this proposition will soon convince you that it is true *regardless of the ways truth and falsity are assigned to its components*. Of course we would pick the explanation which we think is true, but that is to bring in matters which lie outside the question of logical form, and invoke content.

A test for whether the general premise in a putatively explanatory syllogism is a law is to ask whether we would assent to a related counterfactual. Thus the two examples above can be distinguished by the intuition that we would assent to "If anything were iron it would be magnetic" and dissent from "If anything were ceramic it would be magnetic". But if we were to ask for the source of the intuition, from whence comes the assent and dissent, the same point reappears. We know something about the natures of iron and of clay that informs us that they will differ dispositionally in just this way. So even in imagined cases, picked out by the counterfactual grammar, assuming constancy of natures, we will conclude the way we do. Explanation still invokes physical *theory*.

There is a second fundamental objection to this way of construing explanation. It comes from criticisms of an attempt by Hempel (1965) to rescue logicism by adding the requirement of "nomologicality", that is that amongst the premises should be one or more laws of nature. Amongst the many objections to this project the most telling has been the criticism of the important consequence that has come to be known as the "prediction/explanation symmetry". All we need to predict an event, say, is a set of premises from which a description of that event can validly be deduced. We can predict that it will get dark this evening from the premises "It is now day" and "Night always follows day". Both premises are true, or can reasonably be taken to be, so this explanation escapes the problem of Clavius. Obviously those premises do not add up to an explanation. How does this case differ from Pasteur's prediction that anthrax bacilli would be found in the gut of earthworms in those farms where burying dead cattle had failed to stem an anthrax epidemic? Pasteur describes a mechanism of infection, whereas the night/day story merely describes an invariable (so far) correlation. We now have a clue as to how to proceed further. These objections put paid to the logical form account as a plausible theory of the locutionary force of an explanatory discourse. Perhaps we can find a better account in trying to identify the content of typical scientific explanations.

THE CONTENT OF AN EXPLANATORY DISCOURSE

An example commonly discussed in philosophy is that of the explanation of the syndrome or course of a disease. From the point of view of prediction a skilled physician ought to be able to say what will occur as the fever mounts, reaches a crisis and the patient returns through convalescence to normal health. From the initial symptoms it is often possible to predict the course of the illness. But to explain the succession of symptoms a quite different set of considerations is advanced, concerning the disease entity, the infection and the life cycle of the micro-organisms that constitute it, and the subtle and complex responses of the immune system of the sufferer, the work of the T-cells and so on. For prediction we need to know only facts of the same kind as those we wish to predict, in this case observable symptoms. But to explain we need to know the causal mechanism that produces the symptoms. In general the entities that make up the causal mechanism are of a different kind from those we can ordinarly observe, and are known in some other way than that by which we know the kinds of things we can observe as regular antecedents of the disease states. We can see now why positivists prefer to reduce the notion of explanation to prediction. Taking explanation seriously calls for the use of the theoretical imagination to create ideas of beings which are often yet to be observed. The rigid positivism of the old style epistemology of science had no use for the serious contemplation of the status of such beings.

The return to mainstream realism can be led by thinking about the medical sciences, and how they go about verifying explanatory theories. In those sciences explanation is almost wholly by reference to unobserved causal mechanisms. But the great success of the physical sciences in providing the scientific basis for equipment to expand the realm of the observable, such as microscopes, microassaying equipment and the like, encourages medical scientists to take their theoretical constructions seriously, to try to find them by microscopical or other means. It was no good just correlating the onset of malaria with mosquito bites; the explanation was incomplete without the identification of the vector and the plasmodium.

But since, in the first instance, the entities invoked in the explanans are unobservable, how does a scientist manage to think what they are? Here another aspect of philosophy of science must be brought in as an essential ingredient, the theory of theories. Our thoughts of unobservable entities are controlled indirectly by the source-models that a science at a certain state of development customarily makes use of. Great scientific advances are often made by the development and demonstration of the use of a new source-model. It is not unreasonable to see the explaining act in the natural sciences as the invention and use of a suitable source-model to enable the community to conceive of a causal mechanism, generative of phenomena, which is currently unobservable. Of the almost infinite variety of such models I will take the Darwinian evolutionary theory as an example, partly because of its great beauty and incomparable power. Once Darwin had become convinced that the kinds of animals and plants found on earth today were both different from those of the past and united with them by lines of descent, he was faced with the problem of explaining the origin of species. What was the mechanism of evolution? It was no good making any more observations or collecting any more specimens. If the process occurred at all, it was both too minute in its workings and too diffuse in its temporal span to appear before the eyes of any man. The mechanism, that is the explanation of the change of species, had to be imagined. But it had to be imagined within some conceptual framework, or (if one pays attention to the predominantly iconic modes of scientific thinking (c.f. Miller, 1985), within a system of images which would endow it with existential plausibility (Aronson, 1984)). Explaining then is a speech-act which makes use of a discourse which, in its literal meaning, makes reference to beings which are not capable, often, of being observed. In many cases these beings are the components and structures of generative or causal mechanisms.

We have a splendid example of such a complex speech-act in the first four chapters or so of Darwin's *Origin of Species*. The book opens with a description of the ways that farmers, pigeon fanciers and gardeners go about creating new breeds. They take account of *variations* from parent to offspring, and they allow to breed only those creatures which display a variation they want to preserve. Generation by generation this variation spreads through the stock by selective breeding so that a new population appears, differing from the stock from which they sprang. In extreme cases new breeds may wholly replace the old. This well known bit of biology becomes the source-model for Darwin's exposition of the explanation of the origin of species. The explanation works by analogy.

Source-model	Hypothetical mechanism
Domestic variation (observed)	Natural variation (observed)
acted upon by	*acted upon by*
Domestic selection	WHAT?

results in   *results in*

Domestic novelty   Natural novelty
(new breeds)   (new species)

We are led to create for ourselves the key *explanatory* concept, natural selection, to complete the analogical scheme. This pattern is both common and powerful. It is clear that the source-model not only controls the content of the explanatory concept but also provides it with a measure of initial plausibility, so that it can be taken seriously enough to be the basis of exploratory projects designed to see whether indeed such a process, or one sufficiently like it, exists.

An example that exploits the same structure can be found in the way we explain everyday events. That our conception of causation in domestic appliances, for instance, involves both events and mechanisms, is shown in the way we deal with a breakdown. The effect, the dishes having been washed, may fail to occur because a key event has not happened. One may have forgotten to switch on the machine. But the trouble may lie in the mechanism, the ontological tie that binds the Humean concomitant events of "switching" and "coming out clean" together. It may have disintegrated. Manufacturers know this sort of thing too. The non-Humean metaphysics of practical causal knowledge comes out in the fact that most instruction manuals suggest that you check the connection to the power point first, but if all is well there you should call the repair man. In his humble way he grasps the ontological tie that binds causes to effects and is conversant with the inner constitutions of things like timers and pumps. There are all sorts of source-models at work in domestic reasoning. I suppose the fluid theory of electricity is among the most powerful and ubiquitous in the formation of explanatory concepts. (Students of the works of the late James Thurber will remember the poignant case of the elderly relative who treated this model as a literal truth.)

CAUSAL POWERS AND TENDENCIES

But the physical sciences need something more. To see this let us shift to another example. The chemical behaviour of large samples of liquids, solids and gases is explained by reference to the behaviour of unobservables, molecules and chemical atoms, in the interplay of which chemists find the causal mechanisms of chemical reactions. But one might well ask for an explanation of the behaviour of chemical atoms, for instance why do they chum up in the proportions they do? And why are some clusters stable and others not? Lately we have had Carbon 60 as a very surprising molecule. The next level of explanation simply repeats the pattern of the level above. Drawing on the behaviour of positively and negatively electrically charged bodies as a source-model, a further step is taken, in which electrically charged electrons and protons are invoked, the story being filled out with neutral neutrons. The electrical properties of these structures explain the differences in behaviour of chemical atoms. And so on till we reach the current bedrock of "charmed" quarks of different "colours" and "flavours". What is the nature of these bedrock properties? They are nothing but causal powers.

At the end of every explanatory regress we must perforce shift from causal mechanisms to causal powers. So far as we know there is no further level of "mechanism" which will explain the behaviour of quarks. If they exist then their properties are indeed basic dispositions, unanalysable causal powers. Gravity may also be a referent of last resort, explanatorily. To explain the behaviour of falling bodies by reference to gravitational potential may be to cite a basic causal power. Oddly enough, in everyday life, when we don't know or have no idea of the underlying generative mechanism of some process, we may use causal powers as explanatory concepts. Individuals, substances, events, all can have causal powers. But conceptual clarity requires us to distinguish the power to set something going, which an event might have, from the causal power, the source of the subsequent activity. The detonator has the power to set off the dynamite, but it is the dynamite that has the causal power when the demolition of the chimney stack is in question. Powers then are highly relative in their attribution and distribution. This is because at the core of a power concept is some disposition. "This stuff has the disposition to . . . in conditions . . .". Very often the phrase which fills in the first gap in that sentence frame refers to something upon which the stuff in question acts. Different things have different liabilities to be affected by other things. Sulphuric acid has the power to dissolve zinc but not the power to dissolve gold. So to call sulphuric acid a solvent *tout court* is inadequate.

But the concept of causal power has another "ingredient", namely an implication of agency. Many things only act if stimulated. But there are also many things which are potent, that is will act unless prevented from so doing. The causal power schema then has the following form

Active being with tendency   (i) block   (inaction)
                              (ii) release   (action)

So in using a causal powers explanatory format and referring to some active being as the explanation of something requires the explicit statement of the blocking and releasing conditions. Strictly speaking if one cites the gravitational potential as the explanation of a falling body one must add that potential engenders a tendency to fall in the body, and that nothing is stopping it descending.

Physics has followed the Aristotelian mode for the most part. In this mode concepts like charge and field are created, and never more so than in the current explosion of concepts in high energy physics and quantum field theory (c.f. Harré, 1986). There is nothing anthropomorphic about this. It rests on such simple observations as the difference between the coming to move of a stationary billiard ball on a flat table by being struck by one which is moving, and the coming to move of a similar one supported by the hand when that support is removed; or the difference between the causal powers of a piece of soft iron before and after it has been magnetized.

The physical sciences, then, deploy two complementary explanatory formats. In both the format is multi-levelled. In the one a causal mechanism is imagined as the generator of the phenomena to be explained. In the other a causal power, the property of some powerful particular, such as a drop of acid or a stick of dynamite or a charmed quark, is invoked. I have pointed out how in the physical sciences causal mechanism explanatory formats lead to regresses closed only by adversion to basic entities with fundamental causal powers. But it is also the case that invocation of causal powers at the level of observable entities, say the acidity of a drop of acid, is usually backed up by a causal mechanism explanation, dropping down one level to the first explanatory level of the unobservable. Chemists invoke charged ions as the basis of explanatory mechanisms to account for causal powers like acidity. In a most important way, then, the two formats are complementary.

From the point of view of *logical* structure a discourse that cites a correlation and one that cites a disposition (causal power) are identical. Both may look like simple conditional propositions. But the latter is explanatory while the former is not. The difference then must lie in the paucity of content of the one and the richness of relevant content in the other.

REFERENCES

Achinstein P. (1983). *The Nature of Explanation*. Oxford: Oxford University Press.

Aronson, J.R. (1984). *A Realist Theory of Science*. London: Macmillan.

Bromberger S. (1966). "Why questions". In Colodny (Ed.), *Mind and Cosmos*. Pittsburgh: Pittsburgh University Press.

Bunge, M. (1959). *Causality*. Cambridge. Mass.: Harvard University Press.

Clavius, C. (1602). *In Sphaeram de Ioannis de Sacrobosco*. Lyon.

Harré, R. (1986). *Varieties of Realism*. Oxford: Basil Blackwell.

Harré, R. and Madden, E.H. (1975). *Causal Powers*. Oxford: Basil Blackwell.

Hempel, C.G. (1965). *Aspects of Scientific Explanation*. New York: Free Press.

Mill, J.S. (1879). *A System of Logic*. London: Longmans Green.

Miller, A.I. (1985). *Imagery in Scientific Thought*. Boston: Boston University Press.

Scriven, M. (1963). "Explanation and prediction", In M. Frankel and G. Maxwell (Eds), *Minnesota Studies in Philosophy of Science*. Vol. III. Minneapolis: Minnesota University Press.

7 Seeing the Connections in Lay Causal Comprehension: A Return to Heider

Charles Abraham

INTRODUCTION

By adopting an empiricist conception of causation, modern attribution theory, typified by Kelley's (1967) ANOVA model, portrays lay causal comprehension as a process of selecting causes on the basis of covariational analysis This chapter sketches an alternative perspective. I shall argue that understanding the means by which an event is generated, or caused, is prerequisite to its perception as a particular kind of event and that the language we use to describe events conveys particular kinds of causal or generative constructions. The main implication of this position is that a psychology of causal comprehension should focus upon linguistic devices we use to make meaningful connections between persons, entities and happenings. This is not a new departure but a return to the seminal work of Fritz Heider.

NATURALIZING HUME'S PROBLEM

Kelley (1967) based his ANOVA model on Mill's (1872/1973) "eliminative methods of induction" and thereby represented lay causal comprehension in terms of the empiricist definition of causation embodied in the "methods". This particular conception of causation can be better understood by tracing its origins to Hume's (1739) attack on the logical foundation of inductive reasoning. Put simply, Hume's "problem" was that he could see no grounds for assuming that a cricket ball travelling at a certain velocity would necessarily break a pane of glass even if he had observed numerous instances of similar balls breaking similar panes at this velocity. It could, he reasoned, just bounce off. He concluded that while we could observe "constant conjunctions" between causes and their effects we could not then assume any "necessary connection" between such causes and effects. Thus faith in the constancy of causation and inductive reasoning was stripped of any logical justification and ascribed to mere psychological habit or "custom". Mill's methods then, can be regarded as an attempt to rescue scientific practice from the unpredictability of Hume's nightmarish, successionist universe by sustaining the sanctity of inductive reasoning. In this, however, the methods cannot succeed as they are merely systematic procedures for identifying "constant conjunctions". They embody Hume's division of causes from their effects and accept association as the basis of causal comprehension. They make no attempt to reinstate the idea of "necessary connections" and therefore institutionalize rather than undermine Hume's position. When Kelley uses the methods as a means of representing lay causal comprehension institutionalization becomes naturalization. Here the very foundations of naive perception are assumed to be associationist, with lay causal comprehension being based on the observation of "constant conjunctions" without reference to "necessary connections".

Kelley summarizes his model as follows:

> The inference as to where to locate the dispositional properties responsible for the effect is made by interpreting the raw data . . . in the context of subsidiary information from experiment-like variations of conditions. A naive version of J.S. Mill's method of difference provides the basic analytic tool. The effect is attributed to that condition which is present when the effect is present and which is absent when the effect is absent. (1973, p. 194).

We can understand the proposed processes better by referring to Figure 1, a McArthur (1972)-type operationalization of Kelley's model. The perceiver, following Hume, searches for causes of the observed event, namely, Chris's fall. She has available three types of covariational information (that is, information identifying established "constant conjunctions") namely, consensus, distinctiveness and consistency information *(CsDCy)*. In this case the information forms one of the "informational templates" which, according to Orvis *et al.* (1975), unambiguously identify a particular causal source (that is, highlight a single "constant conjunction"). First, the high consensus information tells our subject that being on this path and falling occur together, across persons. The high distinctiveness information tells her that being Chris and falling on paths is not, according to previous observation, associated. Finally, the high consistency information tells her that being Chris and being on this path is associated with falling. This enables our subject to identify a "constant conjunction" between falling and being on this particular path so, following Mill, she makes the inference that something about the path caused Chris to fall.

EVENT	Chris fell on the path.
CONSENSUS INFORMATION (HIGH)	Most people fall on this path.
DISTINCTIVENESS INFORMATION (HIGH)	Chris does not usually fall on paths.
CONSISTENCY INFORMATION (HIGH)	Chris usually falls on this path
INFERENCE	Something about the path causes Chris to fall.
DISPOSITIONAL ATTRIBUTION	The path is very uneven.

Figure 1: The Kelleyan conception of lay causal comprehension as operationalized by McArthur (1972)

One further information-processing move remains, that is, the attribution of "dispositional properties responsible for the effect". Our perceiver may, for example, conclude that the path is very uneven. Kelley does not explain how the perceiver selects these dispositional properties but portrays dispositional attribution as a kind of shorthand for the foregoing analysis. As he puts it:

> The ascription of an attribute to an entry amounts to a particular causal explanation of effects associated with that entry . . . . So all judgements of the type "Property X characterizes Entity Y" are viewed as causal attributions (1973, p. 107).

Thus Kelley follows Hume and Mill in portraying the perceiver as striving to make sense of a succession of essentially unconnected occurrences in terms of observed "conjunctions" or covariations. No "necessary connections" are referred to because the covariational analysis itself is thought to provide an adequate basis for understanding what leads to what in everyday life. I shall argue that, on the contrary, such a model fails to encompass the interpretative processes which render everyday events intelligible in terms of particular kinds of connection.

REVEALING THE CONNECTIONS IN CAUSAL COMPREHENSIONS

From Kant (1781) onwards philosophers have developed refutations of Hume's analysis. Perhaps the most cogent of these is Harré and Madden's (1975) closely argued "theory of natural necessity". The basis of their argument is that in order to conceive of reality we must make assumptions about the natures of persons and entities and, while these assumptions hold, we can be sure that, in certain circumstances, certain entities will, necessarily, behave in particular ways. As they put it:

> Between the nature of a thing and what it can do and undergo there is an ontological tie that binds, and this tie is to be understood in terms of the generative mechanisms that produces the specific response of the particular in given circumstances (p. 53).

In this analysis observation cannot, as Hume supposed, show the ontological ties to be broken; if an entity does not behave as we had expected, it is because it was not, after all, the kind of entity we took it to be. It is not because causation is fundamentally unreliable. Thus by recognizing an entity as a particular kind of entity we delimit the range of causal connections it can, conceivably, be involved in. For Harré and Madden, then, causal comprehension derives from our knowledge of the generative capacities of particular entities and classes of entities. Such knowledge depends upon the categorization and recategorization of entities in terms of the causal or generative processes in which they may legitimately be involved. This is the essence of scientific inquiry and, I shall argue, the purpose of lay dispositional attribution.

Numerous philosophers of science have similarly argued that the identification of causal links presupposes a network of assumptions concerning the natures of entities and the kind of causal connections they can conceivably be involved in. Cohen and Nagel (1934), for example, point out that a scientist relying on Mill's methods to discover the cause of baldness would make little progress because the methods do not offer guidance on which of the plethora of possible associations are worth checking out. Should the investigator, they ask, try to discover if all balding persons were "brought up on cod liver oil?" They conclude that:

> We must . . . start the investigation with some hypothesis about the possible cause of baldness. The hypothesis which selects some circumstances as possibly relevant and others as not is constructed on the basis of previous knowledge of similar subject matter. The hypothesis is not supplied by the canon [that is, Mill's methods] (p. 252).

Miller (1978) makes exactly the same point with reference to the medical practitioner when he says:

> All medical enquiries take place within a more or less circumscribed domain of theoretical commitment in which curiosity is limited by what the investigator regards as possible . . . investigation presupposes suspicion (p. 84)

And Bronowski (1971) rejects associationist philosophies of science as follows:

> Their [that is, Humean philosophers'] theories are still dominated by the belief that science is an accumulation of facts, that a generalization grows of itself from a heaping of instances in a narrow field. They think a scientist is persuaded that light arrives at the eye in a shower of quanta because he does an experiment, does it again and repeats it to be sure.
>
> Alas this is not what any scientist does. He may indeed repeat an experiment two or three times, if its outcomes strikes him as odd and unexpected. But even here he means by odd and unexpected precisely that it conflicts with what other experiments in other fields have led him to believe . . . A set of results is odd and unexpected, in the end it is unbelievable, because it outrages the intricate network of connections that has been established between known phenomena (p. 44)

These texts argue that Hume's problem can be analytically circumvented and that Mill's methods provide an inadequate basis for understanding scientific practice. It is not my intention to detail these arguments but to point out to the reader that the basis of

Kelley's analogy, that is, the idea of the association-seeking scientist, can be seen to be fundamentally flawed. Thus just as Hume failed to take account of the crucial relationship between the perception of an entity as a particular kind of entity and the comprehension of events in which it is seen to be involved in terms of particular kinds of connections, so Kelley's model is unable to embrace naive assumptions about the nature of persons, entities and possible connections. This, I shall argue, renders Kelley's model of lay causal comprehension inadequate in exactly the same manner as Mill's methods fail to represent scientific practice adequately.

THE LAY PERCEIVER AS THEORETICIAN

The inherent assumptions of our causal representations can be revealed by a closer analysis of our understanding of the event-description and information presented in Figure 1. To understand the event-description itself we must mobilize assumptions about the functions of paths and the capabilities of people in general (having assumed, of course, that "Chris" is a person). Additionally we must be able to understand the meaning of the verb phrase "fell on". To illustrate this consider the difference in understanding conveyed by the event-description; "Chris flung herself to the path". The introduction of a different verb phrase changes the assumptions we make about the mechanisms governing Chris's descent and therefore the kind of characterizations of her and the path which are appropriate to comprehending the sequence of connections constituting the event. We cannot, in this case, even with the same $CsDCy$ (consensus, distinctiveness and consistency information), explain the event in terms of the path's unevenness. If "something about the path" caused Chris to fling herself to the ground then it must be something like the path leading unexpectedly on to a firing range, that is, something that provides an intelligible intention for Chris's action. Notice how the word "caused" refers to very different kinds of causal connections or generative relationships in these two cases. In the first case we are concerned with a process of physical mechanism under the control of gravitational forces, while in the second we are trying to comprehend an action under the control of Chris's volition. To understand these two different kinds of event we characterize

Chris and the path so that they "fit into" the connective scenarios communicated by the two verb phrases. This then informs our reading of the *CsDCy*. Thus, while Kelley is right to emphasize the importance of dispositional attributions (or characterizations) in establishing particular causal comprehensions, the Humean basis of the ANOVA model prevents us from representing the cognitive portrayal of relationships and connections which lies at the heart of lay causal comprehension and underpins dispositional attribution.

It is worth noting here that the crucial role of verb phrases in communicating different causal comprehensions was highlighted by McArthur's (1972) study. Despite being limited to explanatory responses such as, "something about the path caused . . ." or "something about Chris caused . . .", subject responses were importantly influenced by the type of verb phrase included in event-descriptions. It is perhaps surprising that these results did not cast doubt upon the importance of *CsDCy* in determining dispositional attributions and focus attention upon the relationships between the meaning of such verb phrases and the structure of subjects' causal comprehensions but, in fact, the study is usually regarded as providing empirical support for the ANOVA model.

The way in which meaningful event-descriptions enable us to construe the generation of events in terms of particular kinds of relationships and connections can be powerfully illustrated by attempting a methods-based, Kelleyan analysis on meaningless, or nonsense, descriptions. The example in Figure 2 has exactly the same logical structure as that in Figure 1 and we can, following Mill, similarly infer that, "something about the brimbly briff caused the brotchety brot to brattle". But what does this mean? It might be fun to speculate that the brimbly briff is very brothy but, apart from the imaginative wanderings which may be elicited by such nonsense-speak, we are none the wiser. We have not achieved an understanding of the event because we are unable to deploy our sense-making assumptions about the natures of the involved entities and casual connections. We do not, in the end, know what we are talking about! By itself then, in the absence of sense-making "theories" or assumptions, the most that an observed covariation can tell us is that there is something to be explained. And indeed, whether or not we can sensibly speak of observing meaningless associations seems questionable.

EVENT DESCRIPTION	The brotchety brot brattled the brimbly briff.
CONSENSUS INFORMATION (HIGH)	Most brots brattle the brimbly briff.
DISTINCTIVENESS INFORMATION (HIGH)	The brotchety brot does not usually brattle briffs.
CONSISTENCY INFORMATION (HIGH)	The brotchety brot usually brattles the brimbly briff.
INFERENCE	Something about the brimbly briff caused the brotchety brot to brattle.
DISPOSITIONAL ATTRIBUTION	The brimbly briff is very brothy.

Figure 2: Nonsense item based on McArthur (1972)

Thus if we are to utilize the person-as-scientist analogy to model lay representations and explanations of causal connections we must examine the "theories" and "hypotheses" lay perceivers use to make sense of their everyday experience. The intelligibility of experience depends upon our ability to conceive of it in terms of particular kinds of connections involving entities with certain kinds of capabilities interacting according to predetermined patterns. Our consideration of Figure 2 demonstrates that without the application of these interpretative processes we are left foolishly wondering about covariation between brimbliness and brattling!

A RETURN TO HEIDER

Turning to an analysis of the "theories" and assumptions of lay perceivers would not be a new approach, but a return to the work begun by Fritz Heider (1958). Heider is often dubbed the "founder" of attribution theory (c.f. e.g. Harvey *et al.*, 1976) yet much of modern attribution theory constitutes a radical departure from Heider's original work. His *Psychology of Interpersonal Relations* encompasses a wide range of ideas which have generated a series of socio-psychological theories from Festinger's (1957) cognitive dissonance theory to Kelley's (1967) attribution theory. The wealth of ideas included in the book allows different readings to be made of different parts and it is not, therefore, surprising that my reading of Heider (1958) differs from Harold Kelley's. I would suggest, however, that a rereading of his original proposals has much to offer the psychologist seeking to represent lay causal comprehension.

Heider saw his task as explicating the meaning-making devices embodied in everyday language. He set about analysing the conceptual structures we use in understanding what leads to what in everyday events. With regard to action, for example, he notes:

> The concepts involved in the naive analysis of action stand . . . in systematic relations to each other just as do the terms of a good scientific system of concepts. Our task will be to formulate this system more explicitly (p. 79)

By looking more closely at the descriptions of everyday events offered by lay perceivers, Heider hoped to reveal the meaning-making devices we use to make sense of our experiences. As he put it much later:

> I had to discover the basic concepts of common sense psychology . . . I had to analyse and think through simple expressions to get out the essential meaning (1976, p. 13)

Heider recognized that causal comprehension was a process of creating meaningful representations through interpretation, and in contrast to mainstream attribution theorists, he concentrated on modelling this "effort after meaning" (Bartlett, 1932).

Using this approach he identified two distinct "theories" underlying lay causal comprehension and called these "personal" and "impersonal causality". These represented two different ways of making sense of an event, with "personal causality" referring to a set of systematically related concepts which collectively mapped out the meaning of intentionality. Thus Heider notes:

> Sometimes the statement, "He did it" is really a short cut for "It was the weight of his body that caused the board to break" but unless intention ties together the cause-effect relations we do not have a case of true personal causality (1958, p. 100)

According to Heider, then, perceivers can draw upon two separate conceptual networks (or schemata) to understand the generation of an event. These require different characterizations of (or dispositional attributions to) involved persons and entities, because they describe very different kinds of generative connections. The availability of these two meaning-making schemata is, I suggest, evidenced by our effortless understanding of the difference in meaning conveyed by "fell on' and "flung herself to".

THREE GENERATIVE SCHEMATA

A number of attribution theorists have acknowledged the importance of Heider's distinction, including Kruglanski (1975), Buss (1978) and Fincham and Jaspars (1980), and a similar distinction is discussed by McArthur (1972). In accounting for her "verb effects" she distinguishes between subjects' comprehension of "manifest verbs" describing "actions" and "accomplishments", and "subjective verbs" describing "emotions" and the formation of "opinions". We can see then that, while Heider and McArthur both refer to naive constructions of causal connections in terms of agency or intentionally, they distinguish these from two different types of perceived connection. Heider refers to lay perceivers' comprehension of physical mechanism while McArthur recognizes our understanding of events in terms of automatic emotional or cognitive reactions.

The distinction between these two types of construction can be illuminated by considering a certain Miss D's letter to an agony columnist.[1] She wonders what she should infer from the fact that her "six-foot, football-playing boyfriend . . . kept blowing his nose" while they were watching "one of those crazy old weepies". What kind of dispositional attributions are appropriate? Is he, she asks, "a bit of a cissy?" The agony columnist clearly working from different preconceptions, dismisses the "cissy" characterization and declares that the boyfriend is a "tender-hearted human being", but then goes on to undermine the validity of this debate by suggesting that "this young man may have a cold coming on". This confuses the issue by suggesting that a set of physical mechanisms (that is, inflammation of the mucous membrane) may be primarily responsible for the nose-blowing. Since "cissy" and "tender-hearted" describe Miss D's boyfriend's emotional reactivity they depend upon nose-blowing being interpreted as the product of an emotional reaction and are rendered inapplicable by this new physical-mechanism interpretation. Here we see just how important it is to distinguish between these two kinds of "non-agency causality". Failing to decide between emotional reaction and physical mechanism, our agony columnist is unable to give any clear advice on appropriate dispositional attributions and so leaves Miss D to ponder the "nose-blowing" unaided!

Combining McArthur's distinction with Heider's then, it is possible to identify three distinct types of causal, or generative, connection which perceivers may use to understand the relationships involved in everyday events, namely, *intentional action, psychological reaction* and *physical mechanism*. These refer to distinct sets of organized concepts which, when deployed, impose a set of meaningful connections on any particular experience and thereby render it intelligible. These connections are, however, different in each case and require different kinds of characterizations of (or dispositional attributions to) involved persons or entities. I have called these sets "generative schemata" (cf. Abraham, 1982) where "schemata" is used in Bartlett's (1932) interpretative sense and distinguished from Kelley's (1972) use of the term to describe stored, covariational databases. I propose to examine the composition of these three generative schemata in greater detail and suggest that this work is of relevance to any analysis of lay comprehension, whether this be undertaken by psychologists or agony columnists!

Heider (1958) undertook a thorough conceptual analysis of our everyday usage of agency concepts such as "can" and "try", and my brief outline of the *intentional generative schema* is based largely on this work. The generative element in this version of causal connectedness is the assumed presence, or activity, of an *agent*. This agent, usually a person, is assumed to be able to *intentionally exert* certain *powers* or abilities in order to alter aspects of the surrounding *environment*. The nature of the powers ascribed to an agent delimits her range of possible action within any given environment (that is, prescribes a conceivable *sphere of action* for that agent). This rudimentary structure is represented diagramatically in Figure 3. The paradigm case here is the perception of environmental change, such as the disappearance of an object, in terms of another's deliberate action, for example, theft. To achieve such an interpretation the perceiver must be able to identify the prerequisite elements, particularly an agent possessing the necessary powers and

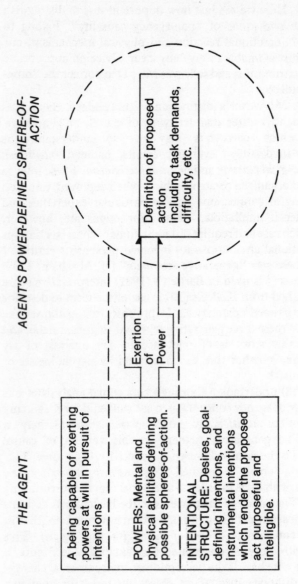

Figure 3

The intentional schema; a description of the interpretive structure of action perception.

intentions whom she believes to have actually executed the action. Thus, in assembling evidence intended to convince others of such an interpretation we attempt to demonstrate means, motive, opportunity and actual involvement.

The *evaluative-emotive generative schema* enables us to understand events in terms of psychological reactions. Here the paradigm case is the perception of behaviour in terms of emotional responses, for example, a fear resulting from an animal phobia. The generative element in this case is the identification of what I have called an *evaluating being*. Ordinarily these will be persons who are recognized as agents but it is not their perceived agency which renders these reactions intelligible. Indeed, it is crucial that the behaviour in question is not thought of as intentionally directed. If it were, we would be considering the perception of a deliberate act of pretence and not a genuine *re*action. Thus this schema introduces an element of automatic and uncontrolled response into our understanding of causal connectedness. The evaluating being is assumed to be capable of *evaluating* entities and persons on the basis of *previous experience* (including exposure to culturally-shared theories and evaluations). Such experience and subsequent conscious and unconscious evaluations are usually viewed as having either a positive or negative flavour. Whatever type of evaluation is made, however, it is assumed to give the evaluating being a certain sensitivity or *potential for reaction* which can then be automatically *triggered* by future encounters with similar entities or persons. These later experiences need not be obviously similar to the sensitizing experiences but must be assumed to be *related to them in the mind of the evaluating being*. Thus we assume a link between the evaluating being's present experience and prior sensitizing experiences. This preliminary analysis is represented diagramatically in Figure 4.

By comparison to our understanding of intentional actions and psychological reactions there seems to be relatively little generalized interpretative structure involved in our comprehension of physical-mechanism connections. All entities and beings assumed to have physical existence may be involved in such mechanisms. Such physical entities must, however, be assumed to have fairly stable *natures* or constitutions. These constitutions and the particular condition of an entity at a particular time (e.g. charged, raised on high . . . etc.) determine the kinds of *physical interactions* which can

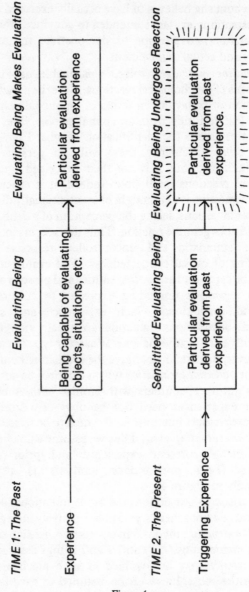

Figure 4
The evaluative-emotive schema; a description of the interpretative structure of the perception of psychological reactions.

conceivably occur between such bodies. The only common feature of such interactions appears to be the transfer or transformation of energy. As Piaget puts it:

> The chief mark of our adult mechanistic conception of the world is that energy is transmitted, this body loses its energy communicating it, that other increases its energy by receiving it from outside. (1930, p. 118)

These entirely automatic and unthinking interactions include billiard-ball collisions and the operation of electromagnetic fields. They may be understood in microscopic detail or in a more imprecise microscopic manner, so that, in the latter case, a substance may simply be characterized as having an inherent physical capacity to sustain certain interactions (e.g. the lay comprehension of gravitational forces, the operation of acids, explosives etc.). The general structure of this kind of causal construction is represented diagramatically in Figure 5.

GENERATIVE SCHEMATA AND DISPOSITIONAL ATTRIBUTIONS: AN OVERVIEW

These three generative schema enable us to view causal comprehension as a process of specifying types of connection rather than causes per se. In the case of our agony columnist, for example, the main question is not whether the "boyfriend" or the "old weepie" is "the cause" of his nose blowing but rather, what kind of event the nose blowing is, that is, what kind of connections account for its occurrence. In answering this question we render the event intelligible and so perceive it as a particular event (for example, "being upset by an old weepie"). If we change our minds, as the columnist suggests, we perceive a different event (for example, "clearing a blocked nose").

Within this view dispositional attributions are not portrayed as "cause identifiers" but rather as characterizations of persons and entities which, given certain background assumptions, enable them to sensibly "slot into" an already-assumed set of generative connections. Such attributions, then, only "explain" an event insofar as they presuppose a generative construction. They "explain" the assumed connections in the sense that they fit local

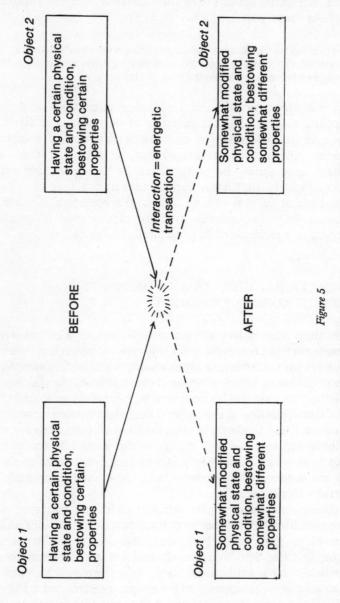

Figure 5

The physical schema; a description of the interpretative structure of physical-mechanism perception.

details into the general structure of presumed, sense-making schemata.

This focus upon construing *types of connections between elements* rather than identifying *discrete causes* distinguishes my approach from Kelley's Mill-based conception and the more recent work of Brown and Fish (1983). Using verb categorization, reminiscent of McArthur (1972), Brown and Fish derive two "causal schemata", which relate closely to my "intentional" and "evaluative-emotive" schemata, but within this framework they retain a Kelleyan conception of dispositional attribution as "cause-identification". Within mainstream attribution theory, however, the work of Jones and McGillis (1976) is a valuable adjunct to the work described here. They see dispositional attribution as "information gain" because it provides characterizations not already present in the background "target" and "category" expectations we bring to our experience. I would argue that these new characterizations bridge gaps between our background assumptions about involved persons and entities and what is required of them by the connection-making structures of the causal schemata we use to conceptualize events.

It must be emphasized that the three schemata are not intended to be a definitive model but rather sketches of what I take to be the basic building blocks of lay causal comprehension. I am not, for example, suggesting that everyday causal comprehensions fit neatly into one or other of the three schemata or that they are deployed in a mutually exclusive manner. Indeed, it seems obvious that even a simple construction, highlighting the use of one schema, such as Miss D's understanding of her boyfriend's problem, presupposes a complex interpretative background drawing upon all three schemata. Further problems arise with psychologists' second-order, causal constructions. Here we find interpretations which recombine elements of the three schemata to form hybrid structures. Peters (1958), for example, points out that the power of Freud's conception of "unconscious wishes" is that it provides us with a set of generative connections describing behaviour, neither as intentional action, or physical mechanism, but as something between the two. Similarly Boden's (1977) discussion of purposeful, computer programs combines familiar connection-making relationships in novel assemblies.

Yet, despite these limitations, reference to the three schemata enables us to explicate the underlying interpretative structures constituting these generative constructions. Thus the primary function of the proposed schemata is to provide a framework within which such deconstructive analysis may be undertaken. By unveiling the connection-making relationships proposed and assumed by lay causal comprehensions, as expressed in explanations, we can identify the role of particular characterizations (or dispositional attributions) in sustaining certain kinds of causal comprehensions. This may be especially important in the investigation of interpretative structures maintaining particular behaviour patterns, for example in examining health beliefs (cf. King, 1983). Such analyses may also be reflexive, revealing the kinds of causal connections embedded in psychologists' second-order understandings of lay behaviour. Skinner (1974), for example, explicitly denounces the utility of the intentional schema in psychological theory-building, declaring that, "there is no place in the scientific position for a self as a true originator . . . of action" (p. 225). This seems rash if lay perceivers are using this kind of construction to understand their own behaviour. Heider's (1946) own balance theory and Festinger's (1957) theory of cognitive dissonance use the evaluative-emotive schema to understand the formation of attitudes and opinions, while Harré and Secord (1972) and Shotter (1975) urge psychologists to view their subjects as agents, acting intentionally. The kind of causal constructions used by psychologists to comprehend behaviour has crucial implications for the characterization of persons and their potential. If these characterizations themselves then become part of lay causal comprehension (cf. Moscovici, 1961) they may be viewed as part of a causal process operating upon the resources available to persons for action-planning. Here the human subject is conceived of as a self-constructing agent (cf. Taylor, 1971; Harré, 1983). In general then, the point of the work is to provide analytic tools which will help us become more aware of the generative connections we use to understand our experiences both as lay perceivers and as second-order psychological theorists.

SOME EMPIRICAL EVIDENCE

In order to assess the relative utility of the ANOVA and "generative schemata" conceptions a series of studies was undertaken

(Abraham, 1982). I shall not attempt to provide reports of these studies within the space constraints of this chapter but merely indicate to the reader the kind of results which emerged.

Methodological considerations

The studies referred to here were modelled upon McArthur's (1972) work but relied upon free-response data so as to facilitate subjects' expression of their comprehensions. This was a particularly important methodological consideration in view of Garland *et al's*. (1975) suggestion that the adequacy of the ANOVA model may have been overestimated because of researchers' reliance upon precoded response formats.

This data was then coded using a series of coders' manuals derived both from definitions of ANOVA and generative schemata concepts, the point of the investigation being to discover which of the categorizations best corresponded to subjects' responses. High intercoder reliability was established for all manuals.

In order to test the usefulness of my schemata I wanted to see if subjects' initial understanding of an event description, in terms of particular causal relationships, would shape further responses in accordance with the interpretative structures of three schemata. Ten McArthur-like event descriptions were therefore precategorized in terms of the particular generative schemata I expected subjects to use in understanding them. These are presented in Table 1. Since the event descriptions are fairly simple it was thought that they would be understood primarily in terms of a single schema and the most intuitively acceptable reading was chosen. It must be noted, of course, that subjects' understanding of such event descriptions is always context-sensitive, so that, for example, although "Chris fell on the path" is precategorized as being understood in terms of the "physical" schema it is quite possible that it would elicit an "intentional" reading in another context.

If subjects were indeed using the three schemata as I expected, then the nature of their responses to any particular event description ought to be predicted by the structure of the precategorized schema. In other words their responses should show evidence that their understanding of, for example, "Chris fell on the path" is structured in terms of the physical schema. To assess this I developed a number of sets of coding categories corresponding to the schemata

Table 1: Event descriptions and their schemata-derived categorizations

Description No.	Event Description	Schemata-derived categorization
1	Chris walked into the post	PHYSICAL (occurrence)
2	Joan put a sticker advocating improved road safety on her car	INTENTIONAL (action)
3	Sue was frightened by the dog	EVALUATIVE-EMOTIVE (emotion)
4	Steve thought the building was very tall	EVALUATIVE-EMOTIVE (opinion)
5	Henry got a birdie on the fifth hole	INTENTIONAL (achievement)
6	Chris fell on the path	PHYSICAL (occurrence)
7	Joan parked her car in Church Street	INTENTIONAL (action)
8	Sue was upset by the letter	EVALUATIVE-EMOTIVE (emotion)
9	Steve thought the concert was fantastic	EVALUATIVE-EMOTIVE (opinion)
10	Henry got a good grade in French	INTENTIONAL (achievement)

structures outlined above. To illustrate these, the categories used to code subjects' dispositional attributions are presented in Table 2.

What kind of information do we need to explain the occurrence of events?

In the first of these studies subjects were asked to list the information they would need to explain the occurrence of described events (see Table 1). Responses were then coded according to Kelley's three "covariational-informational" categories, namely, consensus, distinctiveness and consistency, and also according to ten "schemata-derived-informational" categories, closely resembling the thirteen categories presented in Table 2.

It was found that only 24% of subjects' responses included requests for *CsDCy* information and that only 7.3% of identified requests could be coded according to these three categories. This confirms Garland *et al.'s* (1975) finding that only a relatively small percentage of free-response requests, for explanatory information, are for *CsDCy* information.

When the same requests were coded in terms of schemata-derived categories it was found that 49% corresponded to these categories and that 83% of subjects' responses included schemata-related requests. More importantly, it was found that descriptions' precoding categorizations were a fairly good predictor of the *kind* of schemata-related requests a particular description would give rise to. Thus descriptions precoded as evaluative-emotive (emotions and opinons) tended to elicit requests pertaining to the structure of the evaluative-emotive schema and so on. This meant that descriptions' precoding categorization corresponded to the subsequent coding of requests in terms of schemata structure, so that "evaluative-emotive" descriptions elicited requests categorized according to informational categories derived from the evaluative-emotive schema, "physical" descriptions elicited requests categorized as "physical-schema" requests and so on. In total, 65% of schemata-related requests corresponded to precoding categorization in this way.

It would appear then, that, contrary to ANOVA predictions, subjects do not think covariational information will help them understand why events occurred. This suggests that they may not, after all, be seeking constant conjunctions between causes and effects. It would also seem that subjects are very interested in

Table 2: Schemata-derived dispositional coding categories

Category Number	Schema-Derivation	Coding Category
1.	PHYSICAL	General Physical States and Conditions of Involved Entities and Beings
2.	PHYSICAL	State of Involved Being's Sensory Systems
3.	INTENTIONAL	Volitional Capacities of Involved Agent
4.	INTENTIONAL	Involved Agent's Knowledge and Belief Structures
5.	INTENTIONAL	Types of Intention-Formulations Typifying Involved Agents
6.	INTENTIONAL	Degree of Exertion Typifying Agent
7.	INTENTIONAL	Types of Event-Relevant Task Demands
8.	INTENTIONAL	Range of Agent's Relevant Powers
9.	EVALUATIVE-EMOTIVE	Involved Being's Prior Experiences
10.	EVALUATIVE-EMOTIVE	Involved Being's Prior Evaluations
11.	EVALUATIVE-EMOTIVE	Involved Being's Capacity for Reaction
12.	EVALUATIVE-EMOTIVE	Involved Being's Reaction-Expressive Style
13.	EVALUATIVE-EMOTIVE	Subjects' Own Prior Evaluations of Involved Persons and Entities

information relating to the three schemata, with half of all requests so categorized. Moreover, this interest is specific to the schema in terms of which the event description is initially read so that we can predict the kind of requests subjects will make by consulting the structure of the schema in terms of which an event description is precategorized.

What do dispositional attributions do?

In this study the event descriptions were combined with Orvis *et al.'s* (1975) informational templates so that each item resembled that shown in Figure 1. Each event description was combined, in turn, with each informational template (denoted, in Table 4, by 1A 1B 1C . . . etc.). Subjects were then asked to read these items and explain why the events occurred. Dispositional attributions to, or

Table 3: Percentage of responses to items incorporating similar CsDCy, including dispositional attributions to persons, stimuli and circumstances

CsDCy of Item	Dispositional Attributions to Persons	Dispositional Attributions to Stimuli	Dispositional Attributions to Circumstances
Low-Low-High (P)	71	35	33
High-High-High (S)	56	45	29
Low-High-Low (C)	61	43	34

characterizations of, persons and entities made in the course of these explanations were then coded in two ways. First according to the ANOVA cause-identification categories of person, stimulus and circumstances, and then according to the schemata-derived categories presented in Table 2.

It was found that 92% of subjects' responses included dispositional attributions to persons, stimuli or circumstances. The question, however, is whether or not such dispositional attributions serve to identify covariationally-defined "causes". To answer this question we must consult Table 3, which shows the degree of correspondence between such dispositional attributions and the provided covariational information. The ANOVA model would suggest that the figures along the diagonal of this table would tend towards 100 while the rest tended towards zero, that is, the dispositional attributions would identify the covariation conveyed by the CsDCy information. This is not, however the case, and it was found that only 37.5% of the coded person, stimulus and circumstance dispositional attributions corresponded to the provided consensus, distinctiveness and consistency information in this way. It was also discovered that 31% of these dispositional attributions were found in responses which also contained dispositional attributions to other causal sources. In fact, 36% of

Table 4: Subscriptions to dispositional coding categories across items

Content Categories	Item Number											
	1A	1B	1C	6A	6B	6C	2A	2B	2C	7A	7B	7C
1. Physical Characteristics	2	14	3	1	14	5	1	—	—	2	5	1
2. State of Persons' Sensory Systems	13	7	11	8	3	7	—	—	—	—	—	—
3. Volitional Capacity of Agents	—	—	—	—	—	—	—	—	—	—	—	—
4. Knowledge and Beliefs of Agents	—	—	—	—	—	—	4	6	3	2	—	2
5. Typical Intention Formations of Agents	—	—	—	—	—	—	2	—	2	1	1	—
6. Typical Degree of Exertion by Agents	—	—	—	—	—	2	1	—	—	1	—	—
7. Ease or Difficulty of Task	—	—	—	1	—	—	—	1	—	—	—	—
8. Normal Powers of Agents	2	2	1	1	2	—	1	1	—	—	1	—
9. Prior Experience Characterizing Evaluating Beings	—	—	—	1	—	1	1	—	—	—	—	1
10. Prior Evaluations Characterizing Evaluating Beings	2	—	—	—	—	—	7*	12*	8*	1	—	—
11. Typical Reactivity Potential	1	—	—	—	—	—	—	1	—	1	—	—
12. Typical Reaction or Expressive Style	—	—	—	—	—	—	1	1	2	—	—	—
13. Subject's own Evaluations	—	—	—	1	—	—	1	—	2	—	—	1

Table 4: Subscriptions to dispositional coding categories across items

Content Categories	Item Number																	
	3A	3B	3C	8A	8B	8C	4A	4B	4C	9A	9B	9C	5A	5B	5C	10A	10B	10C
1. Physical Characteristics	1	4	1	—	—	—	12*	11*	3	1	—	—	—	—	—	—	—	—
2. State of Persons' Sensory Systems	—	—	—	—	—	—	3	1	4	1	—	3	—	—	—	—	—	—
3. Volitional Capacity of Agents	—	—	—	—	—	—	—	—	—	—	—	—	—	—	—	—	—	—
4. Knowledge and Beliefs of Agents	—	—	—	—	—	—	3	1	—	2	—	—	—	—	—	—	—	—
5. Typical Intention Formations of Agents	—	—	—	—	—	—	—	—	—	—	—	—	—	—	—	—	—	—
6. Typical Degree of Exertion by Agents	—	—	—	—	—	—	—	—	—	—	—	—	—	—	—	3	—	2
7. Ease or Difficulty of Task	—	—	—	—	—	—	—	—	1	—	—	—	2	9	7	3	5	4
8. Normal Powers of Agents	—	—	—	—	—	1	1	—	1	—	—	1	15	10	3	10	13	3
9. Prior Experience Characterizing Evaluating Beings	—	—	—	—	1	—	4	1	1	1	2	1	—	—	2	4	1	—
10. Prior Evaluations Characterizing Evaluating Beings	7	—	—	4	3	—	—	—	1	11	6	5	—	—	—	2	—	—
11. Typical Reactivity Potential	1	—	1	6	2	1	—	—	—	1	2	1	—	—	—	—	—	—
12. Typical Reaction or Expressive Style	—	—	—	—	—	2	—	—	—	—	—	—	—	—	—	—	—	—
13. Subject's own Evaluations	2	10	5	6	13	5	—	—	1	2	7	7	—	1	1	—	1	—

Key

□ = schema-related category ranges; predicted high subscription rates.

* = very high unpredicted subscription rates.

subjects' responses contained dispositional attributions to two or more Kelleyan "causes". This suggests that these dispositional attributions were not made in response to the provided *CsDCy* information and that their purpose was not to identify discrete "causal sources".

When subjects' dispositional attributions were coded according to the schemata-derived categories it was found that 70% of responses included at least one codeable characterization. The question here is whether or not these characterizations correspond to the structure of the generative schemata in terms of which the event descriptions were precoded. Table 4 shows the distribution of these characterizations across categories and event descriptions. It should be noted that earlier studies had shown that, while responses to "intentional" descriptions tended to include characterizations corresponding to the structure of the intentional schema, there was an important difference between responses to "action" and "accomplishment" descriptions. The former tended to elicit characterizations of agents' knowledge and intentions while the latter elicited characterizations of agents' powers and task difficulty. In response to these findings I made more precise predictions about the kind of characterizations that these two types of "intentional" descriptions would elicit. Specifically the action descriptions (2 and 7) were expected to elicit characterizations corresponding to categories 3, 4 and 5 while the accomplishment descriptions (5 and 10) were expected to elicit characterizations corresponding to categories 6, 7 and 8. We can see, then, that the figures in the boxed areas on Table 4 would be expected to be high (in this case, tending towards 17) while the rest would be expected to tend towards zero. Table 4 shows 71% of characterizations correspond to these predictions. It is also worth noting that 56% of the characterizations which did not correspond to my predictions were elicited by two particular event descriptions (numbers 2 and 4). These turned out to be interesting exceptions! It would seem then, that the generative schemata are not only useful in categorizing subjects' dispositional attributions, or characterizations, but that having decided which of the three schemata subjects are using to understand an event, their structures enable us to predict the *kind* of characterizations subjects will make. This suggests that these characterizations are being used to fit the event into a particular set of causal connections identified by the selected generative schema. This would, of course, explain multiple characterizations (of, for example, the person and the stimulus) as these would serve to sustain connections *between* elements of an event, rather than identify discrete causes.

Discussion

These studies show that the ANOVA model cannot predict the kind of information subjects will ask for when trying to explain McArthur-like event descriptions and, moreover, that the pattern of dispositional attributions to persons, stimuli and circumstances, included in free-response explanations, is not determined by provided covariational information. This strongly suggests that subjects' comprehension of these event descriptions is not adequately represented by the Mill-like procedures underpinning the ANOVA model. The studies also show that the three schemata can be used to precategorize event descriptions in terms of the causal connections they are seen to involve and that, on this basis, the structure of the schemata can be used, with some success, to predict the kind of information subjects will require to explain these events and the kinds of dispositional attributions they will include in their explanations. This suggests that subjects' comprehension of the event descriptions depends upon "seeing" the kinds of connections mapped out by the three schemata and fitting described persons and entities into these connections by means of appropriate characterizations.

CONCLUSION

My argument is that to portray causal comprehension as the observation of temporal covariations between aspects of our environment is to obscure the complex interpretative work required to recognize events as particular kinds of events involving particular kinds of persons and entities. If we are to represent this "work" we must examine the "theories" lay perceivers and scientists use to "see" the connections between persons and entities and characterize them appropriately. This necessitates a focus on the content and meaning of explanations representing perceivers' understandings.

The three generative schemata provide a starting point for such an analysis of lay causal comprehension; a starting point which has already shown its potential in a series of empirical studies. In the longer term however it is clear that the broad distinctions embodied in the schemata will themselves obscure critical differences between our understanding of similar, but distinct, types of causal connectedness. In King's (1983) examination of subjects' "natural explanations" of heart disease, for example, the particular structure of different physical-mechanism explanations (e.g. "poor diet" and "heredity") could have crucial implications for perceivers' adherence to preventive-care programmes. It would seem, then, that the social psychology of causal comprehension must develop representations appropriate to the particular "natural explanations" it encounters in the various fields in which it may be applied. Only by explicating the assumptions underlying our causal comprehensions will we be able accurately to represent the way causal comprehension shapes our perceptions of, and responses to, the environment.

NOTE

1. *Evening Argus,* Brighton, England, 5 February 1980.

REFERENCES

Abraham, S.C.S. (1982). "Towards an interpretative model of causal attribution; a critique of attribution theory". Unpublished doctoral thesis, University of Sussex.

Barlett, F.C. (1932). *Remembering.* Cambridge: Cambridge University Press.

Boden, M.A. (1977). *Artificial Intelligence and Natural Man.* Hassocks, Sussex: Harvester Press.

Bronowski, J. (1971). *The Identity of Man.* New York: The Natural History Press.

Brown, R. and Fish, D. (1983). "The psychological causality implicit in language". *Cognition, 14,* 237–73.

Buss, A. (1978). "Causes and reasons in attribution theory: A conceptual critique". *Journal of Personality and Social Psychology, 36,* 1311–21.

Cohen, M.R. and Nagel, E. (1934). *An Introduction to Scientific Method.* London: Routledge & Kegan Paul.

Festinger, L. (1957). *A Theory of Cognitive Dissonance.* Stanford: Stanford University Press.

Fincham, F.D. and Jaspars, J.M.F. (1980). "Attribution of responsibility; from man the scientist to man the lawyer". In L. Berkowitz (Ed.), *Advances in Experimental Psychology* (Vol. XIII). New York: Academic Press.

Garland, H., Hardy, A. and Stephenson, L. (1975). "Information Search as Affected by Attribution Type and Response Category". *Personality and Social Psychology Bulletin,* 1, 612–15.

Harré, R. (1983). *Personal Being.* Oxford: Basil Blackwell.

Harré, R. and Madden, E.H. (1975). *Causal Powers; a Theory of Natural Necessity.* Oxford: Basil Blackwell.

Harré, R. and Secord, P.F. (1972). *The Explanation of Social Behaviour.* Oxford: Basil Blackwell.

Harvey, J.H., Ickes, W.J. and Kidd, R.F. (Eds), (1976). *New Directions in Attributional Research* (Vol. I). Hillsdale N.J.: Lawrence Erlbaum.

Heider, F. (1946). "Attitudes and cognitive organisation". *Journal of Psychology,* 21, 107–12.

Heider, F. (1958). *The Psychology of Interpersonal Relations.* New York: Wiley.

Heider, F. (1976). "A Conversation with Fritz Heider". In J.H. Harvey *et al.* (Eds), *New Directions in Attribution Research* (Vol. I), Hillsdale, N.J.: Lawrence Erlbaum.

Hume, J. (1739). *A Treatise of Human Nature.* London.

Jones, E.E. and McGillis, D. (1976). "Correspondent inferences and the attribution cube: a comparative reappraisal". In J.H. Harvey, W.J. Ickes and R.F. Kidd (Eds), *New Directions in Attribution Research, Vol. I,* (pp. 389–420). Hillsdale N.J.: Lawrence Erlbaum.

Kant, E. (1781). *Critique of Pure Reason* (trans. N.K. Smith). London: Macmilland.

Kelley, H.H. (1967). "Attribution theory in social psychology". In D. Levine (Ed.), *Nebraska Symposium on Motivation.* Lincoln NBR University of Nebraska Press.

Kelley, H.H. (1972). "Causal schemata and the attribution process". In E.E. Jones, D.E. Kanouse, H.H. Kelley, R.E. Nisbett, S. Valins and B. Weiner (Eds), *Perceiving the Causes of Behavior.* Morristown N.J.: General Learning Press.

Kelley, H.H. (1973). "The processes of causal attribution". *American Psychologist,* 28, 107–28.

King, J. (1983). "Attribution theory and the health belief model". In M. Hewstone (Ed.), *Attribution Theory: Social and Functional Extensions.* Oxford: Basil Blackwell.

Kruglanski, A. (1975). "The endogenous-exogenous partition in attribution theory". *Psychological Review,* 82, 387–406.

McArthur, L.A. (1972). "The how and what of why: some determinants and consequences of causal attribution". *Journal of Personality and Social Psychology*, 2, 171–93.

Mill, J.S. (1872/1973). "System of Logic" (8th edn) in J.M. Robson (Ed.), *Collected Works of John Stuart Mill* (Vols VII and VIII). Toronto: University of Toronto Press.

Miller, J. (1978). *The Body in Question*. London: Cape.

Moscovici, S. (1961). *la Psychanalyse; son Image et son Public*. Paris: Presses Universitaires de France.

Orvis, B.R., Cunningham, J.D. and Kelley, H.H. (1975). "A closer examination of causal inference: the roles of consensus, distinctiveness and consistency information". *Journal of Personality and Social Psychology*, 32, 605–16.

Peters, R.S. (1958). *The Concept of Motivation*. London: Routledge & Kegan Paul.

Piaget, J. (1930). *The Child's Conception of Physical Causality*. London. Routledge & Kegan Paul.

Shotter, J. (1975). *Images of Man in Psychological Research*. London: Routledge & Kegan Paul.

Skinner, B.F. (1974). *About Behaviourism*. London: Cape.

Taylor, C. (1971). "Interpretation and the sciences of man". *Review of Metaphysics*, 25, 1–15.

8 Knowledge Structures and Causal Explanation

Robert P. Abelson and Mansur Lalljee

INTRODUCTION

In this chapter, we are concerned with how explanations depend upon prior knowledge. We view the process of explanation not as an abstract logical calculus, but rather as a commonsense problem of connecting the thing to be explained with some available conceptual pattern, appropriately modified to fit the circumstances. Explanation, in other words, is a form of understanding; it involves recognition of something initially puzzling by assimiliation to that which is familiar. Processes of application of knowledge structures or schemas arise in many areas of cognitive science, and have recently been much discussed (Galambos, Abelson and Black, 1986; Rumelhart, 1984; Rumelhart and Ortony, 1977; Schank and Abelson, 1977).

One might suppose this orientation toward explanation to be straightforward and unexceptionable. Nevertheless, it represents a departure from the dominant paradigms of attribution theory in social psychology. Those paradigms, historically descendent mainly from the theorizing of Heider (1958) and Kelley (1967, 1972, 1973), depict explanation as an essentially logical process in which the explainer's primary task is to establish the locus of causation as lying either in the individual, in the environment, or in some interaction between them. We have elsewhere enumerated a number of criticisms of classical attribution theory (Lalljee and Abelson, 1983; Leddo, Abelson and Gross, 1984; Leddo and Abelson, 1986), and will not pursue these criticisms here. We will instead try to articulate the process of explanation in the terms we find most convincing and natural.

Explanation kernels

For convenience, we label the thing to be explained as the "event", albeit we recognize that not all things worthy of explanation are events. Some are states of nature—"Why do ducks have webbed feet?"—or states of human affairs—"Why are French public schools closed on Thursdays?". Events, however, will be our main focus. We have said that explanation proceeds by the assimilation of the event in question to a familiar pattern of knowledge. Let us denote the familiar explanatory vehicle as the *kernel* of the explanation. Every explanation requires both the selection of a kernel, and the application of the kernel to fit the case at hand. We will give many examples of kernels, but just to get us started and convey what we mean by a kernel, consider a puzzling event discussed by Schank (1986) in his recent book on the nature of explanation. A famous three-year American race horse named Swale was one day suddenly found dead, at the peak of his career. No official explanation has ever been given.

One may speculate at length about this unexpected death, but two ideas seem to come readily to mind: over-exertion and foul play. Each of these constitutes a possible explanatory kernel. The "over-exertion" kernel consists in the knowledge that too much physical activity can kill people—and horses—perhaps by triggering a heart attack. The "foul play" kernel is composed of a cluster of ideas about motivated evildoers with the opportunity and the means to do bodily harm to someone—or some horse. Credible adaptation of either of these kernels to the Swale case would require fitting further details, specifying why Swale in particular might have been subject to a heart attack, or what persons in the racing world might have been in a position to perpetrate foul play.

Two fundamental problems in a theory of explanation are what kinds of things can constitute kernels, and how they are recruited in the service of a particular explanation problem. To make headway on these two problems, it is first useful to discuss distinctions between rather different types of explanation situations. One major distinction (Lalljee and Abelson, 1983) is between *contrastive explanation* and *constructive explanation*. In contrastive explanation, an expected event does not occur, and the explainer's task is to account for this failure. Clusters of expectations are provided by the context, and potential explanation kernels are sometimes easy to enumerate by comparing the failed performance with a corresponding successful performance. In the constructive explanation case, on the other hand, an anomalous event occurs without a clear contextual background. The explainer often must construct a kernel out of thin air, as in the Swale example.

Types of explanation situations

The contrastive/constructive distinction can be further refined into at least three subtypes of each. Table 1 outlines the six types, the first three being contrastive, the last three constructive.

Table 1: Types of explanation situations

Goal	Outcome	Explanation Locus	Comment
Presumed	Presumed failure	Lack of expected action	Explanation often involves reinterpretation of presumed goal. See Lalljee & Abelson (1983) on contrastive explanation.
1. ("Why did actor violate expectations?")			
Known	Failure	Unspecified	A focus of classical attribution theory. Further analysis depends on type of goal which has failed. See Leddo & Abelson (1986).
2. ("Why was goal not achieved?")			
Known	Failure	Failed action	Further analysis depends on type of failed action
3. ("Why did action not succeed?")			
Preserve status quo	Failure	Unspecified	This involves "P-goals" (Schank & Abelson, 1977), and requires constructive explanation.
4. ("How did that happen?")			
Known	Unexpected success	Unspecified	Explanation may involve "hidden resources". Analysis not pursued in present chapter.
5. ("How did so-and-so do it?")			
Unknown	Unknown	Action	Another case of constructive explanation. Analysis not pursued in present chapter.
6. ("What's the purpose of that action?")			

Type 1 was analysed by Lalljee and Abelson (1983). Here an expected sequence of actions in the service of a presumed goal is marked by the puzzling absence of an expected action. The example we used in that paper was of a chap who leaves his bicycle downtown and doesn't lock it. In the present chapter we will present the somewhat richer example of a policeman who fails to arrest a burglar after apprehending and disarming him. This omission contrasts with what one expects, and cries out for explanation.

The successful performance of an action sequence typically involves an intentional chain which begins with a goal and proceeds through a series of steps of planning and execution. When a performance omission is the event to be explained, therefore, the kernel of the explanation could reside in either a goal failure, a planning failure, or an execution failure.

Goal failure means that the goal normally presumed for the performance was somehow not operative. This category can be further subdivided into "goal absence", "goal conflict", "goal reversal", and "goal satisfied".

Goal absence indicates the case in which the main actor, because of naiveté, misunderstanding, or an abnormal state of consciousness, did not intend what one might have presumed. For the scenario of the policeman who fails to arrest the burglar he has apprehended, the explanation kernel could invoke a rookie cop who (somewhat implausibly) didn't realize that he was supposed to arrest burglars after foiling them, or who (again implausibly) from a previous blow on the head temporarily forgot that he was an arresting officer. Goal conflict implies the presence of a competing goal which overrides the pursuit of the expected goal. For example, the officer at the critical moment may have received a radio call to proceed immediately to a scene of ongoing mayhem and murder. Goal reversal covers the tricky contingency of an actor who for ulterior reasons has a goal opposite to the normal goal in the situation. Thus our officer because of bribery may from the start have intended to let the burglar go. Finally, the subcategory "goal satisfied" is meant to suggest a scenario by which the expected goal has already been satisfied. This is not easy to imagine in our policeman/burglar example, but the appropriate kernel would be something like, "The policeman knew that his partner was on the verge of arresting the burglar."

The category of planning failures covers the anticipation of enablement conditions of various kinds. Our unfortunate policeman may have neglected to bring his handcuffs, for example. This category has not been neatly subcategorized, perhaps because there seems such a miscellaneous variety of possibilities, many of which may depend on the type of performance that has been planned. Dyer (1983) has analysed a number of proverbial missteps such as bad timing ("Locking the barn door after the horse is stolen"), lack of contingency planning ("Counting your chickens before they are hatched"), and so on, but these have not been systematically applied to the analysis of explanations. Neither has the category of execution failures (e.g., the paddy wagon broke down) heretofore been clarified.

Execution failures have been a focus of classical arbitration theory approaches to the explanation of performance failures when the details of the action sequence are not given—our Type 2 in Table 1. Weiner, Frieze, Kukla, Reed, Rest and Rosenbaum (1972) have adumbrated the 2×2 classification of internal vs. external, and stable vs. unstable causes for unfavourable (i.e., failed) outcomes, such as flunking a test. The four resulting subcategories of explanation are lack of ability, lack of effort, task difficulty, and bad luck. In a later treatment, Weiner (1979) added the dimension of controllable vs. uncontrollable, creating eight combinations. In a knowledge structure orientation to the explanation process, these subcategories are rather too general and vague. Perhaps "Harry is not good at mathematics" is the best one can do in explaining why Harry failed a mathematics test. But "he/she wasn't smart enough" is not a very edifying explanation for everyday failures such as being late for an appointment, not answering a letter, or getting lost trying to find a new address.

Leddo and Abelson (1986) have compared a number of different concrete planning and execution failure explanations for noncompletion of mundane, scripted (Abelson, 1981) activities such as getting a book from a library, going to a movie, or staying at a motel. One of the prominent subcategories these authors identified was what they called "failure of entry". Many mundane activities are carried out in specific locations to which entry must be gained before the activity can take place. Thus failure to return with a book from a library could be attributable to the library being closed, or failure to stay at a motel could be because all the rooms were occupied. This category is a failure in what Schank and Abelson (1977) referred to as "delta-social control", the transfer of social control to the actor from an institution or another actor.

As Schank and Abelson (1977) have discussed, goal pursuit typically involves the successful completion of a well-structured chain of subgoals. To satisfy an "entertainment goal" (*E*-goal), for example, the actor must gather information (delta-know), get to the right location (delta-proximity), and gain admission (delta-social control). There may in addition be a need to get certain items of paraphernalia (golf balls, opera glasses, etc.) instrumental to the activity. Outcome failure of a goal can often be localized in the failure of one of these component actions, but one might want to know why this action itself failed. This constitutes our third type of explanation situation.

If no very particular expectation has been violated, but an unusual event has occurred, the explainer must develop a kernel from scratch—or rather, from what is known about the facts of similar events. What kinds of things can cause a Swale to die, for example?

Unusual events, such as sudden deaths, often violate a desired aspect of the status quo. They are in that sense goal failures, of the goal type Schank and Abelson (1977) call "preservation goals" or *P*-goals. These goals are unique in that they are usually not actively pursued with persistent plans. Rather, motivated action doesn't typically occur until after the latent *P*-goal is violated. Someone who has lost a wallet experiences the failure of a *P*-goal, and initiates a search to recover it. Often the cause of *P*-goal failure is unclear, and requires explanatory effort. This fourth type of situation will be amplified in detail below.

Two other types of explanation situations will simply be mentioned, but not explored further in this chapter. All the previous types involved goal failure. Failure needs explanation in that motivated activity presupposes an anticipation of success so that (to some extent) failure is always unanticipated. But, as noted by Weiner (1985), success could require explanation, too, if unexpected. How come homely, spineless Hector has won the heart of Lydia, the beauty queen? Or to take real-world examples meaningful to sports fans sharing the authors' respective loyalties, what can explain the recent modest successes of the otherwise feckless San Francisco Giants baseball team, or the Oxford United football squad? A variety of explanatory speculations can be constructed for such cases.

Finally (at least for Table 1), there is the situation of weird behaviour not serving any obvious goal. Why is Eugene lying on the sidewalk, or walking about with a bunch of bananas on his head? The explanatory problem is to find the purpose served by the anomalous behaviour. This type seems difficult to analyse.

EXPLANATION PROTOTYPES AS EXPLANATORY KERNELS

Although it is in many respects useful to distinguish these different explanation situations (and no doubt others not listed in Table 1) there is a common thread that runs through all of them.

The central question in explanation is *what kinds of things cause such-and-such kind of event*. We propose that the answer lies in the concept of *explanation prototypes*. The explainer is assumed to have available a large number of explanation prototypes (*XP*s). These are knowledge structures which capture standard accounts of events characterized by typical bundles of features.

An *XP* can provide the kernel of a constructive explanation, or of a contrastive explanation focussed on a specific failure. What the explainer must do is to locate the characteristic event to which the event to be explained is most similar, and then modify its *XP* if necessary to suit the particular event. For example, HEART ATTACK is an *XP* accounting for a class of significant episodes dangerous to life. One possible solution to the Swale mystery is by reference to HEART ATTACK. However, in the typical heart attack (as commonly conceived), we have a man over 50 who smokes and/or has high blood pressure and/or is overweight, who over-exerts himself and then complains of pains in his chest, whereupon he is rushed to the hospital and is diagnosed as having had a heart attack; he may suddenly die, or he may survive and, with the aid of medication and possibly surgery, resume a more or less normal life. The race horse Swale was not a man over 50 by any means, but could be assumed to be often exposed to the conditions for over-exertion—and possibly also because of repeated stress might be a sufferer from the equine equivalent of high blood pressure. These latter two conditions provide plausible matches to the heart attack

XP, as does the suddenness of death. Thus, "Swale had a heart attack" can be a candidate kernel for the explanation of Swale's death. It only becomes a satisfying explanation if the non-matching details, such as young horse vs. older man, can be relaxed as non-essential, or somehow be modified to be regarded as matching after all. (See Schank, 1986, for a more detailed discussion of this example, or Kass, Leake and Owens, 1986, who have written a computer program with considers several possible explanations of Swale's death. These latter authors, by the way, refer to the modification of non-matching details as "tweaking" a candidate explanation).

PROTOTYPE THEORY IN PSYCHOLOGY

We are ready for a more systematic discussion of the nature and role of event prototypes in explanation, beginning with a brief review of the way prototypes in general are treated in the literature of cognitive psychology. The popularity of the notion of prototypes began with a critique (Rosch, 1973) of the classical concept of the nature of categories. Categories of natural things, such as fruits or birds, and perhaps artificial things such as furniture, had long been regarded as in principle definable by sets of necessary and sufficient features (e.g., *X* is a bird if and only if *X* flies, has feathers, lays eggs, etc.). Examples of exceptional cases (penguins don't fly), ambiguous classifications (tomato as fruit vs. vegetable), and other difficulties led to the seemingly radical suggestion that categories might have no necessary and sufficient conditions for membership. Instead, as Wittgenstein (1953) had originally suggested, a set of category members might be mutually related by "family resemblance". No two members of the family share all relevant features, but each member shares many features with most members. Particular features characterizing large numbers of members (e.g., "sings" and "is smaller than six inches" for birds) are considered most central to the category, and members possessing the most central features (e.g., robins) are most *prototypical* of the category. Prototypicality has a number of strong processing consequences; for example, subjects are faster in verifying that a prototypical case (such as robin) is a member of a category (birds) than that a peripheral case (such as penguin) is a member (Smith, Shoben and Rips, 1974).

The psychological properties of prototypicality are a matter of such discussion and debate (see Smith and Medin, 1981, for an authoritative coverage; also see Wattenmaker, Nakamura and Medin, this volume), but there is little doubt that the concept has taken hold in cognitive psychology. It has also spread to cognitive social psychology: among many applications, Cantor and Mischel (1977, 1979) have used prototypes in the analysis of impressions of personality, and Schank and Abelson (1977) have popularized the concept of scripts (Abelson, 1973, 1976) as prototypical routinized action sequences. (No two trips to a restaurant share exactly the same set of actions, but each trip shares many actions with most other trips). We propose here to extend the applicability of prototypes still further with our notion of explanation prototypes, or *XP*s. The idea has much in common with Schank's (1986) "explanation patterns" (also called *XP*s).

One of the background ideas we need before proceeding further is the *hierarchical* nature of categories. Categories can often be subdivided into subcategories, and themselves may indeed by subcategories of "higher" classifications. Thus both furniture and tools are specializations of the superordinate, "man-made objects"; furniture contains the subcategories of table, chair, bed, desk, etc.; in turn, tables can be subcategorized into kitchen tables, dining-room tables, card tables, coffee tables, etc. (and each of these subcategories could perhaps be further broken down).

Rosch *et al.* (1976) asked the psychological question whether people tend to prefer a particular level of the categorical hierarchy when classifying, thinking about, or discussing objects. That is, when we see a wooden thing with four legs and a seat, do we tend to think and say, "There's a piece of furniture", or "There's a chair", or "There's a kitchen chair"? In this example, the commonsense choice seems to be the middle hierarchical level, "chair". The superordinate level, "furniture", is too vague, and the subordinate level, "kitchen chair", is for most purposes too specific. Indeed, preferred usage of a middle hierarchical level was the result obtained by Rosch *et al.* (1976) for a variety of content hierarchies, using a number of experimental test procedures. Those authors called the preferred level the *basic level* of categorization.

Our claim is that the kernel of an explanation is an account associated with the prototypic event category most applicable to the event to be explained. The kernel *XP* is chosen from a set of contrasting possibilities at the basic level of the event category hierarchy. Let us spell out what we mean by this.

Suppose the event is that Harry, who knew he had his wallet before attending a concert in the park, discovers after the concert that his wallet is missing. What could explain this? The two obvious possibilities are that he lost it, or that it was stolen. What is the natural way to conceptualize these possibilities? Surely we don't want to code these two alternatives as ACCIDENT vs. CRIME. It would be a vapid response to the question, "Why was Harry's wallet gone?" to say, "Because of a crime." That simply does not provide enough information. (Note that classical attribution theory often seems to settle for the overly vague attribution categories of "internal cause" vs. "external cause"). On the other hand, we probably would not want in the first instance to jump to an overly specific conclusion such as, "Harry's wallet was probably lifted by Louie the Dip while Harry was in the ticket queue." Such an account would require a good deal of further knowledge of the situation. This explanation might be given later, as a refinement of an early account, but at the outset the most reasonable level of explanation would seem to be something like, "Harry's wallet was probably stolen by a pickpocket." Here, PICKPOCKETED is the *XP*. It lies at an intermediate level of specificity, like the basic levels for object categories in prototype theory. However, we still have to pin down exactly how to define critical event categories.

The generation of XP sets

It may seem reasonable for PICKPOCKETED to be the raw basis for the explanation of a loss of a wallet, but one wonders what sorts of middle-level categories might arise altogether, for the explanations of myriad other events. Shall we have SKYDIVING, CLAM-DIGGING, BANKRUPTCY, RUBELLA, etc., etc., etc.? We need, in other words, some disciplined way to generate sets of *XP*s. This is a difficult problem, one that besets other applications of knowledge structure theory (Galambos, Abelson and Black, 1986; Schank and Abelson, 1977). Much knowledge of the real world is highly concrete, covering quite numerous objects and events; its mental representation, therefore, is extensive and seemingly non-parsimonious. Furthermore, there are potentially large variations in individual experiences and expertise, leading to considerable variety in knowledge structures between individuals.

A neurologist, for example, after observing a man of 60 who shuffles his feet and very rarely blinks, can attribute these symptoms to Parkinson's disease, an explanation not usually available to the layperson. Obviously we cannot offer a catalogue of *XP*s that covers every piece of knowledge available to every conceivable type of expert. What we will try to do is suggest how widely shared knowledge of common and important types of events might be organized in *XP*s.

We make the major assertion that *XPs are organized to capture the various ways that important but not totally predictable outcomes can occur.* The motivation for this assertion is the commonsense observation that individual and collective explanatory effect will be most extensively and elaborately spent on outcomes that people care about, that they typically want to achieve or avoid but are not completely sure they can. For instance, given the unpleasantness and potential recurrence of the experience of losing one's wallet, one would like to be able to assign a cause on each such occasion. This might help one find it, and could make a recurrence less likely. People cudgel their brains, and ask friends what to do, and generally allocate a great deal of attention to the explanation of the loss of a wallet. Afterwards they may dwell on the recounting of such experiences ("When we visited the ruins at Olympia, I left my purse on this little wall, and the next thing I knew it was gone. Well, . . . etc.").

It is small wonder that well-understood systems of categories should grow up around such characteristic critical events as the loss of possession of a valuable thing such as a wallet. Most people can readily give a set of potential *XP*s for this happening. Although we have not yet gathered the relevant data, it seems a safe bet that respondents asked to provide general explanations given the hypothetical mystery that they have lost possession of a wallet, would produce ideas clustering into a few basic prototypes such as DROPPED-OUT-OF-ITS-PLACE, MISLAID and PICK-POCKETED. One might be inclined to add MUGGING to the list, but we will leave it out for the reason that the victim would know it, if mugged, ending the mystery of the loss. For the critical event of getting stuck in a traffic jam, the *XP* set might include ACCIDENT-UP-AHEAD, CONSTRUCTION-WORK, BAD-ROAD-CONDITIONS, RUSH-HOUR, and HOLIDAY.

There are a couple of things to be noted about sets of *XP*s. First of all, we are (as discussed above) concerned with widely shared knowledge, not with specialized explanations available to particular groups of individuals. One could haggle over what "widely shared" means. For example, a possible XP for a traffic jam might be IT'S-THE-M4. This would be highly meaningful for British readers of this chapter, but mystifying to Americans. By and large, however, our XPs are widely shared in modern, urbanized Western culture.

Second, when one writes out XP sets, one is struck by their concrete particularity. There does not at first blush seem to be an abstract way to match up the members of one XP set with the members of another to create generic XP types. For different critical event categories *(CECs)*, different XP distinctions seem to occur. For example, for the wallet-loss event, it seems important to distinguish DROPPED-OUT from MISLAID, the difference having to do with the kinds of people who might know about the lost wallet, the characteristic locations of the two errors (e.g., while getting into or out of a car vs. while paying for popcorn), and so on. For the traffic-jam case, no comparable distinctions occur. Instead, many of the distinctions have to do with time of day and time of year. ACCIDENT-UP-AHEAD could occur at any time, but RUSH-HOUR and HOLIDAY are specifically time-bound, BAD-ROAD-CONDITIONS is somewhat seasonal, and CONSTRUCTION-WORK occurs in blocks of certain weeks.

But perhaps a judgment of unorganizable particularity in types of XPs for different *CECs* is too hasty. When we try to compare wallet-loss with traffic-jam, perhaps we are comparing plums and grapefruit. These two *CECs* represent different types of explanation situations, arising from different specifications in Table 1. Wallet-loss is an instance of failure of a P-goal (Type 4 in the Table), while traffic-jam is an instance of a failing action (getting from one place to another, or "delta-proximity") for a subgoal of some larger plan (Type 3 in the Table). Perhaps if we confined our attention to XP sets for a homogeneous explanation type, their structural organization would become clearer. (Indeed, it was our desire to seek such structural clarity that motivated the development of Table 1 in the first place). In a way, the purest of our explanation types is Type 4, the violation of preservation goals, because fixing the goal type sharply narrows the relevant considerations. We focus on an analysis of XP sets for this type.

Prototypic explanations for the violation of preservation goals

Figure 1 presents *XP* sets for various *P*-goal failures. These are distinguished according to what the actor loses: an object, a job, a relationship, and so on. The figure is not intended to be anywhere near exhaustive—one can list many other kinds of things individuals can lose, such as a skill, good health, life, or the social control over some activity. There are also other ways the goal of preservation can fail besides through outright loss—objects may break, for example. But we will cover enough cases to suggest what issues are raised in the structuring of *XP* sets.

We do not list *XP*s for general object-loss. If we did, we might try LOST-TRACK OF, and EXPROPRIATED. Such overly general types are not really adequate, as we will see. Compare with the suggested *XP*s for wallet-loss: DROPPED-OUT-OF-PLACE, MISLAID and PICKPOCKETED. As previously noted, it is important for the wallet loser to distinguish dropping a wallet unintentionally from absent-mindedly leaving it somewhere. It is similarly important to specify pickpocketing as a possible cause of a wallet loss rather than just the vague idea that somebody took it. This becomes more obvious when we look at the details inside the respective *XP*s (which we will do later). In any case, object-loss is somewhat too high-level a *CEC* for concise explanation by an *XP*.

On the other hand, we might not want the *CEC* to be low-level. Why should the loss of a wallet be separated as a characteristic event from the loss of a purse, or a gold cigarette lighter, or a book of travellers' cheques? In all these other cases, DROPPED-OUT-OF-PLACE, MISLAID and PICKPOCKETED are possible *XP*s. True, it may be a bit less plausible that a purse would slip unobserved off a woman's lap or shoulder than that a wallet would slip unobserved out of a man's pocket. And a pickpocket might be less inclined to lift travellers' cheques than wallets or purses. But these are matters of slight shifts in the prioritization of the three *XP*s in the several cases, not grounds for rejecting applicability of the set to these various object losses.

These observations imply that the optimum level of abstraction for categorizing this type of object loss is something like "the loss of a valuable object that is carried on the person in public." Other somewhat different object-loss categories such as "the loss of valuables from home" would command different *XP*s: the

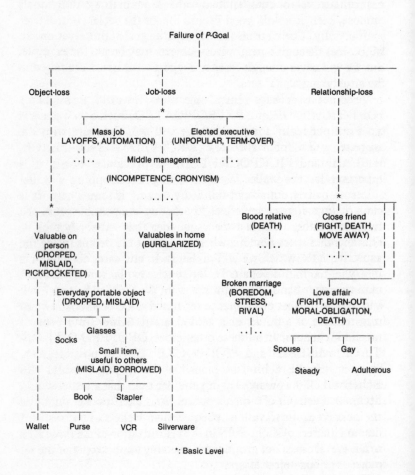

Figure 1

A hierarchy of characteristic critical events, with explanatory prototypes
(XPs in capitals).

overwhelming choice would be BURGLARIZED. If the object-loss category were "the loss of a small, useful object," the major *XP*s might be MISLAID and "BORROWED". Again, the set is somewhat different—the BORROWED explanation arises from the notion that colleagues or family members can sometimes expropriate useful things like a book or stapler without telling you.

What object attributes are important in defining these basic object-loss categories, each governing its own set of *XP*s? There are four: size, value, utility and typical location. Size matters because large things cannot plausibly slip unnoticed out of place, or be mislaid, or be casually borrowed. Value matters because people are motivated to steal valuables, bringing theft to the fore as an explanation for loss of a valuable. Utility matters in motivating casual borrowing. Finally, typical location is relevant to the manner in which thefts are carried out, pickpocketing being qualitatively very unlike burglary.

Let us briefly consider some possible *XP* sets for a different class of *P*-goal failure, the loss of a personal relationship. Three features whose combinations characterize the sample of relationships shown in Figure 1 are attraction, sexual intimacy, and genetic relation. On the face of it, high attraction should make it easy to maintain a personal relationship; sexual intimacy should make it easy or difficult depending on the satisfaction involved; and genetic relation of course requires no action for its maintenance. What *XP*s, then, could apply to the termination of a love affair, characterized by high attraction and satisfying sex? They would have to involve paradoxical patterns belying the apparent ease of relationship continuation, such as FIGHT and BURN-OUT, or overwhelming environmental influence such as MORAL-OBLIGATION, or DEATH, capable of overcoming the positive factors. Similarly, the loss of a close friend could be due to FIGHT, MOVES-AWAY, or DEATH (but probably not to BURN-OUT). By contrast, a broken marriage calls to mind the more or less straightforward alternatives of BOREDOM, STRESS and RIVAL. A relationship with a blood relative can be terminated only by DEATH.

In Figure 1 we also suggest *XP* sets for a few types of job loss, but rather than pursue these new content areas, we return to object-loss and investigate what is *inside XP*s.

THE CONTENT AND FUNCTIONING OF EXPLANATORY PROTOTYPES

Table 2 outlines some component bits of knowledge internal to *XP*s using as an illustration the three alternatives *XP*s for loss of a valuable carried on the person. Each knowledge component potentially has three purposes: to help decide whether this particular *XP* should indeed be selected, to fill in explanatory detail for the event at hand, and to suggest action to remedy the event or prevent recurrence. The central core of each *XP* is the *method* by which the event prototypically occurs, its causal dynamics.

Taking MISLAID first, we note that the causal sequence begins when the lost object, denoted *Y*, is removed at some time during the time period bracketing its loss. The prototypic reasons for *Y*'s removal are to use it, or to permit some action that would be difficult or disadvantageous with *Y* in place, or because it is uncomfortable. For example, a wallet is removed to pay for something, a watch is taken off before washing dishes, or a ring is removed because of raw skin underneath. Instead of being returned to storage, however, *Y* is left where it was taken off (say, on a restaurant table, or by the kitchen sink). Alternatively, *Y* is stuck in with some other object *Z*, such that when *Z* is replaced, *Y* ends up in the wrong place. The victim, however, is not aware of the misplacement. (If the victim were aware, of course, then the loss would not be a mystery).

These causal dynamics provide diagnostic clues to whether and how a mislaying might have happened. The key question the victim asks is whether *Y* is likely to have been removed (presumably, for one of its usual purposes), and if so, where (presumably, in a usual place for that usual purpose). This question is highly general, and would lead to a different selective review of past activities depending on the object that had been lost. Thus a lost wallet would suggest trying to remember payment episodes, a lost purse either payment or nose-powdering, etc . . . The presence of such remembered episodes would greatly increase the likelihood that mislaying is indeed the explanation for the loss, and would presumably propel the victim to inspect the locales of the object usage. The likelihood would be even higher if the "enhancer" of distraction were present at a usage site—for example, if the victim had an argument over the bill while paying at a restaurant.

Note these dynamics are more general than just for valuable

objects. In fact, the *XP* for MISLAID doesn't even specify that the object has the feature, "valuable." The reason for this is that MISLAID can also arise for the other *CECs* of loss of everyday objects, or small objects useful to other people. A washrag or a pair of scissors can be mislaid in much the same way a wallet can be. This generality, by the way, is the reason the actor slot in the MISLAID *XP* is specified as the "remover of *Y*", rather than as the victim. Someone else can mislay the object you can't find, provided they have had access to the object. So the most general mislaying diagnostic is, "Could I or someone else have removed this object lately?"

The DROPPED *XP* is somewhat similar. A small object gets jostled from its usual place, and drops nearby without the awareness of the victim, as when someone drops a wallet getting out of a car. The likelihood is enhanced by careless storage and/or strong jostling. The "actor" is the person responsible for the jostling, or conceivably a natural force such as the wind blowing a piece of paper under a desk. The key diagnostic question is whether and where there were jostles during the period in which the loss occurred. Like MISLAID, DROPPED is general across *CECs*.

Only *PICKPOCKETED* is unique to the category of loss of valuables carried on the person. Its *XP* in Table 2 is more or less self-explanatory, though because it is so richly specific some comment may be in order concerning the default expectations for the various bits of knowledge. A prototypic complete episode of a pickpocketing probably goes something like this: In Times Square on New Year's Eve a shifty character lifts a man's wallet from his back pocket after an accomplice has bumped the man; the shifty character slips the wallet into a folded newspaper and vanishes into the crowd. Now, some of these details could be missing or different. The episode could be in the subway instead of in Times Square, the wallet could be a gold watch, the shifty character could be a gypsy in Paris, and so on. But collectively and individually they are prototypic, and if any of these pieces are present for the event to be explained, they cue the relevance of *PICKPOCKETED*.

All of this having been said, there are still many implicit steps that would have to be made explicit to specify a fully operative knowledge structure theory of explanation. To fit an *XP* to a given case, the explainer must have a great deal of additional knowledge beyond the bare skeletons provided by the *XPs*. To see this clearly,

Table 2: Knowledge components of XPs

(Illustrative *CEC*: loss of valuable object carried on person)

MISLAID *(Y)*

Object features:	Small
Method:	1. *Y* is removed during period that loss occurred (Prototypic reasons: use *Y*; enable an action; *Y* uncomfortable)
	2. (a) *Y* placed on surface near removal, or (b) *Y* gets stuck-in-with *Z*, which was also removed
	3. *Y* is not replaced, as misplacement not noticed, or forgotten (Prototypic reason: scene doesn't invoke habit of replacement)
Enhancers:	Distraction at time for replacement of *Y*
Location:	(If (a) above) Surface near removal of *Y*
	(If (b) above) Place of replacement of *Z*
Actor:	Remover of *Y*
	(Stereotypes: absent-minded professor; elderly person)
Goal:	(Unintentional)

DROPPED *(Y)*

Object features:	Small
Method:	1. *Y* is jostled from its place during period loss occurred (Prototypic manners: Getting in or out of seats; bending over)
	2. *Y* drops near storage place at time of jostle
	3. Drop not noticed (Prototypic reasons: dark; out of sight; no loud sound)
Enhancers:	Careless storage (Prototype: hole-in-pocket)
	Strong jostling
	Hurrying
Location:	Place of jostle (Prototypes: Beside chair or sofa; near car doors)
Actor:	Agent of the jostling
Goal:	(Unintentional)

PICKPOCKETED *(Y)*

Object features:	Small, valuable, carried on person
Method:	1. Person *P* moves close to carrier of *Y* (Prototypic position: behind carrier)
	2. *P* reaches into storage place and removes *Y* (Prototypic places: back pockets; purses) (Prototypic manner: quickly, deftly)

3. Victim does not notice removal
   (Prototypic reason: bumping and shoving in crowd)
4. *P* secretes *Y* and disappears
   (Prototypic prop: newspaper to hide object in)

Enhancers: Deliberate distraction
             (Prototype: confederate bumps victim)
             Careless storage
             (Prototype: vulnerable back pocket)
Location: Crowded place
             (Prototypes: racetrack; subway; outdoor concert or rally)
Actor: *P,* the "pickpocket"
             (Stereotypes: shifty character; gypsies)
Goal: To obtain *Y*

let us amplify matters for the application of MISLAID to a lost-wallet mystery.

First of all, if the wallet was removed to use it, there is the question of the circumstances under which wallets are used. The most obvious answer is, to pay for something; thus the knower must have available (in one form or another) knowledge of all the scenarios in which cash transactions occur. (In Schank's, 1982, terms, these would be all the *MOP*s (activities) in which the PAYING scene occurs). This seems fair enough, but what about things other than money which are typically kept in wallets, such as credit cards, membership cards, ID cards, and laundry tickets? While many of these would be displayed during paying scenes, so that no new hypotheses about the place of the lost wallet would arise, some might motivate wallet removal in their own right. Showing a friend your baby pictures would be a case quite distinct from payment contexts. Further, less likely hypotheses might arise from the possibility that the wallet were removed not for something in it, but for something one might do with it—to be slightly fanciful, perhaps for slipping under a slide projector to prop it up at a desired angle. Then there is the additional possibility that the wallet removal had nothing to do with using the wallet, but rather with enabling something with which the wallet placement was interfering, such as finding coins or a pen deeper down in the pocket or bag.

The next step in the episode is that the wallet is placed on a surface near its removal. But what constitutes a "surface"? A counter top or table top, surely. Does such knowledge matter? Yes, because if the (say) payment scene occurred in an area without available surfaces, it is not likely that the wallet would have been misplaced during that scene. For example, in going to the front door to donate to a charity solicitation, there is no handy way (barring a table in the foyer) to put a wallet down for a moment. We know that people don't normally place their wallets on the floor—(yet another bit of implicit knowledge).

The point need not be much further belaboured. The explainer must be able to recruit knowledge of why people don't notice what they are doing, of how they can be distracted, and so on. And while some of the further knowledge we have listed is general no matter what object is lost, some of it is object-specific. The appropriate places for the removal of watches, or clothespins, or shoes, are not the same as for wallets. Knowledge of how one object might get "stuck in with" another is highly object-specific too.

These observations are not meant to kill off interest in a principled theory of explanation. Rather, they are intended to provide a sense of realism about the cognitive processes involved. It is clear that people do give complex, concrete accounts when offering explanations (Lalljee, Watson and White, 1982), and there is no use in having a theory that tries to avoid the grimy details just because it seems unparsimonious to include them. To our way of thinking, the naive attributor behaves not like a scientist, as some would have it, but like an amateur detective inspecting a set of clues in a given situation. Let us proceed to a specification of how *XP*s (and the implicit knowledge needed inside them) might be used in the process of explaining events.

A process model for the use of *XP*s

Table 3 displays a set of plausible cognitive operations in the service of event explanation. The table is not meant to be taken literally as a serial processing model, as parallel processing and/or sequence inversions are quite conceivable. But we see all of the listed steps as part of the explanation process. The persistence with which the explainer follows these steps, however, depends upon the strength of his or her motivation to find the best (or indeed, any) explanation. We will review the process in general and then apply it to an example.

Given an event to explain, the first step is to characterize the explanation type according to Table 1. (In a complete theory, this table would no doubt be expanded). Second, the critical event

Table 3: Steps in the process of explanation

1. From facts of the event, characterize the explanation type (Table 1).
2. Decide on the appropriate event hierarchy.
3. Locate the basic level *CEC*.
4. Examine all candidate *XP*s.
   (a) Set aside and select another *XP* if poor match of event to *XP* method and/or prototypes.
   (b) Regard as plausible if good match to method and prototype cues. Pass to Step 5.
5. Try to fill in details of plausible *XP*.
   (a) If unsatisfactory, try Step 5 on another plausible *XP*.
   (b) If highly satisfactory, process is finished. If moderately satisfactory, apply Step 5 to another *XP* to try and do better. (But in either case, if conjunctive explanations are contemplated, satisfactory explanations may be cumulated by repeated applications of Step 5.)
6. If no *XP*s survive, relax matching criteria of Step 4 and satisfaction criteria of Step 5. Return to Step 4.
7. If even then, no *XP*s survive, revise Step 3 or Step 2, or query the facts of the event.

category *(CEC)* hierarchy is located. Third, the basic level *CEC* is chosen, based on the features of the given event.

For Type 4 explanations, *P*-goal failures, no hierarchy location is necessary, because the explanation type already presupposes the specific type of goal failure, and (an expanded version of) Figure 1 becomes immediately applicable. For other explanation types, however, several hierarchies potentially might be relevant. Type 3, for example, involving a failed action, depends for its articulation on what subgoal was being pursued when the failed action occurred. An interesting way of classifying subgoals is according to the *D*-goals of Schank and Abelson (1977). These include "delta-proximity" (getting from one place to another) and "delta-know" (finding out about something). A slightly larger set of delta-goals was offered by Abelson (1975), including such exotica as "delta-unit" (attaching or disattaching objects), and "delta-quality" (changing the shape, surface or form of an object, as in cooking or painting). Each of these delta-goals would command its own *CEC* hierarchy. The "failure of delta-proximity" hierarchy, for example, would branch according to mode of transportation, and define such *CEC*s as traffic-jam for road travel, and planes-grounded for air travel.

The other explanation types in Table 1 present extra difficulties in locating focussed *CEC* hierarchies. The contrastive types, 1 and 2, require further narrowing of alternatives to pinpoint the source of the failure, and the constructive types, 5 and 6, present somewhat ill-defined problems. Although we have not pursued these types in this chapter, it is our hypothesis that *CEC* hierarchies are involved in them as well.

The next processing step is to choose from the among the *XP*s associated with the basic-level *CEC*. Since the number of such *XP*s is typically small, this choice could be efficiently made by eliminating implausible candidates, as well as by advancing plausible ones. For any arbitrarily selected *XP*, its plausibility is assessed by matching the method part of the *XP* with what is known about the method in the actual event, and by matching the prototype cues in the *XP* in the event. Thus if a wallet is lost, PICKPOCKETED may be considered plausible if the victim had been in a boisterous public crowd, with sleazy characters much in evidence, but implausible if the time had been spent in a virtually empty hotel lobby with the wallet originally placed inside a jacket pocket inside a trenchcoat. Implausible *XP*s are set aside, and plausible ones are carried forward to a stage of amplified testing of their details.

If the amplified testing of an *XP* is unsatisfactory, another plausible *XP* (should one exist) is tested. If the testing is satisfactory, the process stops—with the qualification that sometimes conjunctive explanations (Leddo, Abelson and Gross, 1984) are responsible, and more than one *XP* might simultaneously apply. This is not too credible for our object-loss examples ("I mislaid my wallet, and I was pickpocketed"). But for some *CEC*s, such as broken-marriage, the explanation could involve *both* BOREDOM and RIVAL, say.

If no *XP* survives through the detailed testing phase, then the criteria for plausibility and satisfactory detail-matching of the *XP*s are relaxed, and the *XP* set surveyed again. Our wallet-loser in the trenchcoat in the sparse hotel lobby might reason that there had, after all, been *some* people in the lobby, including a possibly suspicious man who stood beside him at the magazine counter, come to think of it. As for how a pickpocket could slip a wallet out from inside a trenchcoat, perhaps there *might* be a way. To figure out what way requires an explanation within an explanation, as it were. If pickpocketing is to provide a Type 4 explanation of the wallet loss, then a Type 5 explanation must be supplied for the method.

To give another example of embedded explanation, consider the bizarre case of Harry, who discovers after a concert that the underwear he had on is missing. The two candidate *XP*s for loss of an everyday object like underwear are DROPPED or MISLAID. The former is implausible because jostling would not displace underwear to the ground, and the latter is implausible because one would think a person would remember taking off his underwear. Thus both *XP*s fail on the first pass. When the plausibility criteria are weakened, the explainer might consider MISLAID if an explanation could be found for why Harry would not remember stripping. DRUNKEN STUPOR presents itself, and the hypothesis begins to emerge that Harry was engaged in a boozy sexual escapade, or perhaps a swim in a fountain. This amplified kernel can then be tested against further facts known about the situation. Of course, if in a given case relaxed criteria still produce no satisfactory *XP*, then the explainer must either adopt some more extreme stratagem, or concede defeat. Two other possible cognitive devices are to redefine the event so as to invoke another *CEC* (and therefore new possible *XP*s), or to disbelieve some of the facts of the case. For example, if a belt is discovered to be missing, and MISLAID and DROPPED both fail, the explainer might conjecture that someone thought the belt valuable (ah! . . . a money belt!), activating the PICKPOCKETED *XP*, or that maybe the "victim" never put on the belt in the first place.

An example
For illustration of the process model, we will cover a real example that happened to the first author as this chapter was in preparation:

> Bob is an absent-minded professor. One morning, he carefully hung up his bathrobe and put the new prescription for his urgently needed pills in his shirt pocket along with the list of items to tell the auto repairman. He drove to the auto repair place and, taking his auto identification papers from the glove compartment, went inside. It was very crowded, and he waited in a queue. When his turn came at the service counter, he painstakingly went over the list of desired repairs with the service manager. Then he left his auto key, replaced the identification papers in the glove compartment, and walked to his office. A short while after arriving there, he discovered to his dismay that the crucial medical prescription was not in his shirt pocket. The pocket was empty. He was mystified.

The *P*-goal of retaining the prescription has been violated. Therefore this is a Type 4 explanation, and we refer to the hierarchy of Figure 1. The lost piece of paper loosely fits the notion of an everyday object. (It is probably not valuable or useful to others—but this supposition could be re-examined later if need be). Therefore the *XP*s to try are DROPPED and MISLAID.

DROPPED is not implausible. A shirt pocket is not a foolproof storage place, and the episode involves a lot of getting into and out of cars, and perhaps some bending. Furthermore, a slip of paper would drop noiselessly. Carry forward DROPPED to Step 5.

MISLAID is plausible. The victim is an absent-minded professor, a slip of paper is easy to misplace and overlook, and the counter surface at the auto repair may have something to do with the case. Or the glove compartment. (Or even the bathrobe, though this is unlikely). Carry forward MISLAID to Step 5.

A detailed fit of DROPPED to the episode requires a specification of what could have jostled the prescription from the pocket. Indeed, since the pocket was empty at the end, we need a jostle which also dislodged the list of repair items. This could not have happened before the time at the repair counter, since the repair item list was available then. Taking out the repair list itself could of course have jostled the prescription form, which could have fallen to the floor of the repair shop. But then we need a second explanation for what became of the repair list. Bob would normally save such a list, as the repair requests would have been fresh in his mind, and he would want to keep a record. This leaves us with the hypothesis that the two lists were jostled from the pocket together after Bob left the repair shop. At best, this seems only moderately plausible, since bending to replace the identification papers did not require a deep bend, and no other jostles come to mind. Let us see if we can do better.

The fleshing out of the MISLAID *XP* requires a hypothesis as to why the prescription slip might have been removed. Surely it wasn't to use it, as Bob had not yet got to the pharmacy. It certainly wasn't uncomfortable to have it remain in the shirt pocket. That leaves the idea that it was removed to enable something else, which could have been to locate and remove the repair list. If so, it could absent-mindedly have been left on the service counter, especially since the crowded conditions might have been distracting. But again, that leaves the problem of how the repair list could also have disappeared. Perhaps it, too, was left on the counter, though this seems unlikely in view of Bob's salient motive to save it. The alternative method of misplacement from MISLAID in Table 2 is that the prescription could have been stuck in with something. The repair list seems likely, since it had shared a pocket with the prescription form. But why would the repair list itself have disappeared? . . .

At this point the explainer has no account which is really satisfying. Cycling through the reasoning again with relaxed standards, nothing much changes until we return to the hypothesis that the prescription may have been stuck in with the repair list, and the mystery of what happened to this list. Well, perhaps *it* got stuck in with something (an explanation within an explanation again). What could that have been? The other object in the repair scene was Bob's set of auto identification papers. This provides a useful insight: The repair list might logically (for an absent-minded professor) have been stuck in with the identification papers, and the whole lot returned in their folder to the glove compartment! Conclusion: The prescription is to be found in the glove compartment with the identification papers.

Epilogue: It was indeed there.

Summary

We have suggested that knowledge structures for explanation are organized around outcomes that are both important and not completely predictable. There are several types of explanation situations (Table 1), distinguished by whether the outcome was a success or failure or was unspecified, whether the actor's goal was known or not, and whether the focus of the explanatory problem can be localized in a particular action. Some of these explanation situations are "contrastive", in that the problem is to explain why something did not happen, and others are "constructive", i.e., the need is to account for why something did happen.

We have suggested that the kernels of explanations are provided by explanatory prototypes *(XPs)*. These are pattterns packaged in sets of alternatives attaching to critical event categories *(CECs)* located at an intermediate or "basic" level of description. If the event category is too abstractly specified (say, the actor lost something), the correspondong kernel would be too vague (it was taken by somebody). If on the other hand *XPs* were keyed to highly detailed critical event descriptions (the actor lost a gold cuff-link from his left sleeve), the knowledge storage system would be highly inefficient. In effect, event category hierarchies and explanation pattern hierarchies are parallel. It should be noted, however, that even though the explanation process may start with an intermediate level XP, the actual event to be explained in any given case will carry some amount of finer detail. The initial middle-level XP will be instantiated and amplified to account for this detail, in ways we have described.

Using as an explanation problem type the failure of a preservation goal, we analysed the nature of the optimum level $CECs$ and the corresponding XP sets. We suggested (Figure 1) that the top level of event distinction was according to what sort of thing was lost by the actor: an object, a relationship, a job, etc. The next lower level, the basic one, distinguishes subcategories of losses: valuable objects carried on the person, for example, or small, useful things, or a lover, or a close friend. The XP sets for these various categories arise originally from the application of general knowledge of human motives and behaviour to the concrete case at hand. Valuables are worth money on the market, and people usually desire money; burglars are a set of individuals who will go to great length to acquire money, using specialized means suited to gaining access to valuables; and so on. Explanations grow in the cracks of human difficulties, and this phenomenon can be investigated by articulating the details of concrete explanations and/or the details of concrete difficulties in goal satisfaction.

The contents of an XP include general specifications and prototypic instantiations for the objects, actors and locations involved, the causal mechanics of the critical event, the motives of the actors, and factors which may enhance the likelihood that the XP is applicable.

The explanation process, we hypothesize, involves a sequence of steps starting with the location of a small candidate set of XPs, via a characterization of the explanation type and a search of the most relevant event hierarchy to find the basic level CEC. Once a set of XPs is targeted, each one is matched to the event in question. First comes a rough plausibility check based on features in common between the XP and the event. For any plausible XPs, this is followed by attempts to amplify the details of the suggested kernel. Failure in such attempts drives the explanation process deeper, looking in turn for explanations of anomalies arising during the detail-fitting process. Early or late success, on the other hand, creates one or more satisfactory explanations.

REFERENCES

Abelson, R.P. (1973). "Structural analysis of belief systems". In R. Schank and K. Colby (Eds), *Computer Models of Thought and Language.* San Francisco: Freeman.

Abelson, R.P. (1975). "Concepts for representing mundane reality in plans." In D. Bobrow and A. Collins (Eds), *Representation and Understanding: Studies in Cognitive Science.* New York: Academic Press.

Abelson, R.P. (1976). "Script processing in attitude formation and decision-making". In J.S. Carroll and J.W. Payne (Eds), *Cognition and Social Behavior.* Hillsdale, N.J.: Lawrence Erlbaum.

Abelson, R.P. (1981). "Psychological status of the script concept". *American Psychologist, 36,* 715–29.

Cantor, N. and Mischel, W. (1977). "Traits as prototypes: Effects on recognition memory". *Journal of Personality and Social Psychology, 35,* 38–48.

Cantor, N. and Mischel, W. (1979). "Prototypes in person perception". In L. Berkowitz (Ed.), *Advances in Experimental Social Psychology.* Vol. XII. New York: Academic Press.

Dyer, M.G. (1983). *In-depth Understanding.* Cambridge, MA: M.I.T. Press.

Galambos, J.A., Abelson, R.P. and Black, J.B. (Eds), (1986). *Knowledge Structures.* Hillsdale, N.J.: Lawrence Erlbaum.

Heider, F. (1958). *The Psychology of Interpersonal Relations.* New York: Wiley.

Kass, A.M., Leake, D.B. and Owens, C.C. (1986). "SWALE: A program that explains". In R.C. Schank (Ed.), *Explanation patterns: Understanding Mechanically and Creatively.* Hillsdale, N.J.: Lawrence Erlbaum.

Kelley, H.H. (1967). "Attribution theory in social psychology". In D. Levine (Ed.), *Nebraska Symposium on Motivation,* (Vol. XV). Lincoln, NE: University of Nebraska Press.

Kelley, H.H. (1972). "Causal schemata and the attribution process". In E.E. Jones, D.E. Kanouse, H.H. Kelley, R.E. Nisbett, S. Valins and B. Weiner (Eds), *Attribution: Perceiving the Causes of Behavior.* Morristown, N.J.: General Learning Press.

Kelley, H.H. (1973). "The process of causal attribution". *American Psychologist, 28,* 107–28.

Lalljee, M. and Abelson, R.P. (1983). "The organization of explanations". In M. Hewstone (Ed.), *Attribution Theory: Social and Functional Extensions*. Oxford: Basil Blackwell.

Lalljee, M., Watson, M. and White, P. (1982). "Explanations, attributions, and the social context of unexpected behaviour". *European Journal of Social Psychology, 12,* 17–29.

Leddo, J. and Abelson, R.P. (1986). "The nature of explanations". In J.A. Galambos *et al.* (Eds), *Knowledge Structures*. Hillsdale, N.J.: Lawrence Erlbaum.

Leddo, J., Abelson, R.P. and Gross, P. (1984). "Conjunctive explanations: When two reasons are better than one". *Journal of Personality and Social Psychology, 47,* 933–43.

Rosch, E.H. (1973). "On the internal structure of perceptual and semantic categories". In T.E. Moore (Ed.), *Cognitive Development and the Acquisition of Language*. New York: Academic Press.

Rosch, E.H., Mervis, C.B., Gray, W.D., Johnson, D.M. and Boyes-Braem, P. (1976). "Basic objects as natural categories". *Cognitive Psychology, 8,* 382–439.

Rumelhart, D.E. and Ortony, A. (1977). "The representation of knowledge in memory". In R.C. Anderson, R.J. Spiro and W.E. Montague (Eds), *Schooling and the Acquisition of Knowledge*. Hillsdale, N.J.: Lawrence Erlbaum.

Rumelhart, D.E. (1984). "Schemata and the cognitive system". In R.S. Wyer, Jr. and T.K. Srull (Eds), *Handbook of Social Cognition*. Vol. I. Hillsdale, N.J.: Erlbaum.

Schank, R.C. (1982). *Dynamic Memory: A Theory of Reminding in Computers and People*. New York: Cambridge University Press.

Schank, R.C. (1986). *Explanation Patterns: Understanding Mechanically and Creatively*. Hillsdale, N.J.: Lawrence Erlbaum.

Schank, R.C. and Abelson, R.P. (1977). *Scripts, Plans, Goals, and Understanding*. Hillsdale, N.J.: Lawrence Erlbaum.

Smith, E.E. and Medin, D.L. (1981). *Categories and Concepts*. Cambridge, MA: Harvard University Press.

Smith, E.E., Shoben, E.J. and Rips, L.J. (1974). "Structure and process in semantic memory: A featural model for semantic decisions". *Psychological Review, 81,* 214–41.

Weiner, B. (1979). "A theory of motivation for some classroom experiences'. *Journal of Educational Psychology, 1,* 3–25.

Weiner, B. (1985). "'Spontaneous' causal thinking". *Psychological Bulletin, 97,* 74–84.

Weiner, B., Frieze, I., Kukla, A., Reed, L., Rest, S., and Rosenbaum, R.M. (1972). "Perceiving the causes of success and failure". In E.E. Jones, D.E. Kanouse, H.H. Kelley, R.E. Nisbett, S. Valins and B. Weiner

(Eds), *Attribution: Perceiving the Causes of Behavior.* New York: General Learning Press.

Wittgenstein, L. (1953). *Philosophical Investigations.* New York: MacMillan.

9 Relationships Between Similarity-based and Explanation-based Categorization*

William D. Wattenmaker, Glenn V. Nakamura and Douglas L. Medin

I. INTRODUCTION

Why do we have the categories we have and not others? This very old question about the structural basis of concepts and categories has recently received renewed attention. In this chapter we approach this issue by asking what makes categories psychologically cohesive.

Traditional answers to the question of what makes categories coherent have relied on the notion of similarity. The consensus has been that concepts should be analysed into constituent components or features, that patterns of matching and mismatching features across concepts provide a metric of similarity, and that similarity relationships constitute the structural basis of categories. For example, *robins* and *eagles* are placed in a different category from *collies*, because *robins* and *eagles* share a number of properties (e.g., wings, two legs) not true of *collies*. Except for the proviso that properties be perceptible to humans, the essential claim of similarity-based approaches to categories is that we have the concepts we have because that's the way the world is structured.

The success of similarity-based approaches to concepts is well documented. Work of Rosch and others arguing that our concepts mirror the correlational structure of the environment has led to a revolution in our view of concepts and categories that has pervaded not only psychology (see Medin and Smith, 1984; Mervis and

* The research described in this paper was supported in part by NSF Grant BNS 84-19756 and by National Library of Medicine Grant LM 04375. We thank Lawrence Barsalou, Dedre Gentner, Denis Hilton, Andrew Ortony, Larry Rendell, and Brian Ross for helpful comments and discussions relevant to this paper.

Rosch, 1981; Smith and Medin, 1981, for reviews) but also linguistics, philosophy, anthropology, and artificial intelligence. The idea that concepts have fixed definitions comprised of singly necessary and jointly sufficient features has been superseded by the view that many concepts are structured in terms of characteristic rather than defining features.

Despite its impressive successes as an account of the structural basis of categories, the similarity-based approach to concepts has recently been severely criticized (Murphy and Medin, 1985; see also Medin and Wattenmaker, 1987; Wattenmaker, Dewey, Murphy and Medin, 1986, for related arguments). We believe that many of these criticisms are well-founded, so much so that we see no way to salvage the view that concepts are structured solely in terms of similarity. The first part of this chapter will briefly describe the similarity-based approach to conceptual structure and then highlight certain problems or shortcomings that we believe are intimately linked to this view.

The upshot of our criticisms of the similarity-based view of concepts is that the focus on the structure of the environment comes at the cost of neglecting the nature of the organism which develops and uses concepts. Part of the answer to why we have the categories we have is that we are the sort of organisms we are. This leads to an alternative approach to concepts which we refer to alternatively as the knowledge- or explanation-based approach to conceptual structure. This approach emphasizes that people's prior knowledge and theories about the world serve to structure concepts and provide *explanations* for *why* certain instances are members of a concept. This explanation-based approach to concepts is in keeping with the spirit of other chapters in this volume that in one way or another address themselves to alternative conceptions of causal explanation.

In the second main section of this chapter we discuss how an explanation-based approach to concepts handles many of the problems associated with similarity-based approaches. We will argue that peoples' theories serve to constrain which properties or features of a concept are selected or made salient, provide the basis for both intra- and inter-conceptual relational structures, and guide inductive inferences and mental simulation.

Assuming that the above arguments can be made in a compelling manner, one way in which this chapter might be read is that there are two approaches to conceptual structure and that the preponderance of evidence favours one of them (the explanation-based one). But things are not so simple. Many of our criticisms of similarity-based induction, namely that the notion of similarity is too unconstrained, seem equally applicable to explanation-based induction. If there are no constraints on theories, then to say that concepts are organized in terms of theories may be circular. The final sections of this chapter take a second look at similarity and a second look at explanation. We shall argue that there are alternative conceptions of similarity, more structural in character, that provide a basis for integrating similarity- and explanation-based approaches.

The major theme of this chapter is that the road to future progress in understanding human conceptual behaviour lies not with the nature of the world alone nor with the nature of human beings alone, but rather with the *relationship* between intelligent organisms and their environment. This view leads naturally to an interleaving of the notions of similarity and explanation. Similarity and explanation may be mutually constraining, we argue, and there may be some intriguing parallels between similarity-driven and explanation-driven induction. Before developing this more integrated view, however, we need to provide more by way of background.

II. THE SIMILARITY-BASED APPROACH TO CATEGORY STRUCTURE AND CONCEPTUAL COHERENCE

The most pervasive and intuitively plausible explanation of conceptual coherence is that objects, events or entities coalesce to form concepts because they are similar to each other. In this approach, similarity relations among objects in the environment determine the structure of concepts, so that similar objects are placed in the same class and dissimilar objects are placed in different classes. This similarity structure among external objects or events yields distinct clusters, and concept formation is simply a process of internalizing these natural discontinuities.

Although the consensus has been that similarity provides the *metric* for structuring categories, and that similarity can be defined in terms of matching and mismatching properties, there is disagreement concerning which aspects of similarity underlie category structure.

A. The classical view

One view of category structure (inherited from Aristotle) is that natural language concepts are characterized by simple sets of defining features that are singly necessary and jointly sufficient to determine category membership (e.g., Katz and Postal, 1964). A candidate exemplar either does or does not possess these defining features and thereby is or is not a member of the category. The major problem with the classical view is that research suggests that the majority of natural concepts are not organized around defining features but rather are structured in terms of sets of typical or characteristic features (see Medin and Smith, 1984; Mervis and Rosch, 1981; Smith and Medin, 1981, for recent reviews).

B. The probabilistic view

The rejection of the classical view of categories has been associated with the ascendance of the probabilistic view of category structure (Wittgenstein, 1953). The current consensus has it that categories are "fuzzy" or ill-defined, and that they are organized around a set of properties or clusters of correlated attributes that are only characteristic of category membership. Membership in a category can thus be graded, rather than all-or-none, where the better members have more characteristic properties than the poorer ones. In an attempt to be specific about the structural basis of graded categories, Rosch and Mervis (1975) had subjects list properties of exemplars for a variety of concepts such as *bird*, *fruit* and *tool*. They found that the listed properties for some exemplars occurred frequently in the concept while others had properties that occurred less frequently and, most importantly, the more frequent an exemplar's properties were, the higher its ratings for typicality in that category. Rosch and Mervis formalized the notion that categories are organized by a principle of *family resemblance*. They developed a measure for the prototypicality of an example that increases with the frequency of the properties it shares with members of its own category and decreases with the frequency of properties it shares with members of contrasting categories (cf. Tversky, 1977, pp. 347–9). Less formally, family resemblance increases with within-category similarity and decreases with between-category similarity. Family resemblance is highly correlated with the speed with which an exemplar can be categorized as well as with other typicality effects (see Rosch and Mervis, 1975).

In related work, Rosch and her associates (Rosch, Mervis, Gray, Johnson and Boyes-Braem, 1976) found that one level of abstraction, which they call the *basic level*, is more fundamental than either more specific subordinate categories or more abstract superordinate categories. For example, by their criteria, *chair* would be a basic level concept, but *furniture* and *rocking chair* would not be. These claims are reinforced by a variety of empirical results (see Mervis and Rosch, 1981). For example, basic level categories are the ones first learned by children, most likely to be shared by people of different cultures, and most rapidly classified in reaction time experiments.

There have been numerous attempts to be more specific about the structural underpinnings of basic level categories. For example, Rosch *et al.* suggested that basic level categories maximize both component cue validity (the probability that an entity belongs to category *j* given that feature *i* is present) and within-category similarity relative to between-category similarity. Neither claim stands up to closer scrutiny. Cue validity is maximized for the most abstract or general categories and it is impossible to simultaneously maximize within-category similarity and minimize between-category similarity (Medin, 1983; Murphy, 1982). These problems notwithstanding, the ability of the family-resemblance (or probabilistic) view to address findings that are problematic for the classical view, coupled with converging operations that reinforce the notion of a basic level, makes a good case for the idea that our categories mirror the correlational structure of the environment.

Despite considerable support for the probabilistic view, we believe that evidence from two major sources reveals that the probabilistic view is fatally flawed. The first source of evidence is primarily empirical and grows out of our attempts to be more specific about the structural basis of family resemblance categories. Here the central problem is the practice of equating concepts with lists of independent attributes or features. The second source of evidence is mainly theoretical or conceptual and it questions the fundamental notion of similarity. Our criticisms apply not only to the Rosch and Mervis operational definition of family resemblance but, more generally, to all current similarity-based approaches to conceptual coherence (see Murphy and Medin, 1985).

1. Empirical problems for the similarity approaches to family resemblance categories

a. *Family resemblance sorting.* According to a family resemblance principle, categories are organized around exemplars that are prototypical of potential categories. In Rosch's words, the idea is "that potential prototypes will tend to become centers of categories in free sorting" (Rosch, 1975, p. 196). That is, if we construct artificial categories by selecting prototypes and generating examples to create a family resemblance structure, then these same categories should be reproduced when people are allowed to construct their own categories from these examples. This prediction is a natural consequence of viewing concepts as comprised of sets of independent features.

The idea that people will prefer to sort entities into categories organized around a prototype was examined in a recent set of studies in our laboratory (Medin, Wattenmaker and Hampson, 1987). Figure 1 presents an abstract description of a set of 10 entities and two alternative means by which they might be sorted into two equal-sized categories. The dimensions correspond to types of components or features and 1 and 0 correspond to values on these dimensions. For example, D1 might be colour and 1 might correspond to a red stimulus and 0 to a green stimulus. The abstract notation, 1111, might correspond to a stimulus consisting of one large red triangle and the notation, 0000, to a stimulus consisting of two small green circles.

The sort on the bottom left side of Figure 1 is labelled as family resemblance and the topmost example in each category represents the prototype or best example of the category. Each of the other examples would match the best example on three of its four values. An alternative sorting strategy is to partition the examples on the basis of values on a single dimension (in the example in Figure 1, the first dimension, or colour). If all components are roughly equal in importance, it is easy to see that the family resemblance sort maximizes the average within-category similarity minus the average between-category similarity. For the family resemblance partitioning there is an average of 9.6 within-category matches (the first example has 12 matches to other category members and the other four examples have 9 matches to other members; self matches are not counted) and an average of 6.4 between-category matches, yielding a difference of 3.2 matches (mismatches will show a mirror-

DIMENSION

Example	D_1	D_2	D_3	D_4
1	1	1	1	1
2	1	1	1	0
3	1	0	0	0
4	0	1	0	0
5	0	1	1	1
6	0	0	0	0
7	0	0	1	0
8	1	0	1	1
9	0	0	0	1
10	1	1	0	1

Family Resemblance Sort		One-Dimensional Sort	
Category A	Category B	Category A	Category B
Dimension	*Dimension*	*Dimension*	*Dimension*
D_1 D_2 D_3 D_4	D_1 D_2 D_3 D_4	D_1 D_2 D_3 D_4	D_1 D_2 D_3 D_4
1 1 1 1	0 0 0 0	1 0 0 0	0 1 0 0
1 1 1 0	0 0 0 1	1 1 1 1	0 1 1 1
1 1 0 1	0 0 1 0	1 1 1 0	0 0 0 0
1 0 1 1	0 1 0 0	1 1 0 1	0 0 1 0
0 1 1 1	1 0 0 0	1 0 1 1	0 0 0 1

Figure 1
Abstract notation for the ten examples from the sorting experiments.
D_1, D_2, D_3 *and* D_4 *refer to component dimensions and the values 0 and 1 represent the two alternative features (e.g., red versus green in the dimension of colour). The partitioning on the bottom left represents a sort consistent with family resemblance principles, and the partitioning on the bottom right represents a sort consistent with the use of a single dimension.*

Note: From "Family resemblance, conceptual cohesiveness, and category construction" by D. L. Medin, W. D. Wattenmaker and S. E. Hampson, 1987, *Cognitive Psychology, 19*, p. 246. Copyright 1987 by Academic Press, Inc. Reprinted by permission.

image pattern and can be ignored in this example). For the one-dimensional partitioning there is an average of 9.2 within-category matches and an average of 7.2 between-category matches, yielding a difference of 2.0 matches. Comparing the two sorting strategies it is clear that the family resemblance partitioning produces greater within- relative to between-category similarity for the situation where the constituent dimensions are equally weighted.

The general procedure involved asking participants to examine the stimuli carefully and place them into two equal-sized groups in "a way that seems natural or sensible." The exact stimulus material employed varied from study to study. Figure 2 illustrates one such set. The cartoon-like animals map directly on to the abstract structure in Figure 1. For this particular set the exact realization of some value (e.g., "striped") varied from animal to animal. The figure shows the animals grouped by what would be a family resemblance sorting with the respective prototypes for each group clustered in the centre.

The results of our sorting studies are easy to describe. We failed to find any evidence whatsoever that people construct categories that have a family resemblance structure. Across a variety of different stimulus materials, instructions, category structures and task demands we never observed family resemblance sorting. Instead, people showed a strong preference for unidimensional sorting despite our varied efforts to prevent subjects from sorting on the basis of a single dimension. Even when we took measures to prevent unidimensional sorting by constructing stimuli that had three values on each dimension and requiring people to sort the examples into two categories, we still did not observe family resemblance sorting.

A possible response to these results is to argue that, although family resemblance categories do not emerge in sorting tasks, in learning situations family resemblance structures are more natural. As we shall see, however, learning studies reveal parallel findings.

b. *Linear separability.* One way to conceptualize the process of classifying stimuli on the basis of similarity to prototypes is that it involves a summing of evidence against a criterion. If an instance has a criterial sum of weighted properties it will be classified as a bird, and the more typical a member is of the category the quicker the criterion will be exceeded. The key aspect of this prediction is

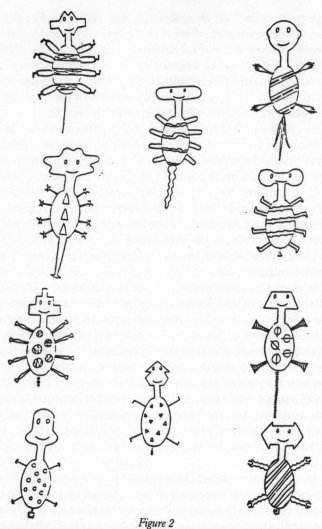

Figure 2
One instantiation of the abstract structure indicated in Figure 1. The four dimensions
are body markings (spot vs. stripes), head shape (round vs. angular), tail length (short
vs. long), and number of legs (4 vs. 8). The drawings are grouped by a family
resemblance principle.

Note: From "Family resemblance, conceptual cohesiveness, and category
construction" by D. L. Medin, W. D. Wattenmaker, and S. E. Hampson, 1987,
Cognitive Psychology, 19, p. 250. Copyright 1987 by Academic Press, Inc.
Reprinted by permission.

that there must exist some additive combination of properties and their weights that can be used to correctly partition instances into members and nonmembers.

There is a formal similarity between this constraint and linear discriminant algorithms used in machine pattern recognition (e.g., Nilsson, 1965). If exemplars from two different categories have n properties, then the categories are said to be linearly separable if one can find a set of weights for the n properties such that a linear discriminant function yields higher values for all instances of one category than for those of the other category (Sebestyn, 1962). For a prototype process to work in the sense of accepting all members and rejecting all nonmembers, the categories must be linearly separable. Technically, categories that are not linearly separable should be impossible to learn according to this perspective. However, given that subjects may employ auxiliary processes (e.g., memorization) when confronted with repeated failure, these theories can be interpreted as only making the weaker claim that non-linearly separable categories should be very difficult to learn.

Although linear separability is an important constraint in formal models of classification, there has been very little work attempting to see if linear separability is a meaningful constraint on human classification learning. Of course with natural categories this constraint cannot be examined unless one can ascertain the underlying components of properties of exemplars. To avoid the ambiguities associated with specifying the components of natural categories, researchers interested in structural constraints resort to constructing artificial categories where presumably the component properties can be specified to create the category structures that are of interest.

Figure 3 illustrates categories that are or are not linearly separable. The stimuli consist of values on four components described in terms of a binary notation. The essential difference between the *LS* (top) and the *NLS* (bottom) categories is that the *LS* categories can be separated on the basis of characteristic features. Every Category A member and no Category B member has three of the four characteristic values for Category A (value 1). Thus each exemplar in both categories could be correctly classified by summing the typical values. If the exemplar contains three out of four typical values for Category A then it is a member of Category A; if the exemplar contains less than three typical values of Category A

Linearly Separable Categories

	CATEGORY A DIMENSION					CATEGORY B DIMENSION			
EXEMPLAR	D_1	D_2	D_3	D_4	EXEMPLAR	D_1	D_2	D_3	D_4
A_1	1	1	1	0	B_1	1	1	0	0
A_2	1	0	1	1	B_2	0	0	0	1
A_3	1	1	0	1	B_3	0	1	1	0
A_4	0	1	1	1	B_4	1	0	1	0

Categories Not Linearly Separable

	CATEGORY A DIMENSION					CATEGORY B DIMENSION			
EXEMPLAR	D_1	D_2	D_3	D_4	EXEMPLAR	D_1	D_2	D_3	D_4
A_1	1	0	0	0	B_1	0	0	0	1
A_2	1	0	1	0	B_2	0	1	0	0
A_3	1	1	1	1	B_3	1	0	1	1
A_4	0	1	1	1	B_4	0	0	0	0

Figure 3

Abstract representation of the alternative categorization tasks used in the studies of linear separability. Each task involved eight stimuli varying along four dimensions.

Note: From "Linear separability and concept learning: Context, relational properties, and concept naturalness" by W. D. Wattenmaker, G. I. Dewey, T. D. Murphy, and D. L. Medin, 1986, *Cognitive Psychology, 18,* p. 177. Copyright 1986 by Academic Press, Inc. Reprinted by permission.

then it belongs in Category *B*. A similar algorithm using the number of typical Category *B* values would also lead to unambiguous classifications.

The categories that are not linearly separable have a similar overall distribution of values (Category *A* has five more typical values than Category *B* in both the *LS* and *NLS* cases) but they cannot be partitioned by summing the typical values. For example, exemplar *A*1 has more values characteristic of Category *B* than of Category *A*. Similarly, exemplar *B*3 has more values typical of Category *A* than of Category *B*. A weighted additive function that would correctly partition the category members does not exist. The categories are not linearly separable.

If linear separability is a meaningful constraint on human classification, then people should find the classification task outlined at the top of Figure 3 easier to master than the task at the bottom of Figure 3. To once again make a long story short, however, across a variety of instructions, stimuli and category sizes we were able to find no evidence that linear separability acted as a constraint on people's classification learning (e.g., Medin and Schwanenflugel, 1981).

c. *Related findings.* Probabilistic view theories treat concepts as relatively static and context-independent. The concept *bird*, for example, is thought to be instantiated with the prototype or best example of a bird independent of the prevailing context. Roth and Shoben (1983), however, have shown that typicality judgments vary as a function of particular contexts. For example, college students in the United States judge tea to be a more typical beverage than milk in the context of librarians taking a break, but this ordering reverses in the context of truck-drivers taking a break. In addition, Barsalou (1983) observed that people frequently appear to construct new categories as they become necessary to achieve a current but novel goal. For example, if someone is going on a camping trip for the first time he or she may construct "ad hoc categories" for *places to go camping, things to take camping*, and so on. The ability to construct new categories further illustrates people's highly dynamic and flexible ability to construct representations that meet contextual constraints. Barsalou (1985) also demonstrated the standard typicality effects for ad hoc or goal-derived categories but in this case the underlying basis for typicality was not similarity to a prototype but rather proximity to an ideal value. For example, for the category, *things to eat on a diet,* typicality judgments were a function of how closely an example conformed to the ideal of zero calories. Again, these observations do not fit with the context-free, similarity-driven abstraction models that characterize the probabilistic view.

2. Conceptual problems for similarity

a. *The flexibility of similarity.* There are a number of reasons to believe that similarity is simply too unconstrained a notion to offer a complete account of conceptual cohesiveness. Consider for example Tversky's (1977) theory of similarity that defines similarity as a function of common and distinctive features weighted for salience. One difficulty with constraining similarity is that in this formulation similarity relations among a set of entities will depend on the particular weights given to individual properties. This is problematic in that Tversky (1977) has demonstrated that the relative weighting of a feature varies with stimulus context and experimental task (see also Gati and Tversky, 1984). Thus there is no unique answer to the question of how similar one entity is to another. To make matters worse, Ortony, Vondruska, Foss, and Jones (1985) have argued that Tversky's model is *too constrained* (!) in that it assumes that a given feature has the same salience regardless of the entity in which it occurs.

A second problem with defining similarity in terms of common and distinctive attributes is that no constraints have been provided for determining what features will be selected. Thus, as Murphy and Medin (1985) pointed out, the number of attributes that *plums* and *lawnmowers* have in common could be infinite: both weigh less than 1,000 kg, both are found on earth, both are found in our solar system, both cannot hear well, both have an odour, both can be dropped, both take up space, and so on. Any two entities can be arbitrarily similar or dissimilar depending on what is to count as a relevant attribute. In fact, Watanabe (1969) offered a formal proof known as "the theorem of the Ugly Duckling" showing that there is no objective justification for preferring any one partitioning of entities over other possibilities. An implication of this proof is that, logically, any two classes are as similar to each other as any other pair of classes.

b. *Attributes as building blocks.* The Rosch and Mervis (1975) measure of family resemblance in terms of matching and mismatching properties is a convenient simplification, and served their purposes rather nicely. This approach implicitly assumes, however, that the properties listed by subjects can be treated as primitives which can be added together independently. However, most concepts are not a simple sum of features (e.g., Armstrong, Gleitman and Gleitman, 1983; Wattenmaker, Dewey, Murphy and Medin, 1986). All the features that are characteristic of a bird do not make a bird—unless these properties are held together in a bird structure. The properties typically listed for the concept bird—laying eggs, flying, having wings, having hollow bones, building nests in trees, having feathers, and singing—each represents a complex concept with both internal structure and an external structure based on inter-property relationships. Building nests is linked to laying eggs, and building them in trees poses logistic problems whose solution involves other properties such as wings, hollow bones and flying. Therefore, it seems that the properties associated with many lexical concepts are anything but an independent set of non-decomposable primitives. A person who simply memorized the attributes of a concept "bird", for example, would have a very odd idea of a bird. Simple listings of independent features lead to a very different *notion* of a bird because information about specific relationships of category features to each other is missing.

A consequence of assuming that categories consist of collections of independent properties or unspecified property relationships is that it does not include information about operations, transformations and relations among properties. In this conception, categorization involves a passive matching of independent attributes to a summary representation, or a passive matching of attribute combinations to an exemplar representation. Rips and Handte (1984) discuss an example where people agree that an object five inches in diameter is more similar in size to a *coin* than to a *pizza* but nonetheless is more likely to be a pizza than a coin. One possible interpretation of these results is that people's real-world knowledge about the size of coins as mandated by law is intruding on the categorization decision. Thus the categorization decision is based on the application of real-world theories to the task, rather than a simple, passive process of attribute matching.

In many instances categorization might involve making a number of inferences and causal attributions. For example, jumping into a swimming pool with one's clothes on is in all probability not directly associated with the concept *intoxicated*. However, observing this behaviour might lead to classifying the person as drunk. Clearly one's concepts are intimately related to one's theories, and a concept may be instantiated when it can explain an event and is consistent with causal schemata rather than when it matches an object's attributes.

3. Summary

Although there is clear evidence that many natural categories are fuzzy, the similarity-based approach has been unsuccessful in clarifying the structural underpinnings of these findings. Although family resemblance measures derived from attribute listings do predict typicality judgments, there appears to be something fundamentally wrong with family resemblance as a measure of conceptual coherence. When we incorporate family resemblance structures into artifically constructed categories, people do not sort by family resemblance nor does the presence or absence of a structural constraint associated with the family resemblance view, linear separability, have any discernible effect on people's category learning. In addition, there are at least three major problems with similarity-based approaches which treat attributes as independent: (1.) there are no clear constraints on feature weighting associated with concept changes; (2.) similarity will depend crucially on which out of a potentially infinite set of attributes or features are selected; and (3.) relational properties associated with structured descriptions are ignored. Although we maintain that similarity cannot explain conceptual coherence, as will become evident later, we do not wish to imply that a similarity-based approach is completely wrong or useless. Our primary argument is that in order to explain the richness of conceptual structure it is necessary to consider concepts in terms of the broader goals and general world knowledge that the categorizer possesses. We now turn our attention to a more direct discussion of the importance of theoretical and causal knowledge in categorization. Later on, we will have a second, more constructive look at similarity.

III. A KNOWLEDGE-BASED APPROACH TO CONCEPTUAL COHERENCE

Our thesis is that representations of concepts should be thought of as embedded in theories people have about the world. In this section we will attempt to show that viewing concepts in this way can account for many problems that a similarity-based approach fails to achieve.

A. Family-resemblance constructions and theories

1. *Family resemblance sorting.* In an earlier section of this chapter we described a series of failed attempts to obtain family resemblance category constructions. Family resemblance is defined in terms of matching and mismatching independent features, and consequently in these experiments the features that we employed had few clear inter-property linkages. A knowledge-based approach, however, emphasizes the importance of causal and theoretical structures in conceptual coherence and is more consistent with the idea that a network of inter-property relationships links properties to each other and provides conceptual cohesiveness (see Murphy and Medin, 1985, for an amplification of this argument). If this is so, then it may be a mistake to look for family resemblance sortings in contexts where the component properties bear little or no conceptual relationships to each other. To examine this possibility in a second set of sorting studies, we used properties that had salient inter-property relationships (Medin, Wattenmaker and Hampson, 1987). In these experiments we used either trait descriptions that were related to a basic personality dimension (e.g., introversion vs. extroversion) or an occupational stereotype, or alternatively we used cartoon-like drawings of animals where the particular properties could be related to each other in terms of environmental adaptations. In each of these cases some underlying theme or theoretical knowledge exists that can potentially serve to integrate the individual properties. When these materials were used, for the first time we were able to observe category constructions that had an underlying family resemblance structure. These results contrast sharply with the previous experiments, in which family-resemblance constructions were never observed. These findings are consistent with the following claim: categories that have a family resemblance structure may derive their coherence not from overlapping characteristic properties but from the complex web of causal and theoretical relationships in which these properties participate.

2. *Linear separability.* According to the view we have been

developing, whether or not some structural property is important should depend on the type of knowledge structure in which it is embedded and the inter-property relationships appropriate to that context.

What type of inter-property encoding is compatible with linearly separable categories and a summing strategy? Presumably it is important that all the features must be perceived to reflect some common element. For example, consider an object with the following properties: "made out of metal", "has a regular surface", "medium size" and "easy to grasp". Out of context, each of these properties is distinctive, and although one can think of many possible inter-property relationships, no one appears to be particularly salient. Consider, however, the situations where one might be looking for something to use as a substitute for a hammer. In this context each of the properties can be readily linked to the superordinate concept "hammer substitute", and the notion of integrating or summing components to determine overall suitability may become more sensible. On this interpretation, *LS* categories might become easier to learn either because participants would find it natural to add up the number of hammer-like properties or because they might mentally construct a (hammer-like) object from each description and make categorization decisions based on how well the object might serve as a hammer substitute. In fact, Wattenmaker, Dewey, Murphy and Medin (1986) found that presentation of the hammer theme did facilitate learning *LS* categories.

In general, we have found (Nakamura, 1985; Wattenmaker, Dewey, Murphy and Medin, 1986) that learning *LS* categories is facilitated when knowledge structures are activated (e.g., the "hammer substitute" idea) that encourage subjects to encode properties in relation to a superordinate theme and to sum across the dimensions in order to make a categorization decision. Of course, not all interproperty relations or property-theme relations are consistent with a summing strategy. Wattenmaker *et al.* ran other studies where conjunctions of features were made salient by relevant knowledge structures, and under these conditions the learning of nonlinearly separate categories was facilitated. Thus it is not the case that ease of learning can be specified in terms of the configuration of independent features inherent in the category structure. Rather the types of inter-property linkages that are promoted by relevant knowledge, and the compatability between these linkages and the structure of the categories, are the key determinants of learning difficulty.

B. Correlated attributes and causal knowledge

It has often been suggested that conceptual coherence derives from the presence of correlated features. Rosch, Mervis, Gray, Johnson and Boyes-Braem (1976) and Rosch (1978), for example, proposed that natural categories divide the world according to clusters of correlated attributes that "cut the world at its joints." Basic level categories are said to maximize the correlation structure of the environment by preserving these feature correlations. A problem with this correlated-attribute perspective is that there are so many possible correlations that it is not clear how particular correlations are detected (see Keil, 1981). Furthermore, the similarity-based approach fails to distinguish between simple correlations and correlations that derive from underlying causal mechanisms.

To pursue this issue, Medin, Wattenmaker and Hampson (1987) examined the possibility that people would be more likely to construct categories around correlated attributes that could be causally related than around correlated attributes that could not be causally related. For example, in one experiment the stimulus materials were medical symptoms, and subjects could construct categories with symptom pairs that either could be causally-linked (e.g., dizziness and earache) or symptom pairs that would be more difficult to link causally (e.g., sort throat and skin rash). Similarly, in another experiment the stimulus materials consisted of descriptions of animals, and again subjects could base their partitionings on correlated properties that could be causally related (e.g., brightly coloured and poisonous) or correlated properties that were more difficult to relate causally (e.g., long-tailed and slow).

In both experiments people demonstrated a strong preference to sort on the basis of correlated attributes for which a causal or explanatory link could readily be made, and verbal reports indicated that subjects used these causal linkages to justify their constructions. In addition, people chose to sort on the basis of correlated attributes rather than a single dimension only in the case where the correlation was causal in nature. Clearly, causal knowledge plays a fundamental role in conceptual coherence by selecting correlated attributes and in specifying their relationship.

There is also evidence that theoretical expectations can dominate empirical relationships in the perception of correlations. Chapman and Chapman (1967, 1969) presented evidence that therapists and undergraduate subjects perceived correlations between test results and psychological disorders when in fact there were no correlations or the correlations were in the opposite direction. For example, in the draw-a-person test, observers have the belief (part of their personal theories) that suspiciousness of others will be revealed by how the eyes are drawn, and a belief of this sort prevents observers from detecting the empirical correlations. Many of the features we believe to be correlated are probably generated by theoretical knowledge rather than based on observation.

C. Theories and attribute selection in natural concepts

In an earlier section we discussed the difficulties associated with specifying what attributes are selected. We would like to argue that attributes are selected based on people's general world knowledge. For example, one way to investigate the types of attributes that are associated with some concept is to examine the types of attributes that subjects list for a concept. Indeed, this procedure has been employed by Rosch and Mervis (1975) who found that listed attributes can be used to predict accurately both goodness of example ratings and reaction times to verify category membership. Conceivably, the types of attributes people list in this type of a task should be heavily constrained by the relation that a concept has to broader knowledge. That is, rather than listing every possible attribute of a concept, people will provide only those features that are particularly salient as dictated by background knowledge (see Tversky and Hemenway, 1984, for a related discussion). For example, people are unlikely to list flammable as a property of money, not because it does not burn but because flammability is not central to the role money plays in our theories of economic interaction. However, flammability would be more likely to be listed as a property of wood because of the importance of burning wood in human activities.

The central point is that the majority of attributes a concept has are seen as irrelevant and are not even considered (e.g., flammable for money). It is the place of the concept in the network of everyday activities and knowledge that determines whether or not we associate a particular feature with a concept. It seems that attributes are not in any sense "given" but rather derive from the role of the concept in broader knowledge, functions and goals. In addition, attribute listings tend to leave out important information such as the relational properties that we have argued are important in structuring concepts.

If attribute listings fail to capture the complete structure of concepts, why is it that attribute listings predict goodness of example ratings? One possibility is that both attribute lists and goodness of example ratings are constrained by the same theories. Indeed, Barsalou (1985) found not only that exemplars of goal-derived categories (e.g., things to take out of one's house in case of fire) have typicality ratings that correlate with the degree to which they satisfy the relevant goal, but additionally, natural categories might be organized in terms of dimensions that reflect the interaction between people's goals and activities and the concept. For example, for the concept fruit, "how much people like it" was significantly correlated with exemplar goodness even when the effects of frequency and family resemblance were partialled out.

Although the issue of attribute selection is not important in laboratory studies using impoverished stimulus materials such as red triangles and blue circles, it becomes a dominant factor when one introduces a richer set of stimulus materials. This is amply illustrated by some recent research on rule induction carried out by one of us (Glenn V. Nakamura). The basic task consisted of presenting pre-classified examples taken from more than one category and asking people to come up with a rule that can be used to determine category membership. The category examples were children's drawings associated with the draw-a-person test used in clinical assessment. For a fixed set of drawings, the category labels were varied. For example, one group of participants was told that the drawings were done by mentally healthy versus disturbed children, another group was told that the drawings were done by creative versus non-creative children, and still another group was told that the drawings were done by farm versus city children. The results cannot be described simply in terms of the relative salience of a fixed set of properties, because category labels and descriptive units were not independent. For example, participants in one condition might note that the humans drawn by farm children all had at least some animal parts in them (e.g., a pig-like nose), but when the same drawings were labelled as creative or mentally disturbed no participant mentioned the presence of animal parts.

These results support an important point based on Kant's distinction between the productive use of imagination (embodying innate perceptual constraints) and the reproductive use of imagination (involving relating particular experiences). Kant's terms (Kant, 1788/1933) correspond closely to Wittgenstein's distinction between "seeing the object" and "seeing the object as." The same object (e.g., a triangle) can be *seen as* a geometric drawing, a wedge, a mountain, a triangular hole, a threat, an arrow, and so on (see also Barresi, 1981). We think this distinction is also important for the draw-a-person stimuli. Actually, in each of the different labelling conditions people stated rules at an abstract level and used the inferred properties of the drawings as support. For example, in the case of drawings supposedly done by farm children the rule might be that "each drawing reflects some aspect of farm life." One drawing might be seen to have a pig-like nose, another to have a farmer's work clothes, and so on. These observations suggest that the drawings do not manifest some fixed set of properties so much as "support" a set of descriptions that derive from the interaction of the drawings with particular observers.

D. Fixed semantic structure and dynamic theories

We have been emphasizing that existing models of categorization have focussed exclusively on similarity relations while ignoring inter-property and inter-concept relations. It should be noted that much of the research in semantic memory based on network models has attempted to represent these relationships. However, this approach has some characteristic shortcomings.

Johnson-Laird, Herrmann and Chaffin (1984) argue that it is difficult to capture the flexibility of human memory in terms of fixed semantic structure. Much of our knowledge is computed by extension to real-world examples rather than pre-stored. To borrow one of their examples, people know that a tomato is more "squishable" than a potato, although it would seem implausible that this fact is directly represented in semantic memory. Additionally, relational properties like "squishable" are highly dependent on context, and the operations of freezing the tomato and boiling the potato would reverse the observations. In order to account for the flexibility that is possible with human memory, it is necessary that these mental simulations be constrained by world knowledge and people's causal theories about the world. This knowledge allows us to distinguish between transformations that are irrelevant to some relation, from those that are relevant (e.g., boiling versus spray-painting potatoes for the operation of squishing). Theories are dynamic and represent mental models of the world based on perception, memory and imagination.

E. Summary
In this section we have attempted to show that people's theories and knowledge of the world play a major role in conceptual coherence and that many issues that are problematic for a similarity-based approach can be explained by a knowledge-based approach. For example, we argued that categories derive their coherence not from sets of matching or mismatching properties, but rather from a complex interleaving of causal and theoretical relationships in which these properties participate. Causal knowledge works to make certain patterns of correlated properties more salient than others and to provide an underlying basis for their relationship. Furthermore, the role of a concept in everyday knowledge and activities constrains which of a potentially infinite set of properties is associated with the concept. Viewing concepts as embedded in theories appears to answer many of the difficulties associated with similarity-based approaches to concepts.

IV. INTERLEAVING OF SIMILARITY AND EXPLANATION

Despite the ability of the explanation-based approach to handle these problematic issues, many readers perhaps still cling to the intuition that similarity does influence categorization and that much of the time entities are placed in the same category *because* they are similar. We agree with the first part of this intuition but not the second. In fact, in this section and the following one we attempt to forge a rapprochement between explanation-based and similarity-based categorization. We will discuss a variety of phenomena such as representativeness, mental simulation, homeopathy and contagion, remindings, and the transfer of knowledge between domains, that reveal interactions between similarity and explanation. In each of these cases similarity will be observed to intrude into explanatory systems. However, in most instances this will be a different type of similarity. It will be a similarity that is primarily characterized by interrelated features that are generated by underlying explanations and theories rather than by sets of independent features.

A. Similarity and decision-making

There is a ubiquitous tendency for people to focus on the resemblances or similarities between two events in order to make predictions about class membership. This reliance on similarity has a direct impact on the formation of causal explanations. When two events are similar to each other there is a strong tendency to assume that the events are associated, and this association is often assumed to be a causal one (especially in the case where one of the events precedes the other). It is very easy to move from an observation of similarity to a conclusion of causality.

Tversky and Kahneman (1973) refer to the tendency for similarity to influence people's informal decision-making and judgments as the representativeness heuristic. This use of similarity may fly in the face of logic. For example, people judge that it is more likely that a person is both over 55 and has a heart attack than the simple event of having a heart attack. This suggests that likelihood judgments are based on similarity to some prototypic victim of a heart attack.

As a further illustration consider the following example (from Kahneman and Tversky, 1982). Two people share a cab to the airport where they are to take separate flights which happen both to be scheduled for an 11:00 a.m. departure. Traffic is unusually heavy and the associated delays cause them to arrive at the airport 45 minutes late. One person finds out that his plane left on time and the other learns that his plane was delayed and departed just five minutes earlier. Which person is likely to be more unhappy about missing his plane? Other things being equal, most people would agree that it would be the person whose plane had been delayed. Kahneman and Miller (1986) interpret this example in terms of mental simulation and possible worlds. It is easier for the person who just missed his plane to imagine similar possible worlds in which he would have been able to catch the plane than it is for the other person. Again, similarity seems to intrude on reasoning and causal explanation. Note however that the similarity which enters this scenario generation and evaluation of possible worlds is a more complicated type of similarity.

B. Homeopathy and contagion

The impact of more direct perceptual similarity on the development of causal explanations is evident in the structure of people's naive theories. For example, in *The New Golden Bough*, Frazer's (1959) analysis of cultural belief systems led to the principle of homeopathy (cause and effect tend to be similar). One manifestation of this principle is homeopathic medicine. For example, in the Azande culture the cure for epilepsy is to eat the ashes of the burnt skull of the red bush monkey. Why? Because the red bush monkey happens to exhibit seizure-like stretching motions in the morning. Thus, the cure (and often the cause) is seen to resemble the symptoms. Similarly, the Azande cure for ringworm is to apply fowl's excrement (the ringworm looks like the excrement). There are numerous other examples of homeopathic medicine, such as in curing jaundice with yellow substances, stopping bleeding through the use of red stones, and curing skin growths by rubbing across the growth with a downward motion at the instant a shooting star is viewed.

Similarity also affects explanations in other ways. For example, people often make the implicit assumption that there should be similarity between the magnitudes of effects and causes. If the effect is large the cause should be large, or if the effect is complex the cause should be complex. Thus, as pointed out by Einhorn and Hogarth (1986), when germ theory was first introduced it met with a great deal of resistance and disbelief due to the discrepancy in the magnitude of the causes and effects. It was inconceivable that tiny invisible organisms (a small cause) could have such powerful and devastating effects as illness and death (a large effect).

Another set of factors that influence the form of causal explanations was referred to by Frazer as contagion (a cause must have some form of contact to transmit its effect). Thus once an arrow pierced a man it was believed that the fate of the man was held by the arrow. If the arrow was subsequently damaged, for example, then the wounded person would be caused great suffering. Similarly, in many cultures items that have had physical contact with a person (e.g., clothes, strands of hair, and teeth) were believed to assume the characteristics of the person. Thus the Papuans of Tumeleo search desperately for any scrap of their clothing that may have been caught on a branch, for if an enemy were to find this scrap the person would be at the mercy of the enemy. In general, the more contiguous events are in time and space, the more likely it is that they will be perceived as causally related (e.g., Michotte, 1963; see also Shanks and Dickinson, this volume). If these examples seem exotic, see Rozin, Millman and Nemeroff (1986) for evidence that contagion operates in contemporary Western cultures as well.

It should be noted that whilst factors such as similarity, temporal order, and contiguity influence the development of causal explanations, their influence is constrained by broader knowledge. For example, if one has contact with a person afflicted by a cold and starts to sneeze thirty minutes later, biological knowledge prevents a causal attribution despite the influence of factors such as temporal order, contiguity and similarity.

Shweder (1977) maintains that resemblance, not co-occurrence, is the fundamental conceptual tool of everyday thinking in all cultures, not just so-called primitive cultures. That is, instead of relying on empirical observations of co-occurrences, people depend on conceptual similarities or resemblance in forming beliefs. Thus, commonsense notions like permissive child-rearing practices lead to anarchy or liberal political views, and that people who are leaders will have high self-esteem, are based on conceptual similarities rather than observations of co-occurrences. Whilst some of these characteristics might in fact covary, the basis for their purported relationship is conceptual similarity rather than scientific explanation. Thus in Shweder's view the Azandes' perceived connection between ringworm and fowl's excrement is much like our perceived connection between self-esteem and leadership in that both are based on resemblances rather than on the observation of co-ocurrence.

c. Similarity and access to explanations

Similarity is likely to have a significant effect on explanations in another way. Given the importance of similarity relations in retrieval (where similarity is defined in a theory-based way that allows for the encoding of relational properties), it is likely that explanations that are applied to a novel event are likely to be constrained by similar events and their associated explanations. Thus, if a characteristic of a person *Y* reminds you of a previously known person X and an attribution had been made to explain this characteristic of person X, then the same attribution is likely to be applied to person Y. In support of the importance of reasoning from prior episodes, Read (1983) found that in some cases people rely on single, similar instances in making causal attributions.

One important question in this mode of transferring explanations is what principles govern access to prior episodes. Is access determined by superficial similarities or more abstract, perhaps causal, relations? Gentner and Landers (1985) examined this issue in a recent study and found that the degree to which a story cued recall of a previously read scenario was more dependent on literal or surface similarity rather than on higher-order similarities defined in terms of causal relations (see also Ross, 1984). Judged aptness of analogy depended on these higher-order relations. Similarity-based access to explanations may lead to the application of incorrect explanations to situations, or at least constrain the range of explanations considered.

This line of work highlights the transfer of knowledge from domain to domain based on either superficial similarity or higher-order similarity based on causal relations. Consistent with this idea, analogies can be viewed as having the ability to influence the form of theories. Consider, for example, theories about extroversion and introversion. In terms of a reservoir metaphor, extroverts are viewed as having excess energy that is expressed socially. If one takes a homeostatic system as a metaphor, however, then extroverts would be viewed as being chronically under-aroused and thus seeking social stimulation. The point of this example is that theories and explanations might be constrained by the structure of knowledge in other domains, and *access* to this knowledge seems to be influenced by similarity.

By now we may have left the reader in a somewhat uneasy state. We started this paper by criticizing the notion of similarity and arguing that concepts are organized around people's theories about the world. Yet in discussions of explanation-based categorization and reasoning, similarity was observed to influence the structure of explanations. We have not, however, come full circle. The similarity intruding into explanation and the similarity to be considered in the next section are not necessarily the similarity that defined concepts in terms of independent attributes. Before discussing this alternative notion of similarity we shall first provide a framework or rationale that links similarity and explanation.

V. INTEGRATION OF EXPLANATION AND SIMILARITY

Our main idea can be conveyed with a simple example. It is not the case that two people are twins *because* they are very similar to each other. Rather, two people may be very similar to each other *because* they are twins. That is, similarity can be seen as the product of a deeper underlying (in this case, genetic) mechanism.

Our notion is akin to the distinction between the core and identification procedure (e.g., Miller and Johnson-Laird, 1976). The core of a concept contains abstract defining features that bring out relations between a concept and other concepts. The identification procedure consists of perceptual and more characteristic features that are used to pick out instances of a concept.

It is important to be specific about our ideas here because the kinship to core versus identification procedures could be misleading. First of all, we do not take the distinction to correspond to the difference between metaphysics and epistemology. We view both surface similarity and notions about underlying mechanisms as matters of epistomology, not metaphysics. Second, there may be a tendency to view identification versus core properties as being analogous to the *combination* to a safe versus the *contents* of the safe. By this analogy the two types of properties have little to do with each other. Instead, we maintain that core and identification properties often are intimately linked and that the core properties may give rise to identification properties. For example, the concept *man* can be defined in terms of core features like "adult, male, human", and identification properties like hair length, presence of a beard or moustache, or characteristic gait may be used to decide that some person is a man. These properties are not unrelated inasmuch as being male is partly a matter of hormones that influence physical attributes such as facial hair, and being male in our Western culture at least partly constrains other properties such as hair length and characteristic gait.

We are not arguing that the similarity view is after all correct.

Appearances can be deceiving, and members of the same category (e.g., bean bag chairs and kitchen chairs) need not necessarily look alike. Our claim is that similarity is more a good heuristic than an iron-clad guide to categorization.

The view we are espousing represents a form of psychological *essentialism*. As used by Linnaeus, the essence of a concept is its "real nature" or that which makes the thing what it is. In Aristotelean logic the essence gives rise to properties that are inevitable consequences. We are going to have to use the notion of essence a little more loosely because we want to extend our scope beyond natural kinds to artifacts such as chairs. For artifacts the basic idea is that the intentions of the builder, the goals of the user, and the functions which an object must satisfy serve to structure and give definition to the concept and help constrain more superficial or surface properties.

Several implications seem to follow fairly naturally from this form of functional essentialism and the notion of conceptual cores. First of all, this view is antithetical to independent attributes. Cuvier, a contemporary of Linnaeus, argued that every organized being forms a whole and that each part taken separately indicates and implies all the others. By this rationale, family-resemblance categories may be organized not so much in terms of surface features but in terms of underlying principles. For example, characteristic properties of the category *bird*, such as having hollow bones, feathers, wings, building nests in trees, and even singing can all be seen as adaptations to allow for or respond to consequences of flying. Our studies which finally succeeded in obtaining family resemblance sorting can be interpreted as an indication that the apparent use of family resemblance rules may be masking the use of a deeper principle that some core factor or cause is present which probabilistically leads to surface structure (family resemblance features).

Once the notion of independent properties is abandoned it becomes natural to think in terms of relational properties. Gentner (1983) has argued that analogies and metaphors are organized around relational properties rather than attributes. As an illustration of this idea, consider the Rutherford analogy between the atom and the solar system. In Gentner's formulation, features that belong to a system of mutually interconnected causal relations are likely to be transferred from one domain to another. For example, properties such as "revolves around" (planets, sun), "attractive force" (sun), "distance" (sun, planets) and "more massive than" (sun, planets) are all causally connected based on our understanding of central force systems. Thus these causal relations will be transferred to our understanding of an electron, and properties such as yellow and hot will be ignored. Thus Gentner's model defines similarity in terms of patterns of causal relations between features rather than in terms of independent features. Given that theories lead to the development of inter-property linkages and that the encoding of objects is generated by our theories, it seems that it is important to define similarity in terms of the relational properties in which features participate. There is no compelling reason why similarity notions must be linked with the practice of treating features as independent.

Just as Gentner has argued that higher-order relations are more important than lower-order relations, so also is it natural to argue from our view of psychological essentialism that some properties are more central to a concept than others. For example, Asch and Zukier (1984) presented subjects with discordant or apparently antagonistic descriptions of a person (e.g., generous, vindictive) and asked the subjects whether the descriptions made sense. These discrepancies were nearly always readily resolved and one of the consequences of these modes of resolution was that one attribute might emerge as more important than the other. For example, when the attributes were *generous* and *vindictive*, a typical resolution was to focus on the vindictiveness as central and to assume that generosity only derived from ulterior motive. Intuition also suggests that a property that is equally true of two different concepts may be more central to one concept than to the other. For example, to our knowledge all *bananas* are curved and all (conventional) *boomerangs* are curved, but a *straight banana* would continue to satisfy the notion of a banana in a way that a *straight boomerang* would not.

These observations suggest that by linking similarity to explanations, goals, and causal structures we can arrive at just those kinds of similarity that will prove helpful in understanding how people learn about and use concepts. Perhaps this notion of similarity makes intuitive sense, but to avoid logical nonsense, however, we shall need to go a step further. So far we have argued that more central properties or explanatory principles may give rise to superficial similarity, but we still need to have organisms sensitive to the right kinds of similarity. Otherwise the theorem of the Ugly Duckling, and Nelson Goodman's strictures on similarity, will still leave us in a quandary.

A. Tuning of similarity

What we have said so far suggests something about the kinds of similarity that it might be useful to attend to, namely those that derive from underlying cores, essences or causal principles. An organism tuned to the relevant forms of similarity would be able to store information that preserved explanatory principles. If humans are somehow attuned to the right kinds of similarity (through the nature of our perceptual and conceptual systems and through the influence of one's culture and environment), then there would be close links between similarity and explanation. (See Lebowitz, 1986a, b, for related arguments from an artificial intelligence perspective.) Appropriately constrained similarity would allow a novice to set up useful categories even in the absence of knowledge of underlying principles.

Recent research in developmental psychology is highly consistent with this general claim. Infants and young children are novices in many domains and being sensitive to appropriate types of similarity may help them to construct just those categories that will be useful later on. What kind of similarity do novices need? If young children were, in general, highly selective and focussed on a single stimulus dimension, then they might attend to the wrong dimensions and miss the relevant ones. Furthermore, although some patterns of correlated attributes are no doubt important, Keil (1981) points out that there are many possible correlations and no guarantees that children would find the appropriate ones. A surprisingly powerful strategy (pointed out and argued for by Brooks, 1978, and Kemler-Nelson, 1984) is to respond in terms of overall similarity. For example, Medin (1983) demonstrated that storing instances and accessing them in terms of one form of overall similarity (interactive rather than independent) leads to sensitivity to correlated attributes in the absence of any explicit analysis of correlation or co-occurrence.

In support of this general argument, it has often been argued that as children get older they exhibit a developmental shift from holistic representations based on overall similarity to analytic representations (e.g., Kemler and Smith, 1978; Smith and Kemler-

Nelson, 1984; Vygotsky, 1962). Holistic representations preserve characteristic features along several dimensions rather than relying on a single defining feature. In support of this idea Kemler-Nelson (1984) found that five-year-olds had more difficulty learning categories defined by a single feature than categories defined by overall similarity, but this was not true for ten-year-olds. In some related research, Keil and Batterman (1984) have found evidence for a developmental shift in the representation of word meanings from collections of characteristic features to more nearly defining features. For example, kindergartners (5-6 years old) preferred a description of an island as a place that is warm, and has coconut trees, palm trees, and girls with flowers in their hair, even though the technical definition of an island was violated in the description. In contrast, fourth graders (9-10 years old) preferred a description that had none of the characteristic features of an island, but contained the crucial information that the land was surrounded by water on all sides. There is also evidence that infants respond in terms of overall similarity (e.g., Bornstein, 1984; Offenbach and Blumberg, 1985; Younger and Cohen, 1985) even before they have an explicit notion of what a stimulus dimension might be (Smith, 1986). Furthermore, children find classification tasks involving superordinate categories, where overall similarity is not such a good guide, to be more difficult than tasks involving basic level categories (Horton and Markman, 1980; Rosch *et al.*, 1976).

Evidence with adult subjects is also consistent with these ideas. Wattenmaker and Medin (1987) found that if adults learn about examples through a procedure that encourages responding on the basis of overall similarity, then family-resemblance constructions can be obtained even in the absence of conceptual or theory-driven underpinnings. Specifically, in this paradigm (borrowed from Brooks, 1978) subjects initially learned to associate a label with each of the examples (short descriptions of hypothetical people) and when this paired-associate task was mastered, participants performed the sorting task with only the associated labels and not the original examples. This initial learning forced subjects to process the individual examples as bounded entities rather than dissecting the examples into their components. In a study using similar procedures Wattenmaker (1987) found that complex correlations between features influenced categorization even when the correlation was not selectively encoded and could not be verbalized. Both of these results suggest that if subjects are attuned to the right kinds of similarity, holistic representations based on overall similarity can preserve useful categories even when the underlying principles are not understood. In many cases, we have argued, there will be deeper principles linked to or generating superficial similarity. Therefore organisms that are biased or predisposed to form concepts on the basis of overall similarity will have an appropriate parsing for a later stage when greater knowledge will allow a deeper basis for categorization.

The one exception to this general claim concerning the importance of overall similarity indirectly serves to support it. Overall similarity is a good general-purpose heuristic but certain relationships in our environment have presumably been stable for many thousands of years. Examples might be the distinction between animate and inanimate objects and certain principles of physical causality such as the fact that solid objects do not move through the space occupied by other solid objects. These forms of stability ought to permit perceptual analyses that are either innate or acquired very early on. Indeed there is evidence that such selectivity (and not just overall similarity) for these types of information is present in very young infants (e.g., Baillargeon, Spelke and Wasserman, 1985; Gelman and Spelke, 1981; Gibson and Spelke, 1983; and Leslie, 1982).

VI. CONCLUSIONS

In this chapter we have argued that a similarity-based approach to conceptual coherence is insufficient to explain the richness of conceptual structure, and opted instead for a knowledge-based approach to conceptual coherence. A knowledge-based approach emphasizes that coherence derives from both the internal causal structure of a conceptual domain and the position of the concept in the complete knowledge base. Concepts are viewed as embedded in theories, and are coherent to the extent that they fit people's background knowledge or naive theories about the world.

In discussing theory-based categorization, however, similarity was often observed to constrain and structure explanations. We were therefore led to explore formulations of similarity that are consistent with an emphasis on flexibility and theory-driven categorization. Our proposed rapprochement between similarity and explanations is that explanations form part of the deep structure which defines deep similarity (relational structures) and may generate surface similarity. This modified notion of similarity may constrain explanation by influencing patterns of association (especially causal associations) and by constraining access to prior explanations. The notion of an underlying explanatory structure seems to direct us toward just those forms of similarity that are likely to be useful in conceptual functioning.

Where does all this exposition leave us with respect to the question of conceptual coherence? We believe that a complete account of conceptual coherence will require an understanding of a similarity-based component and a knowledge-based component. Superficial similarity is not an infallible guide to categorization but it is right enough often enough to provide a useful heuristic. Even so, we may be guilty of overstating our case in that whilst surface similarity probably has a role to play in the categorization of natural kinds and artifacts, it may be of little use in structuring concepts such as verbs (see Gentner, 1981). In any event, even perceptual similarity seems to require relational properties and not just attributes. Inter-property relationships are important ingredients at the level of similarities and rules as well as at the level of knowledge or theories.

Our preferred reading of our thesis is not that there is a pendulum between similarity- and explanation-based categorization that swings one way or another depending on whim or fancy, but rather that we are slowly tracing our way up a spiral with ever more accurate conceptions of similarity and explanation.

REFERENCES

Armstrong, S.L., Gleitman, L.R. and Gleitman, H. (1983). "What some concepts might not be". *Cognition, 13,* 263–308.
Asch, S.E. and Zukier, H. (1984). "Thinking about persons". *Journal of Personality and Social Psychology, 45,* 1230–40.
Baillargeon, R., Spelke, E.S. and Wasserman, S. (1985). "Object permanence in five-month-old infants". *Cognition, 20,* 191–208.
Barresi, J. (1981). "Perception and imagination". Paper presented at the

Conference on the Philosophy of Perception and Psychology. Montreal, Canada.

Barsalou, L.W. (1983). "Ad hoc categories". *Memory and Cognition, 11,* 211–27.

Barsalou, L.W. (1985). "Ideals, central tendency, and frequency of instantiation as determinants of graded structure in categories". *Journal of Experimental Psychology: Learning, Memory, and Cognition, 11,* 629–54.

Bornstein, M.H. (1984). "A descriptive taxonomy of psychological categories used by infants". In C. Sophian (Ed.), *Origins of Cognitive Skills.* (pp. 313–38). Hillsdale, N.J.: Lawrence Erlbaum.

Brooks, L. (1978). "Nonanalytic concept formation and memory for instances". In E. Rosch and B.B. Lloyd (Eds), *Cognition and Categorization.* (pp. 169–215). Hillsdale, N.J.: Lawrence Erlbaum.

Chapman, L.J. and Chapman, J.P. (1967). "Genesis of popular but erroneous psychodiagnostic observations". *Journal of Abnormal Psychology, 72,* 193–204.

Chapman, L.J. and Chapman, J.P. (1969). "Illusory correlation as an obstacle to the use of valid psychodiagnostic signs". *Journal of Abnormal Psychology, 74,* 271–80.

Einhorn, H.J. and Hogarth, R.M. (1986). "Judging probable cause". *Psychological Bulletin, 99,* 3–19.

Frazer, J.G. (1959). *The New Golden Bough.* New York: Criterion Books.

Gati, I. and Tversky, A. (1984). "Weighting common and distinctive features in perceptual and conceptual judgments". *Cognitive Psychology, 16,* 341–70.

Gelman, R. and Spelke, E. (1981). "The development of thoughts about animate and inanimate objects: Implications for research on social cognition". In J.H. Flavell and L. Ross (Eds), *Social Cognitive Development.* (pp. 43–66). New York: Cambridge University Press.

Gentner, D. (1981). "Some interesting differences between verbs and nouns". *Cognition and Brain Theory, 4,* 161–78.

Gentner, D. (1983). "Structure-mapping: A theoretical framework for analogy". *Cognitive Science, 7,* 155–70.

Gentner, D. and Landers, R. (1985). "Analogical reminding: A good match is hard to find". Paper presented at the International Conference of Systems, Man and Cybernetics. Tucson, Arizona.

Gibson, E.J. and Spelke, E.S. (1983). "The development of perception". In J.H. Flavell and E.M. Markman (Eds), *Cognitive Development.* (Vol. III, pp. 1–76). P.H. Mussen (Series Ed.), *Handbook of Child Psychology.* New York: Wiley.

Horton, M.S. and Markman, E.M. (1980). "Developmental differences in the acquisition of basic and superordinate categories". *Child Development, 51,* 708–19.

Johnson-Laird, P.N., Herrmann, D.J. and Chaffin, R. (1984). "Only connections: A critique of semantic networks". *Psychological Bulletin, 96,* 292–315.

Kahneman, D. and Miller, D.T. (1986). "Norm theory: Comparing reality to its alternatives". *Psychological Review, 93,* 136–53.

Kahneman, D. and Tversky, A. (1982). "The simulation heuristic". In D. Kahneman, P. Slovic and A. Tversky (Eds), *Judgment under Uncertainty: Heuristics and Biases.* (pp. 201–08). Cambridge: Cambridge University Press.

Kant, I. (1788/1933). *Critique of Pure Reason.* Trans. Norman Kemp Smith. London: Macmillan.

Katz, J.J. and Postal, P.M. (1964). *An Integrated Theory of Linguistic Descriptions.* Cambridge, MA: MIT Press.

Keil, F.C. (1981). "Constraints on knowledge and cognitive development". *Psychological Review, 88,* 197–227.

Keil, F.C. and Batterman, N. (1984). "A characteristic-to-defining shift in the development of word meaning". *Journal of Verbal Learning and Verbal Behavior, 23,* 221–36.

Kemler, D.G. and Smith, L.B. (1978). "Is there a developmental trend from integrality to separability in perception?". *Journal of Experimental Child Psychology, 26,* 460–507.

Kemler-Nelson, D.G. (1984). "The effect of intention on what concepts are acquired". *Journal of Verbal Learning and Verbal Behavior, 23,* 734–59.

Lebowitz, M. (1986a). "Not the path to perdition: The utility of similarity-based learning". Manuscript submitted for publication.

Lebowitz, M. (1986b). "Integrated learning: Controlling explanation". *Cognitive Science, 10,* 219–40.

Leslie, A.M. (1982). "The perception of causality in infants". *Perception, 11,* 173–86.

Medin, D.L. (1983). "Structural principles in categorization". In T. Tighe and B.E. Shepp (Eds), *Perception, Cognition, and Development: Interactional Analyses.* (pp. 203–30). Hillsdale, N.J.: Lawrence Erlbaum.

Medin, D.L. and Schwanenflugel, P.J. (1981). "Linear separability in classification learning". *Journal of Experimental Psychology: Human Learning and Memory, 7,* 355–68.

Medin, D.L. and Smith, E.E. (1984). "Concepts and concept formation". *Annual Review of Psychology, 35,* 113–38.

Medin, D.L. and Wattenmaker, W.D. (1987). "Category cohesiveness, theories and cognitive archeology": In U. Neisser (Ed.), *Concepts Reconsidered: The Ecological and Intellectual Bases of Categories.* Cambridge: Cambridge University Press.

Medin, D.L., Wattenmaker, W.D. and Hampson, S. (1987). "Family resemblance, concept cohesiveness, and category construction". *Cognitive Psychology, 19,* 242–279.

Mervis, C.B. and Rosch, E. (1981). "Categorization of natural objects". *Annual Review of Psychology, 32,* 89–115.

Michotte, A.E. (1963). *The Perception of Causality.* New York: Basic Books.

Miller, G.A. and Johnson-Laird, P.N. (1976). *Language and Perception.* Cambridge, MA: Harvard University Press.

Murphy, G.L. (1982). "Cue validity and levels of categorization". *Psychological Bulletin, 91,* 174–7.

Murphy, G.L. and Medin, D.L. (1985). "The role of theories in conceptual coherence". *Psychological Review, 92,* 289–316.

Nakamura, G.V. (1985). "Knowledge-based classification of ill-defined categories". *Memory and Cognition, 13,* 377–84.

Nilsson, N.J. (1965). *Learning Machines.* New York: McGraw-Hill.

Offenbach, S.I. and Blumberg. F.C. (1985). "The concept of dimensions in developmental research". In H.W. Reese (Ed.), *Advances in Child Development and Behavior.* (Vol. XIX, pp. 83–112). New York: Academic Press.

Ortony, A., Vondruska, R.J., Foss, M.A. and Jones, L.E. (1985). "Salience, similes, and the asymmetry of similarity". *Journal of Memory and Language, 24,* 569–94.

Read, S.J. (1983). "Once is enough: Causal reasoning from a single instance". *Journal of Personality and Social Psychology, 45,* 323–34.

Rips, L.G. and Handte, J. (1984). "Classification without similarity". University of Chicago. Unpublished manuscript.

Rosch, E. (1975). "Cognitive representations of semantic categories". *Journal of Experimental Psychology: General, 104,* 192–233.

Rosch, E. (1978). "Principles of categorization". In E. Rosch and B.B. Lloyd (Eds), *Cognition and Categorization.* (pp. 27–48). Hillsdale, N.J.: Lawrence Erlbaum.

Rosch, E. and Mervis, C.B. (1975). "Family resemblances: Studies in the internal structure of categories". *Cognitive Psychology, 7,* 573–605.

Rosch, E., Mervis, C.B., Gray, W.D., Johnson, D.M. and Boyes-Braem, P. (1976). "Basic objects in natural categories". *Cognitive Psychology, 8,* 382–439.

Ross, B.H. (1984). "Remindings and their effects in learning a cognitive skill". *Cognitive Psychology, 16,* 37–416.

Roth, E.M. and Shoben, E.J. (1983). "The effect of context on the structure of categories". *Cognitive Psychology, 15,* 346–78.

Rozin, P., Millman, L. and Nemeroff, C. (1986). "Operation of the laws of sympathetic magic in disgust and other domains". *Journal of Personality and Social Psychology, 50,* 703–12.

Sebestyn, G.S. (1962). *Decision-making Processes in Pattern Recognition.* New York: Macmillan.

Shweder, R.A. (1977). "Likeness and likelihood in everyday thought: Magical thinking in judgments about personality". *Current Anthropology, 18,* 4.

Smith, E.E. and Medin, D.L., (1981). *Categories and Concepts.* Cambridge, MA: Harvard University Press.

Smith, J.D. and Kemler-Nelson, D.G. (1984). "Overall similarity in adults' classification: The child in all of us". *Journal of Experimental Psychology: General, 113,* 137–59.

Smith, L.B. (1986). "From global similarities to kinds of similarities: The construction of dimensions". Paper presented at the Workshop on Similarity and Analogy, University of Illinois (June).

Tversky, A. (1977). "Features of similarity". *Psychological Review, 84,* 327–52.

Tversky, A. and Kahneman, D. (1973). "Availability: A heuristic for judging frequency and probability". *Cognitive Psychology, 5,* 207–32.

Tversky, B. and Hemenway, K. (1984). "Objects, parts, and categories". *Journal of Experimental Psychology: General, 113,* 169–93.

Vygotsky, L.S. (1962). *Thought and Language.* Cambridge, MA: MIT Press.

Watanabe, S. (1969). *Knowing and Guessing: A Formal and Quantitative Study.* New York: Wiley.

Wattenmaker, W.D. (1987). "Nonanalytic concept formation and sensitivity to correlated attributes". Manuscript in preparation. University of Illinois.

Wattenmaker, W.D., Dewey, G.I., Murphy, T.D. and Medin, D.L. (1986). "Linear separability and concept learning: Context, relational properties, and concept naturalness". *Cognitive Psychology, 18,* 158–94.

Wattenmaker, W.D. and Medin, D.L. (1987). "Family resemblance and nonanalytic category construction". Manuscript in preparation. University of Illinois.

Wittgenstein, L. (1953). *Philosophical Investigations.* G.E.M. Anscombe. Oxford: Basil Blackwell.

Younger, B.A. and Cohen, L.B. (1985). "How infants form categories". In G.H. Bower (Ed.), *The Psychology of Learning and Motivation.* (Vol. XIX, pp. 211–47). New York: Academic Press.

Author Index

241